Contact Center Management

Jan Smets

CONTACT CENTER MANAGEMENT

FROM COMPLAINTS SERVICE TO VALUE CENTER

LANNOO CAMPUS

This book was originally published
as *Contact Center Management,* LannooCampus Publishers (2016).

D/2018/45/330 – ISBN 978 94 014 5410 0 – NUR 801

Cover and interior design: Peer De Maeyer
Translation: Ian Connerty

LannooCampus Publishers is a subsidiary of Lannoo Publishers,
the book and multimedia division of Lannoo Publishers nv.

LannooCampus Publishers
Erasme Ruelensvest 179 box 101
3001 Leuven
Belgium
www.lannoocampus.com

TABLE OF CONTENTS

Foreword

Jan Smets is quite rightly known as an excellent writer and speaker on all matters relating to contact centers. Not only because he can tell us what is going to happen during the next fifty years, but also because he has kept our feet planted firmly on the ground for decades with his own inimitable, inspiring and funny but scientifically rigorous style. I know from personal experience that his message of 'get the basics right' is still as valid today as it has always been. What's more, it is a message that many organizations still need to take to heart. This book will allow them to do so – and that is surely one of its major merits.

When Jan told me that his publisher was interested in making an English translation of his first book and that there was a possibility for sponsoring by third parties, I immediately approached a number of the leading organizations in our field, who in recent years have put a lot of effort into innovation and progress on the supplier side. With the acquisition of Interactive Intelligence, Genesys has sent out an unmistakable signal that 'cumbersome' and 'expensive' platforms will soon be a thing of the past. Verint specializes in customer and employee engagement, combining a human touch with automation and robotics to create a seamless and efficient experience for both staff and customers. VANAD is an internationally and fast-growing contact center 'jack-of-all-trades'. Together, they show that outsourcing remains a valuable business model, and not just for cost reasons. It was logical that these innovative companies should wish to participate as a sponsor in Jan's book. Our thanks to them for their willingness and generosity.

In essence, there has been little change to the fundamentals of Remote Customer Interaction over the past few decades. It was – and still is – about distance channels and value creation. The challenge is and will remain how to find the best balance between human contact on the one hand and the ways in which organizations and technology can contribute to providing better solutions on the other hand. In the future, these solutions will need to go beyond simply answering specific customer questions, and for this the human dimension remains indispensable. People may no longer understand everything about computers, but computers will never understand everything about people. Feeling and creativity will never come from a system, and certainly not in that combination.

There are more than enough companies around the world to demonstrate that Remote Customer Interaction is a strategic value driver. The European

Union has also made clear with GDPR and the new contact center ISO standard that customer contact is a worthwhile profession and deserves to be respected as such. I am in no doubt that this inspirational book contains enough telling examples and valuable information to consign Calimero to the pages of contact center history forever.

Good contact centers are a win for all stakeholders: the people who work in them, the customers who deal with them, the organizations that use them and everyone else besides. Why? Because a contact center is the best source of knowledge and relevant information about the most important activity of each and every organization: taking care of its customers.

I wish you lots of pleasure in reading this first international book by my good friend Jan.

David Gybels
CEO, The House of Contact Centers

Introduction
Contact center management: from complaints service to value center

Contact center management

This is a book about contact center management. As you might have guessed. If not, the title would have been utterly silly.

The following pages are intended to be a traveler's guide through a very specific branch of management. Don't expect reams of meaningless theory or politically correct slogans. Using real examples from daily practice, supplemented with dozens of useful tips, we will explore in an original, instructive and (hopefully) entertaining way the typical questions that play a crucial role in the life of any contact center:

- In what ways can a contact center truly generate value for the customer and the company? Can the semantic discussion regarding 'cost center' versus 'profit center' finally be settled?
- Are social media the beginning of the end for the classic contact center?
- How should a contact center be managed in order to achieve increased customer satisfaction?
- How can the performance of a contact center be monitored and interpreted by choosing the right KPIs? How can the real value of some of the current fetish indicators be properly assessed, subject as they are to the fashionable trends of the moment?

This book has not been written as a technological manual. You will find no instructions for using specific systems and applications. Instead, its purpose is to step back and take a broader look, to reflect on strategic visions, and to translate their key elements into concrete management decisions.

At the same time, it wants to do even more. In the final analysis, it is above all a story about dealing with customers, about how you can create or (if you are not careful) destroy emotional value in real conversations with other human beings day after day. In this sense, the book is relevant for anyone involved in customer experience and can serve as a practical supplement to the avalanche of theoretical literature that already exists on this subject.

Nowadays, it is impossible to imagine any sales, marketing or customer service process without the support of a contact center. Such centers are created to deal in the most efficient way possible with the large volume of customer interactions inherent in those processes. Even though they each have their own specific role and typical characteristics, any story about contact center management is therefore inevitably also a story about marketing, sales and service.

Or as Brian Cantor has expressed it: 'All contact centers, regardless of size, specific functions or channel capabilities, are united by a simple reality: they represent a link between brand and customer.'[1] Linking the brand and the customer... How cool is that!

Finally, this book is also about the efficient management and guidance of organizations. Business processes are often spread over many different silos, separated by hierarchical walls and functional divides. The distance from and to the contact center is sometimes too great, so that there is a risk that some of the added value will be lost. It is my ambition in the following pages to be something of a bridge-builder, spanning the gulfs that often exist between different sections of the same organization.

In this sense, the book is not exclusively targeted at contact center managers. As a result, its reading requires no prior in-depth practical knowledge of the field. At most, contact center managers might be able to skip a few pages here and there or read through others more quickly. But I take it for granted that all my readers, whatever their specific function, share a passionate interest for strategy, customer experience, sales, marketing or management ... Something for which you already have my sincere respect.

This book is not about typically Belgian situations. Sure, the examples and quotes often stem from Belgian contact centers or organizations. Because that is where I have first-hand experience to share, and not just rehashed stories to copy. But if there is one thing I have learned over the years, when talking to peers at international conferences or congresses, it is that we all struggle with the same universal issues. This makes me believe that the lessons presented here are not bound by Belgian borders.

Work to be done

According to research conducted by the House of Contact Centers between 2005 and 2014, almost 70% of Belgian contact centers think that they are not performing as well as they would like.[2] On average, contact center managers give their organization a maturity score of 2.2 out of 5, whereas their ambition is to achieve a score of 3.7. The House of Contact Centers itself regards 3.5 as the norm for 'good', but seeks nonetheless to raise its customers to a level of 4.

Please don't see this as 'proof' that customers in Belgium are being poorly served.[3] It is best regarded as a drive to do better and a sign of sufficient self-knowledge in the field to know that there is still room for improvement.

Since the end of 2006, I have been closely involved with the Expert Class in Contact Center Management. This has given me a privileged insight into the determination displayed by contact center managers to learn and evolve in a positive direction. The Expert Class also proved to be an ideal forum in which to translate my wide-ranging practical experience with Belgacom and bpost in a series of concepts that I could test against other insights. Contact centers are still a relatively young business phenomenon, for which no such thing as 'universal truth' already exists. Precisely for this reason, it was doubly interesting and informative to do some 'sound-boarding' during Expert Classes with my fellow professionals, who were able to talk shop from the perspective of a proven reality rather than based on commercial rhetoric.

It was this series of lectures and lessons that nurtured my desire to one day put down some of my findings in writing.

Thank you!

I am extremely grateful to the illustrator Marijke Meersman for the push she gave me to finally get this book off the ground. It was she who put me in contact with the good people at LannooCampus. We had worked together in the past. In years gone by, Marijke was the designer of many beautiful postage stamps, an activity for which I am also responsible at bpost. Now we are once again 'partners in crime', but this time for something completely different.

Of course, my heartfelt thanks also go to Hilde Vanmechelen, Niels Janssens, Hans Housen and Lotte Demeyer of LannooCampus, for their expert guidance through a process that for me was new and unfamiliar. My respect for real writers has increased to no end as a result. Their wise counsel but also their endless patience and ruthless feedback kept my determination going to see this project through. Likewise, a deep bow also to Annemie Vandaele and Mitchell Pontzeele for their initial editing of the text. Thank you, Mr. Connerty and Haico Kaashoek for the English translation.

Thank you to David Gybels and Inge Vissers for their invitation to take part in the Expert Class, but also for their unconditional support at all times, without which this book would never have been published. Nor its English version, for that matter. For the latter, I also want to express my deepest gratitude towards Marije Gould, Menno Schuurman, Michel Delfosse, Merijn te Booy and Ad Nederlof.

My fellow lecturers and students contributed in no small measure to the content of the following pages, primarily by allowing me to crystallize my ideas through discussion. The chapter about reporting is largely based on their feedback during one of the Expert Class modules. Without them, there would quite literally have been no story to tell.

It goes without saying that this story has also been colored by my own experiences working in two of the largest in-house contact centers in Belgium. Belgacom and bpost are the glasses through which I have viewed the world for the past 20 or so years.

If you only take away one lesson when you reach the end of this book, I hope it will be that 'one size' very definitely does not 'fit all'! Do not expect to find ready-made answers to all your problems in the following six chapters. It bears repeating that this book is not intended to be a manual to be copied. Focus instead on its ideas, examples, and best/worst practices, which hopefully you will then be able to integrate into your own reality.

And if, while reading, your bullshit meter tilts into the red zone, please don't be afraid to let me know. This, like all other feedback, is more than welcome...

To help offset the effects of my own narrowness of vision, I am honored that a number of my personal sources of inspiration were also willing to contribute their own ideas and comments. This allowed the end result to be raised to a much higher level. I am therefore eternally grateful and indebted to (in alphabetical order):

Benedikte Paulissen, *Telenet*,
Benno Schiffer, *Verint*,
Christophe De Clercq, *Eneco*,
Christophe Degrez, *Eneco*,
David Gybels, *THOCC*,
François Rousillon, *KBC*,

Geoffrey Peyttier, *THOCC*,
Gert Linthout, *Möbius*,
Gerry Cools, *Proximus*,
Horst Remes, *OneStone*,
Koen Van Gerven, *bpost*,
Kris Vervaet, (then) *EDF – Luminus*,
Nathalie Werbrouck, *Proximus*,
Rudy Moens-HansTops, *bpost*,
Stefan Sterk, (then) *Carglass*,
TomVandeCruys, *Lampiris*,
Koen Delvaux, (now) *Joyn*.

Standing on the shoulders

Isaac Newton already said that it is easier to see further if you can stand on the shoulders of giants.

In the past, I have been fortunate enough to work with a number of people who can truly be regarded as the giants of their profession. Hence, a sincere 'thank you for everything' to Alain, Antoine, Benedicte, Bart, Bernard, Carina, Carla, Christian, Claudine, Danny, David, Dirk, Etienne, Evi, Frank, Fred, Geert, Gerry, Hannelore, Hans, Ingrid, Isabelle, Jan, Jean-Marc, Jethro, Joris, Katleen, Kathleen, Katia, Katrijn, Klara, Laure, Lien, Marc, Marinus, Marleen, Martine, Nathalie, Nikki, Paul, Pascale, Patrick, Philippe, Sid, Stéphanie, Stef, Wim and all the many others with whom I have been able to help write a small piece of contact center history. The practical examples that follow are as much their work as mine, perhaps even more so...

This applies equally to the many hundreds of contact center agents at Belgacom and bpost, the unsung heroes of customer contact, who actually do every day what others only talk about. Hats off to you all!

Thank you also to Mary-Lynn, Baudouin, Jacques, Philippe, Geert, Koen, Marc, Kurt for the inspirational leadership, coaching and opportunities you have each given me over the years.

Contact center management is a passion. Whenever I meet new colleagues from the sector, it always seems as though we have been infected by the same virus, of which the symptoms include obsessive customer orientation, operational pragmatism and constructive (self-)criticism. This not only makes the exchange of ideas that much easier, but also that much more pleasant. It is impossible to even begin to summarize the countless planned and chance encounters that have taken place throughout my career, let alone all the congresses, seminars, receptions, work meetings, discussions, presentations, documents and other writings, each of which in their own way has continued to inspire me over the past two decades. I can only hope that I have provided the correct references, when appropriate. I offer my sincere apologies for any oversights I might have made in this respect, and would be pleased to receive any corrections that may be necessary.

Where the heart is – and stays

But leaving aside this professional passion, the heart is only truly at home... at home!

From today onwards, I start repaying the enormous debt I owe to Carla and Jonas for giving me the freedom to sacrifice some – in fact, quite a lot – of our precious quality time to wrestle with the challenges of the blank page and the often equally blank mind. And this in addition to the many hours of 'real' work, which also eat into our time together but have at least provided me with the story that I hope to tell in the following pages.

Jonas, papa's book is finally finished. Again.

How about a game of Fifa on Playstation? But only if you let me still be KV Mechelen...

Jan Smets
jan.smets@skynet.be

1

THE CONTACT CENTER DEFINED

Introduction

'Let's start at the very beginning. A very good place to start ...'

European research: Belgian contact center sector

A European white paper from 2013[4] recorded the following statistical data for the Belgian contact center sector:

- 96,500 people employed;
- 2.15% of the active working population;
- 10% level of penetration in companies;
- Market value of 5.6 billion euros.

Each day in Belgium, almost 100,000 contact center employees do their utmost to answer the questions of customers and help them with their problems.

This means millions of individual contacts, day after day, in a tiny country like Belgium alone.

Given these numbers, it might seem that there is little need to start with a clear definition of a contact center. Surely with all these daily experiences, everybody must be able to form their own picture of what a contact center is and how it works, or not?

That might be true to some extent, but only on condition that 'everybody' is actually aware that he or she came into contact with such a center in the first place. According to a recent research study,[5] contact with companies has become so self-evident for customers that people don't even always remember exactly when and how it happens.

If it is possible to speak of a general contact center 'image' in the public mind, this image usually reflects deeply ingrained prejudices that exist both inside

'If you talk about a call center, people often think of a gulag full of telephone slaves carrying out monotonous and soul-destroying work, while being constantly monitored, measured and assessed. And often combined with irregular and anti-social working hours, in an environment dominated by STRESS.'

Extract from an internal bpost HR document (including capitals)

and outside the organization. These clichéd prejudices say that, by and large, customers do not like contact centers. They are not happy with the long waiting times and the impersonal service they receive. Contact center staff are perceived as hating their work, which they carry out under the supervision of a management that would like nothing more but to outsource the whole lot as fast and as cheaply as possible, preferably to somewhere abroad.

If you do a Google search on the term 'I hate contact centers', you will get around 175 million results. Do a similar search with 'I hate my contact center job' and you will get almost 165 million results. The contact center is often seen as the 'ugly duckling' of the business world.

In an effort to counter this impression, the sector-specific professional literature is often guilty of what might be called 'pamphletism'. Definitions focus on claiming a particular role, position and importance, rather than concentrating on a clear description of the concept 'contact center' in itself. Expensive words are the norm, with little clear will or desire being shown to clarify what the words actually mean.

A degree of objectivity would therefore be useful. It is important to set out the parameters within which the rest of our story will take place. But instead of searching for the ultimate definition, it is more beneficial – and a lot easier – to

'Contact center': a concept in search of a definition

Wikipedia keeps it short and simple: 'A contact center is a department specialized in dealing with customer contacts through various channels of communication.' It is this diversity of channels that distinguishes a contact center from a call center. According to the same source, the latter is: 'A department or organization specialized in dealing with telephonic communications. A distinction is made between inbound and outbound traffic. The main characteristics of call centers are the large number of employees (agents), the strict distribution of tasks, strong central direction and a high level of efficiency.'

Notice how the unsuspecting reader is immediately spoon-fed a number of 'characteristics' that conjure up the clichéd image of the gulag-telephone factory. And how a 'contact center' is immediately given a different emotional coloring than a 'call center'.

The Contact Center Management Dictionary[6] also places the emphasis on different channels of communication when it speaks of a contact center as 'a general name for an organization or part of an organization that focuses on maintaining contacts with customers/clients. These contacts take place through various channels of communication by which two-way traffic is possible: internet, e-mail, text messages, telephone, fax, letter, chat'.

More recent definitions place greater stress on the 'noble' role of the contact center or the high degree of specialization involved.

In a series covering a number of direct marketing topics, a contact center was defined as a 'company or department, which, amongst other things, deals with incoming and outgoing communication processes (for example, telephone calls, e-mails, chat) for marketing purposes using trained personnel, supported by telecommunications and information technology'.[7]

Finally, in a 2009 publication David Gybels of the House of Contact Centers described a contact center as 'a specialized department or an organization in its own right that is responsible for dealing with large numbers of customer contacts via direct channels: telephone, e-mail, text messages, IVR (Interactive Voice Response) and WWW. Contact centers are supported by the use of sophisticated technology, are partially automated, can be organized virtually and serve as a multi-functional service center with a central position within the organization. Contact centers are value drivers. They make a direct contribution to income, customer satisfaction, CRM, the gathering of market information and the optimization of services and processes.'

Amen. Go in peace...

identify the fundamental building blocks that all contact centers have in common and to then determine the way in which they are managed.

The three main building blocks, which you can see in figure 1 (page 19), are the core of the belief on which the rest of this book is based. As such, they are worth spending a few pages on. Those of you who are already converted to the contact center faith can skip to the start of the next chapter or else can read on and nod knowingly in agreement as our story unfolds. The choice is yours.

The essence of contact centers: three universal building blocks

In my opinion, the work of a contact center always involves dealing with:

Figure 1: the three universal building blocks of contact centers

- large volumes, in which 'large' must be interpreted in relation to the total size of the operations;
- non-physical;
- customer contacts, where the term 'customer' includes both internal and external customers, as well as the notion of 'user' (the customer of a customer).

A contact center is the most efficient organizational structure to deal with large volumes of customer contacts when they do not involve a physical element. Amen.

As soon as a specific group of people within an organization are charged with handling virtual customer contacts, a contact center has been created. As far as I am aware, there is no scientific 'lower limit' to determine how 'big' a center must be or how many staff it must have before it can be regarded as a 'proper' contact center. Having said that, some specific contact center instruments, such as WorkForce Management, are deemed only to be effective from 20 to 30 employees upwards. In her book *The Real-Time Contact Center*, Donna Fluss even sets the bar as high as 100 employees.

It should be clear, of course, that we are talking about more than the occasional telephone contacts of a receptionist or an administrative assistant.

Our three building blocks assume the non-physical nature of the contacts. Although many people like to claim the contrary, the contact center does not have exclusivity when it comes to interaction with customers. In reality, it is often not even the largest contact channel. At bpost, for example, the post offices have an annual volume of customer contacts that is thirty times greater than the volume of the organization's contact center. And I'm not even considering the multitude of contacts made by postmen and -women during their daily delivery rounds.

Even so, it is the virtual nature of contact center work that makes it possible to concentrate on 'large volumes'. This creates the necessary degree of freedom to take maximum advantage of economies of scale. For example, it would be unthinkable in a retail environment to set up a gigantic store in a cheap and remote corner of Europe and then expect every customer on the continent to find their way there. But this is perfectly possible – in fact, it is a tried-and-tested recipe – for contact centers. Irrespective of its physical location, a contact center is the place where all virtual contacts are brought together.

As a result, it is not unreasonable to expect that this concentration should lead to the development of a significant degree of expertise.

As we have seen, some definitions explicitly link the contact center to information technology. The temptation to do this is understandable. Many tools are indeed highly sector-specific and characterize the way some contact centers are organized and run. I am increasingly gaining the impression that many vendors/suppliers simply see the contact center as a mere collection of technological applications (preferably their own). But these applications are no more than an enabler of the contact center concept, not its essence. They are part of a 'chicken-or-egg'-like discussion relating to the volume aspect of a contact center's work. Technology makes possible the scaling-up of services, without losing manageability. At the same time, the reliable and complex support of large volumes requires the use of sophisticated technology.

The virtual nature of the contacts is crucial for determining the processes of the contact center. In a later phase, it will also be the decisive factor for defining the role and position of the center. If an activity cannot be carried out efficiently 'at distance', it needs to be questioned whether this activity even belongs in a contact center.

On the other side of the contact relationship there is always a customer, either internal or external. This third building block implies that in everything that follows we will need to find a balance between efficiency and value creation.

Front office and back office: the yin and yang of the contact center

Referring to a contact center as opposed to a call center makes it possible to recognize the mix of communication channels. The concept of a call center places the emphasis too explicitly on the front office, the part of the organization that is in direct contact with customers.

In the following pages, the back office – 'the part of a (contact center) organization that deals with support and largely administrative processes'[8] – will also be regarded as a core element in the functioning of a contact center.

Viewed in operational terms, the front and back office are inextricably interwoven. Searches, complex questions, complaints, etc. that would delay the customer for too long in the front office are referred to the back office for further follow-up. This second-line function means that the back office forms an integral part of the contact. In many organizations some offline channels of communication, such as letters, faxes and certain e-mails, are passed directly to the back office. When this happens, there is no longer a structural barrier between the first and second line processing of contacts. The integration is complete.

In operational reality, the front and back office are the yin and yang of the contact center: the origin of the workload of the latter is found in the work carried out by the former.

Figure 2: the yin and yang of the contact center

The more contacts the front office can deal with autonomously to the satisfaction of the customer, the better it will be for the back office, since the influx of complaints and follow-up tasks will be significantly reduced.

At the same time, the speed and quality of service provided by the back office will determine how many repeat calls the front office will receive from the same customers. A recent study[9] has revealed that some 20% of the questions received in customer service departments and call centers are the result of issues that have not been dealt with properly by the back office.

In other words, the front and back office are conceptually two sides of the same coin.

This can be anchored organizationally in different ways.

Some companies create separate organizational units, at most sharing a common management. The reasoning in this case argues that the difference in skills, personnel, follow-up, style and focus are so great that a far-reaching form of specialization is justified. Other companies prefer to opt for a maximum degree of flexibility in their use of staff resources by integrating front and back office functions, so that tasks in both offices can be carried out by the same personnel. In this case, the terms 'front' and 'back' describe a range of activities, not separate organizational departments.

I admit – regularly and loudly – to being a fervent advocate of the second option. My practical experience has taught me that significant gains in capability and effectiveness can be made if personnel can be switched from one task to another. This makes possible the optimization of results, especially when there are seasonal variations in the workflows of both offices.

Whichever choice the organization makes, it is vital in both scenarios that the contact center management focuses on the full picture and must not allow the activities of one office to be optimized simply by passing on work to the other office.

Outsourcing the contact center: only the tasks, not the responsibilities

The rest of our story will concentrate on the management of contact center activities; in other words, on the 'what', 'how' and 'why', and not necessarily on 'by whom'. Even so, this last question deserves to be answered, albeit briefly, since in recent years it has had an enormous influence on the way the sector is viewed by outsiders.

The contact center landscape is populated by a combination of in-house setups (the contact center as part of the company) and the so-called facilitating

The outsourcing of contact center activities: not a marginal phenomenon
In 2013, the previously mentioned European research study[10] divided the Belgian contact center landscape between 74% in-house and 26% outsourced.
42% of the companies that took part in the study said that they would consider outsourcing at least a part of their contact center activities.

or external contact centers (outsourcers who perform the role of the contact center on behalf of another company).

The outsourcing of whatever activity is almost a discipline in its own right, and one which can often give rise to highly principled and highly emotional debates. In this respect, the outsourcing of contact centers is no exception; quite the opposite. It is a more sensitive than average subject that often touches a raw nerve.

This is related in part to the fact that contact centers characteristically employ a relatively large group of staff.

As a result, for some organizations the political and social context is so delicate that it is almost impossible to start any meaningful dialogue about outsourcing.

The fact that the activities of a contact center are focused on 'dealing with customers' is another emotional bone of contention.

One school of thought argues that a contact center is such a strategically important part of the company's core business that it is unwise in any circumstances to relinquish control of it to outsourcers. A second school looks at contact center activities from the perspective of core competencies. In this case, the reasoning argues that the management of a contact center requires skills that are so far removed from the company's own management strengths that it is better to entrust the task to outsiders who possess the necessary specialized knowledge to do the job properly.

Whichever choice you make, it is worth noting that neither school of thought questions the strategic importance of customer contacts as such.

It is also important to remember that the possible outsourcing of 'large volumes of non-physical customer contacts' does not relieve the company of its obligation to monitor that the job is done properly. The final responsibility for providing good customer service remains indisputably with the company, and not with the outsourced contact center.

For this reason, it is inevitable that the company will still need some level of contact center management competencies in-house, in order to make this monitoring task possible.

In short, just because you have outsourced a large part of your contact center work, this does not mean that you can afford to close this book and forget about it. No matter how they are organized and run, contact centers are still an important part of your business, and the more you know about them, the better. A very good place to start, indeed...

SOUNDBITE

To outsource or not to outsource, that is the question – but to do it well also requires some careful thought.

François Rossillion (senior expert in distribution for the Belgian financial institution KBC Group) prefers to talk of 'strategic sourcing' rather than insourcing or outsourcing.

For him, strategic sourcing is 'the realization of strategic objectives through the making of well-considered choices between doing certain tasks yourself or outsourcing them to third parties'.

In other words, the question about which resources and aids a company should use needs to be addressed long before the question of possible outsourcing becomes a matter for consideration.

'The top management of any enterprise first needs to accurately identify its own core activities and competencies. This is where the bulk of the available capital and resources most urgently need to be invested, since this is where they will provide the biggest competitive advantage and create the most added value. This identification process will result in a distinction being made between core activities and non-core activities. You need to do the core activities yourself. They should never be outsourced. Non-core activities may be outsourced, but only under certain conditions.'

In the Expert Class in Contact Center Management, François discusses the different arguments for and against outsourcing. These arguments are not geared specifically to the activities of a contact center, but can just as easily be applied to them.

They can be summarized as follows:

Management focus and capacity

- Resources (investments, people, infrastructure) are concentrated on core activities. The management maintains a clear focus on the things it does well or from which it can gain a competitive advantage.
- Outsourcing can be an important catalyst for (internal) change.
- A limited internal capacity for innovation can be supplemented with external expertise.
- When a third party is better able to manage certain (operational) risks, outsourcing can be part of a risk management strategy.

Better operational quality and faster 'go-to-market'

- Quality improvements can be realized through partnerships with a (specialized) third party.
- There is access to an agreed and contractually binding level of service provision.
- It is possible to 'purchase' access to operational expertise, knowledge and a broader pool of specific talent, without the need to first build up all these resources internally.
- Capacity management is optimized, with a high degree of flexibility that is seldom possible in-house. This in turn facilitates the ability to change course more quickly.

Cost management

- Standard processes become more like commodities, which can be bought in wisely.
- There is a fall in the global service cost for the organization; for example, through access to lower labor costs, particularly when 'off-shoring' (outsourcing abroad) is an option.
- The cost structure changes for the better, because fixed (internal) costs can be made variable.
- Particularly in cases of off-shoring, tax benefits and other interesting sources of local funding can help to cut costs even further.

'For me, the question of management focus is the first and most important reason for outsourcing,' says François Rossillion. 'Research has confirmed that this is also the reason most commonly cited (55%) by companies that outsource. But it is an illusion to have blind faith in outsourcing as a guarantee for success – and this is equally true for contact centers. Other research (Gartner, 2003) has demonstrated that 50% of outsourcing relationships do not achieve the desired result or even fail completely.'

Here are the five most common reasons for failure:

1. The desired results were not clearly defined in advance. There were no Service Level Agreements (SLAs) or else they were badly formulated;
2. Highly restrictive contracts allow the partner too little room for maneuver, leading to endless disputes and discussions;
3. There is insufficient operational direction (also on the part of the outsourcing company);
4. Initial decisions are taken on the basis of an unbeatable low basic price, but there is often later a need to bear additional (and unbudgeted) costs when unforeseen problems arise;
5. Technology and processes do not immediately result in better quality. Outsourcing is not a magic wand that removes all underlying problems without the need for further investment.

'The activities of a contact center can certainly be outsourced, but it is important to do it for the right reasons and, above all, in the right manner.'

2

CONTACT CENTER MANAGEMENT: BALANCING EXERCISE IN A SPECIFIC CONTEXT

The management of a contact center involves a combination of classic management challenges in a specific context.

Components of contact center management

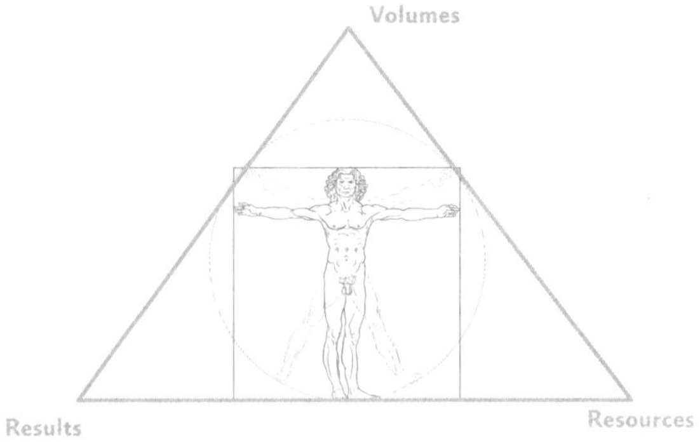

Figure 3: the balancing act of a contact center manager

The classic components of contact center management involve a non-stop balancing act. There are three elements that constantly influence each other: volumes, resources and results. The results are the outcome of the allocation of resources in relation to the volume of contacts.

In 'volumes' the skill of the contact center manager's art lies in an ability to predict the number of inbound and outbound contacts. It also involves the ability to influence these volumes and not simply accept them passively as an inevitable and unchangeable given.

'Resources' refer to the available personnel and technology, as well as the necessary level of experience possessed by the workforce and all aspects related to the decisions about who, what and when.

'Results' relate to both the service aspect and the content quality. This implies the need to differentiate, so that the 'result' can be interpreted differently in function of different target groups.

Finding the right balance between these three components is the universal challenge of every form of management. Once again, this is not something confined exclusively to contact centers. However, contact center management does require translating this challenge in a manner that matches the specific nature of the contact center environment.

Contact center management in search of a definition: part 2
The Incoming Calls Management Institute describes inbound call center management as 'the art of having just the right number of well-trained and well-supported agents in just the right place at just the right time for the purpose of dealing with an accurately predicted workload to the required level of service and with the required degree of quality'.

This is a highly workable definition, but it places a heavy emphasis (and burden of responsibility) on the question of workforce management. This is the management skill of timetabling the use of available staff resources in the best possible manner on the basis of the predicted incoming volumes. We will return to this concept again later on. At this stage, we can simply note that the skeptic might argue that not much skill is involved when volumes can be predicted with such accuracy.

During my Belgacom years, the task of contact center management was pragmatically described in presentations as 'ensuring that the right customer is directed in the right manner to the right available member of staff, who knows what he/she must do and then does it well'. This definition shifts the emphasis to the need for possible (customer) differentiation and operational excellence, also at the level of the individual contact center agent.

The biggest difference with other branches of management is perhaps the 'real time' aspect of the work, which means that almost every decision can be judged immediately on its merits. Few other sectors are measurable with such immediacy. This creates huge pressure in relation to the need for speed of reaction, the immediate evaluation of that reaction in terms of 'good' or 'bad', and the rapid identification of the right solutions.

The contact center manager between hammer and anvil

The contact center manager deserves a bit of respect and a whole lot of empathy for the very specific function he occupies.

He is positioned at the busy junction where:

- customer expectations and the service provision of the company will match or clash, with the manager facilitating the former or managing the fall-out of the latter;
- customer expectations and the organization of customer service are confronted with the concerns and varying competencies of a relatively large group of personnel. Contact center managers need to build a bridge between these two extremes, while realizing that their people management skills will be tested to the full when the bridge is put under severe operational pressure;
- traditional cost minimization must be reconciled with the need for value and service, which together form the non-negotiable core task of every contact center manager;
- different building blocks and underlying mechanisms need to be harmonized into a smoothly functioning whole... Or not...

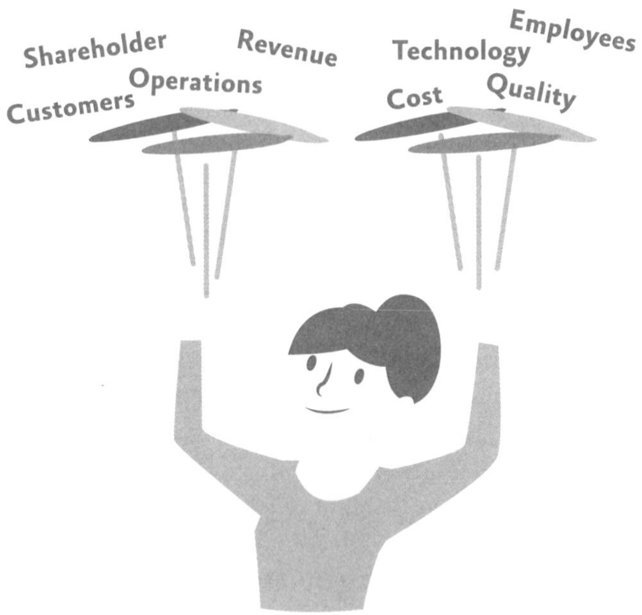

Figure 4: the contact center manager juggling plates

In other words, the contact center manager is like a plate juggler in a Chinese circus, who needs to keep an improbable number of plates spinning in the air all at the same time. But in contrast to a circus performer, he doesn't always feel he's getting a lot of applause or cheers.

The nature of his work means that it is possible to measure in real time how many plates are still in the air and how many have come crashing to the ground.

It is therefore vital to know the exact place and to correctly estimate the exact value of each plate. To do this, we first need to map out the role and position of the contact center as a whole.

3

ROLE AND POSITION OF THE CONTACT CENTER

'If you don't know where you're going, every road will take you there ...'
Confucius

Now that we have unambiguously defined what a contact center is, we can move on to discuss its role and the added value it can create. The first key point to remember is that the way in which a contact center should be run is closely related to the expectations you have of it. So, it's key to always start with the 'why'.

Start with the why[11]

The discussion about the role and position of a contact center is similar to the discussion about the gender of angels. Is it a cost center or a profit center? Or is it something else altogether?

This is not merely a semantic discussion. It is symptomatic of the way in which the entire sector so often seems to wrestle with the fundamental reasons for its existence. Frequently, this has a kind of Calimero-like inferiority complex as its root cause and/or consequence.

When we were discussing possible definitions, it was already obvious that some of them were charged with an apparent need to claim a specific role, which would give the contact center the same degree of importance as other business departments, such as sales and marketing.

Vendors and consultants tend to play on this air of unease and uncertainty in their dealings with contact center managers, filling them with an almost evolutionary sense of guilt. In their discourse, an inbound, service-oriented call center is depicted as a Neanderthal-like phenomenon in the modern business world, a pure accounting cost at a very early (one might even say primitive) stage of development.

As a result, there is often a feeling among contact center managers that, if their center is to survive and eventually create value, it will need to evolve quickly.

In this kind of context, the graphic displayed in figure 5 risks sending the wrong message:

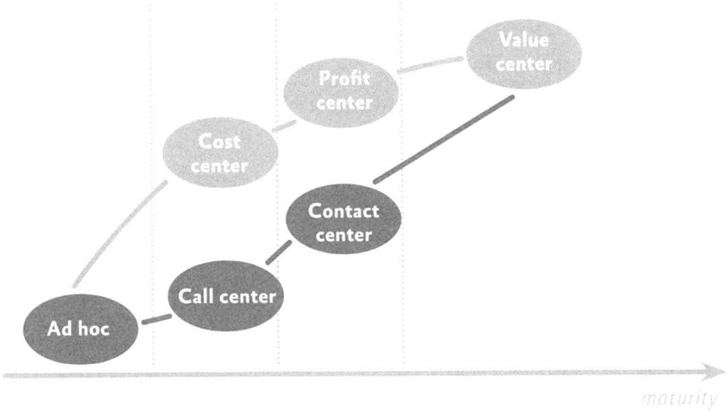

Figure 5: the clichéd view of contact center development[12]

This leads me to develop an alternative model as a counterweight to the clichéd view and as a guideline for a more balanced and successful evolution. This model, which will be used as our reference throughout this chapter, is depicted in figure 6.

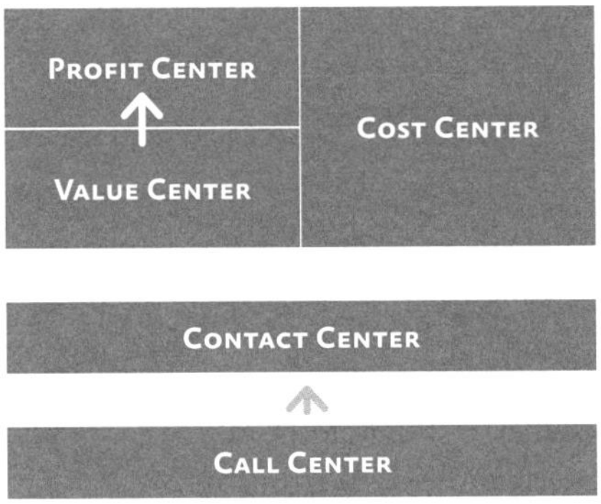

Figure 6: Jan's model for contact center positioning

It avoids a number of 'either… or' discussions. It also tries to avoid the often emotionally charged semantics associated with those discussions.

There is no shame or 'dishonor' attached to the performance of certain basic call and contact center functions. So why should we see a need to disguise their reality?

The reasoning is actually quite simple:

- a call center can – but not necessarily must – become a contact center, providing it significantly expands its different channels of communication;
- a call/contact center is always a value center, because it always has an impact on the emotional state of mind of customers;
- if the center takes on an explicit sales role, it can be regarded as a profit center;
- but given its DNA, a call center will always remain a cost center.

Each of these roles brings its own obligations. 'With great power comes great responsibility' is not an adage for Spiderman alone!

From call center to contact center: from POTS to PANS[13]

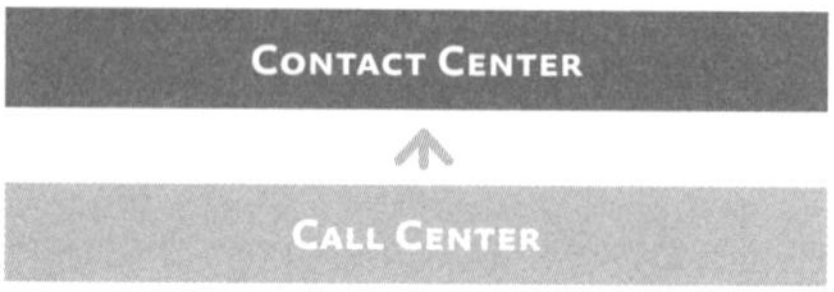

Figure 7: from call center to contact center

A call center can – but not necessarily must – become a contact center, providing it significantly expands its different channel of communications.

The term 'call center' has lost popularity in recent years. Nowadays there is an unmistakable air of stigma attached to it. This is an unhappy reminder of excesses in the past, when aggressive telesellers forced their random attentions on unsuspecting or even unwilling consumers.

In these circumstances, a rebranding can be useful, so that the transition from 'call center' to 'contact center' is quickly made. But there is more.

As we have already seen, the concept of a contact center excludes the back office population to a significantly lesser extent than does the call center concept. Moreover, it reflects the fact (as we saw in our various definitions) that interaction with the customer nowadays takes place though several different communication channels and not simply through the medium of the telephone, as was usually the case in years gone by. In addition to the ultra-traditional channels – letter and fax, as well as telephone, which are still popular with some customers – recent years have seen the dramatic rise in the importance of:

- the internet, websites, e-mails and web forms,
- text messages,
- video-conferencing and Skype,
- co-browsing,
- social media,
- chat.

Figure 8: the numerous channels of communication in the call... er... contact center

The offline nature of a number of these channels means that they are most probably supported by agents in the back office. This again underlines the importance of including it conceptually as an integral part of the contact center set-up.

There are various reasons for this proliferation of communication channels. The first and most obvious explanation is technological progress. When American marketeers first started exploring call centers as a tool in the 1920s, most of the communication channels available today did not exist.

But there is also a contact center variant of 'keeping up with the Joneses' at play.[14]

Companies copy practices from other companies or slavishly follow the hype of the day. They want to keep up with – or even stay ahead of – the game, but more often than not they are more afraid of being left behind. They are happy to go along with what everyone else is saying: 'If that's the way customers want to communicate nowadays, surely you don't want to miss the boat?' Well, do you?

Exploit before you explore

Well... no. 'Look before you leap' – or, if you prefer, 'exploit before you explore' – is a much better approach. If the purpose of your contact center is to help customers as quickly as possible in the best possible way, then there is nothing

The 'Catch 22' of communication channels

Combining 'fast' and 'good' is a challenge in any activity.

The less traditional channels of communication have changed the balance between the need for 'formal' quality and the need for speed of response.

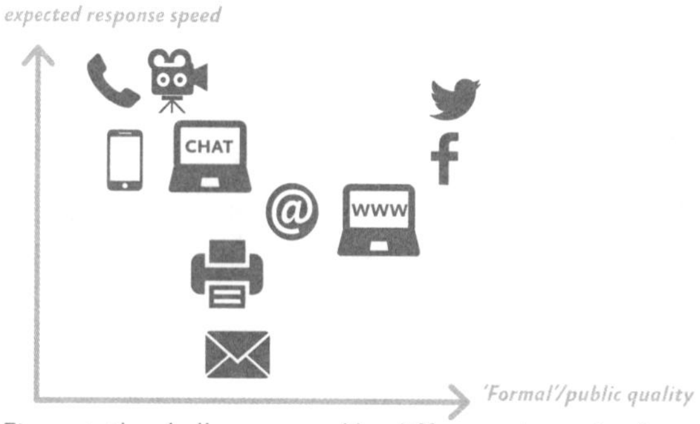

Figure 9: the challenge posed by different channels of communication

A customer who has sent you an angry letter, even if supported in his complaint by a legal representative, will usually give you the time to send him a formal reply, which you, in turn, will first have checked by your legal advisors.

In contrast, an answer given on the telephone is expected to be immediate. This conversation, however, is normally confined to just the caller and the agent, so that any mistakes that happen are not immediately made public.

The new media have made feedback loops much shorter, so that interactions now arrive more quickly and more easily in the public domain. In other words, the traditional balance has been disturbed, so that the traditional organization of call centers, geared primarily to allow a rapid response to telephone calls, has also been disturbed.

This paradox often leads to the setting up of dedicated teams for individual channels, but this is usually at the expense of efficiency and flexibility.

In other words: Catch 22.

wrong in directing the customer to the channel that will allow you to best meet his needs. After all, to use another quaintly old-fashioned phrase, 'it is for his own good'. And he might just thank you in the end.
This directing of customers to the most appropriate channels can and should (must?) take operational limitations into account. Isn't it better to do a few things really well rather than do many things passably?

The more communication channels you have, the greater the number of challenges you will need to face, both in terms of practical organization and the competencies required by your personnel. Historically, most contact center operatives were appointed to the job almost exclusively because of their verbal skills. Few other criteria were deemed to be important.

So, the first lesson is this: to begin with, make sure you fully exploit the possibilities of the communication channels you already have. Make sure that these channels are working to maximum efficiency before you start introducing new ones. Opening all sorts of new channels without giving it proper thought might seem as though you are responding to customer expectations, but if these channels are poorly run they will have the opposite effect to what you intended.

'So, what about the wishes of the customer?' I can hear some of you ask. Believe me, you will know soon enough if you end up in a situation that your customers regard as unacceptable. This will give you the opportunity to change your communication strategy before any lasting damage has been done.

Do social media mean the end of the traditional contact center?

Social media... Nowadays, it is impossible to avoid them in any debate about the future of contact centers. Any discussion on any aspect of the customer experience inevitably seems to gravitate towards this 'social' dimension. I have lost count of the number of experts and consultants who preach that the sector will soon succumb to the dominance of Twitter and other Facebooks. They are quick to condemn companies who 'miss the boat', predicting they will end up booking a one-way ticket to Jurassic Park instead. For a contact center manager, it takes a firm degree of self-confidence to weather this storm of criticism.

The 'expert' reasoning is deceptively simple. Customers are spending an increasingly large part of their life in the public glare of social media. It is the weapon that has allowed them to seize power in their relationships with suppliers. This means that customers will no longer be willing to conform with the internal procedures of companies or to 'slavishly' choose the channel of contact that a particular company (for whatever reason) prefers. They want to converse with companies – and their contact centers – in the online arena where the largest part of their life is now played out. Companies should accept this fact and respond to it actively – if they know what is good for them...

Be honest, how often have you heard arguments of this kind in recent years? Hundreds of times, I am willing to bet.

What's more, technology vendors are almost falling over each other to show how their solution is capable of processing, routing and even prioritizing social feeds, either in a separate environment or as part of an existing platform.

According to this logic, providing customer services and (above all) dealing with customer complaints via social media – known in the jargon as 'social care' – has become the new normal.

This is not a hype, or so these prophets of online modernism claim, but rather an irreversible evolution in the manner in which customers converse with each other and, therefore, in the way they want to converse with companies in the future. Attempting to resist this tide of progress will at best result in pitying looks and at worst in outright condemnation. But one thing is certain: the future looks bleak for any company that dares to ignore the writing on the wall...

The emperor's clothes

Sounds pretty gloomy, doesn't it? But is it true? Personally, I am not so sure. To my mind there is something fundamentally wrong about the way this reasoning is applied in practice.

Please don't take this as a diatribe against social media in general.

The enormous power of the medium as a platform for social conversations is undeniable. Moreover, viewed from a marketing perspective, social media are one of the big success stories of the first two decades of the 21st century in the field of company interaction with customers. There are whole libraries full of case studies to prove it.

Unfortunately, those who preach the blessings of social care in general are also attempting to force those 'blessings' onto contact centers, but for the wrong reasons. So perhaps the time has come to cry out that the emperor isn't actually wearing any clothes.

Pundits who claim that social care is not a hype are literally wrong. The word 'hype' means 'something that receives exaggerated attention'.[15] In view of the level of penetration of a platform like Twitter, which is currently estimated at around 7%,[16] the massive amount of attention currently being focused on customer reactions via this and other similar channels is very clearly exaggerated to a disproportional extent. In short, social care in a contact center context is unquestionably a hype. If, for example, we examine the levels of management attention originally given in an organization like bpost to different communication channels, a mathematical analysis would lead to the conclusion that one customer tweet weighed more heavily than 150 customer telephone calls!

'In 2012, customer care via social media seemed like a good idea. So did dancing Gangnam Style.'

In November 2012, these were the exact words on one of the opening slides of my presentation to the National Contact Center Congress. My aim was to reproach the assembled contact center community for the lemming-like manner in which they were following the social care hype, in much the same way that millions of YouTube visitors at that time were going crazy for the whacky Korean singer Psy and his 'Gangnam Style' dancing.[17] In later versions of the same presentation, I replaced 'Gangnam Style' with 'Harlem Shake', 'twerking', 'La La Land' and 'Bum Bum Tan Tan'. But the basic point remains the same; hypes seem like a good idea at the time, but that idea often soon wears off.

The dance reference was no coincidence (although as I get older I am finding it increasingly difficult to keep up with all the latest trends). It refers to a highly appropriate and telling metaphor, first coined by Dr. Nicola Millard, a futurologist at British Telecom. She used it at a congress to advise delegates about the best way to deal with social media. She compared this challenge with a visit to a dance club:

- At the very least, you need to observe; to see what music is being played and how people are dancing to it. What is hot and what's not? Who is dancing with whom? For companies, this monitoring exercise is the equivalent of an Olympic minimum. Observe what your customers are saying about you, your market and your competitors. Who are they saying it to? With what emotions and what degree of intensity? The highly public nature of social media makes it easy to follow conversations, both in terms of content and tone. This has become a free but nonetheless powerful tool in market research; in fact, many now believe it is the future of market research.
- Joining in with the dancing requires more skill and daring. If you don't want to make a fool of yourself in public, you need to be sure you know all the

right moves before stepping out onto the dance floor. You don't want to be shaking when you should be twerking. The metaphor is clear: as far as companies are concerned, participating in conversations only works when you know how to do it and do it well.

- Before you start dancing real close with someone, you need to make sure that the object of your attention will allow it and appreciate it. Otherwise, you might end up quite literally with red cheeks, or something even worse. Before attempting as a company to break into conversations on social media, make certain that your public will value your contribution rather than resent it; otherwise, your good intentions will boomerang back in your face.

Today, you can see many companies that still make some very awkward moves on social media. They try to get themselves in the spotlight but don't really know what to do when they get there. This usually suggests that their digital strategy has been copied from others: 'Everyone else is doing it, so we'd better do it as well!'

Tweeroes

By now, I expect that some of you have your eyebrows well and truly raised. No matter how clumsy social care might currently be, surely it is still a positive evolution, isn't it? If a customer is using the social media megaphone to tell everyone and their brother just how incompetent your company really is, it can only be a good thing that you have the option to intervene and save your company's online reputation, can't it?

Well... not necessarily. It all depends.

Depends on what? Primarily on what problems need to be solved.

We have all heard it at conferences or during presentations: the heroic stories of sorely tested customers, driven to despair by their fruitless search at all levels of the organization to find the solution to their problem. In desperation, they finally vent their frustrations on social media, where their public cry for help is finally picked up by a watchful community manager, who moves heaven and earth to put matters to right, restoring the company's image and at the same time converting the customer into a fervent online brand ambassador!

Win-win!

Applause all round.

Hmm.

'KLM sucks'

Another example I often use in my presentations is based on an anecdote told by the Dutch marketeer Merijn Te Booij from Genesys.[18] As I recall it, the story revolves around his wife, who had to return to the Netherlands for a funeral. She booked a flight online via the Dutch airline KLM, but at the last moment needed to change her reservation. It sounds simple – but it wasn't. No matter what she tried, she was unable to make the change, neither online nor via the contact center. In response, an irritated and frustrated Te Booij posted a tweet: 'KLM sucks!' The airline, which has a good reputation for its active use of social media, picked up this comment online, contacted Te Booij directly through one of its conversation managers and got the problem sorted out in no time at all. As a result, this episode is now much quoted as an example of how a potentially damaging situation was rescued by a constructive online intervention.

Agreed, it is indeed a good illustration of the way in which an active social care policy can redress negative customer experiences. If the necessary support systems are in place, this policy can be both efficient and effective.

But viewed from the perspective of a contact center, the Te Booij story was an accident waiting to happen.

At an emotionally sensitive moment, the primary reservation channel – the website – was apparently unable to offer an option to carry out a transaction based on a reasonable and logical need of the customer. Getting in touch with the contact center also failed to resolve the problem, not even after the matter was passed up to supervisor level. The reason for this failed response was almost certainly related to the rigidity of the guidelines imposed on the contact center personnel, guidelines from which they did not dare to deviate. But when the social community team – which belongs to a different part of the organization – finally got involved in a last-ditch effort to rescue KLM's reputation, suddenly a different set of rules and regulations applied. They were allowed to do what the contact center could not.

In other words, the whole episode could have been avoided if the first two contact channels – the website and the contact center – had been allowed the same range of possibilities as the social community team. True, the world would have been denied an amusing anecdote, but the actual customer experience would have been much, much better.

Show me a success story of this kind, and I will probably show you a story in which the traditional channels failed, not because these channels are badly organized or because the agents failed to do their best, but simply because they were not allowed to do whatever was needed. Wouldn't the customer actually get a better service if the primary channel is properly equipped to meet his needs?

The mother of all examples – 'United Airlines breaks guitars' – is an excellent case in point. You probably already know the story, but if not, you can always join the 18 million others who have viewed it in recent years on YouTube.[19]

After the American band 'Sons of Maxwell' boarded a United Airlines flight at Chicago, one of the other passengers told them that the UA ground crew had been throwing their guitars cases around during the transfer of their luggage. When lead singer Dave Caroll discovered on arrival at their destination that his costly Tailor guitar had indeed been damaged, he started off on a long journey through the airline's many different processes and procedures, in the hope of finally securing an apology and some compensation.

After failing to secure either, he decided to protest through his music. He posted a song on YouTube – *'I should have flown with someone else, or drive by car, cause United breaks guitars...'* – and it quickly became an online sensation. He followed this up with two more songs in a similar vein, with a growing number of fans and publicity. Experts argue that this contributed to the huge drop in the price of United-shares during this period.

Later, Dave Carroll wrote a book[20] about his adventures and the almost unbelievable sequence of incompetent reactions by the United Airways service team. Today, he is a valued speaker about the way that one man's voice really can make a difference, if only it can get itself heard. Caroll has millions of hits on YouTube, although I secretly suspect that a large part of these come from the congresses and presentations where he is pushed forward as 'proof' of the absolute necessity for companies to join in with the new online world of social media.

Okay, it's an undeniably great story, and even a good song. But once again it is possible to ask whether things might have turned out differently – and better – if Mrs Irlweg, the head of UA's complaints department mentioned in the song, had done something more than just stick rigidly to the company's guidelines.

What if United's contact center had had the freedom to find a commercial solution to the complaint?

What if Mrs. Irlweg had been able to say 'yes' to Dave Caroll, instead of 'no, no, no!' The episode would have passed without notice.

So why don't managers in contact centers use this kind of story more, just to make precisely that point?

Reputation before experience

For many companies, the focus on social care is clearly more about polishing their public image than about providing an optimal customer experience. This becomes more apparent when the company's management of social media is located in a different part of the organization than the contact center – usually in either the marketing or communication department. This often results in a very different emphasis, with a higher degree of freedom of action. Liberated from concerns about fairness or the creation of precedents, extra efforts for the customer are now made with enthusiasm. Generally applicable conditions and/or internal procedures are willingly sacrificed on the altar of public reputation.

This kind of thinking is sometimes also applied to customer differentiation. In his book *CRM at the Speed of Light*[21] Paul Greenberg introduced the notion of a 'customer referral value', an indication of the range of impact of a customer's network and therefore his ability to help or harm your good name. He regards this as a better alternative to the traditional 'customer lifetime value' – the net value that a customer can generate during his entire association with the company over many years – as a means of differentiating the extent to which a company will make extra service-efforts in order to satisfy the customer's expectations.

Of course, the notion of service adjusted to reflect the value of the customer is nowadays a relatively normal phenomenon in the business world. However there is a risk that this is taken to a whole new level. Are we approaching a situation in which the more people who can hear you when you scream blue murder, the better the service it will get you? This is starting to look a lot like episodes from *Black Mirror* coming to life...

'All customers are equal, but some customers are more equal than others', or something like that. Suddenly, even George Orwell's pigs seem like amateurs...

The poisoned chalice

By offering a 'higher' level of service in this manner, there is, of course, a risk that the company will create a kind of pull effect, which will automatically suck

bpost has a near-miss with its own 'breaks guitars' scenario

In May 2012, bpost escaped from its own smaller version of 'United breaks guitars'. Somebody posted a text on Facebook about a dog that had been run over by a postal delivery van. This was immediately picked up by a number of sympathizers and reposted. For a time, it looked like the situation might go viral, but fortunately the storm blew itself out before things went that far.

Jo's dog was run over on her own property by a postal delivery van and the driver was such a coward that he just left the poor animal lying there and drove away without saying a word. Zina was a beautiful little pug who wouldn't harm a fly :(Jo put in a complaint to the post service but today heard that her complaint is unfounded!!! WTF!!! Please share this for Zina in the hope that some big cheese in the post office might eventually get to hear about it. Shame, shame, shame on you, bpost! RIP Zina, commiserations Jo.

You should be ashamed of yourself to treat people in this way when they have just lost something dear to them. The old saying is truer than ever!!! THE MORE I LEARN ABOUT PEOPLE, THE MORE I LIKE ANIMALS!!!

Like • React

bpost NL Hello Mieke. bpost deeply regrets this incident. We have contacted the local police and following their investigation it seems that we cannot be held responsible. We have notified this to the customer directly. Kind regards

Like • React

Figure 10: united at bpost - almost

It is certainly possible to question the wording of the answer. No doubt it is legally accurate and factually correct to refuse acceptance of liability for the incident. Even so, in terms of our previous dance metaphor it still looks like a pretty odd move - although honesty compels me to confess that this mail dates from the early years of online conversations, before the emergence of more customer-oriented community managers.

Be that as it may, in my opinion it was still possible - with a little empathy and a bit of creative thinking - to do much better. This is the kind of complaint where you need to look beyond the fixed procedures, which are not designed to cover statistical exceptions of this nature.

But ... that answer must be no different from the answer that would have given if the tragic fate of Zina was communicated to the company by letter or telephone. Consistency of response throughout the different channels is crucial.

people into that channel. Or as one of my managers recently put it: 'Nowadays, if I need xxx, I don't call them by phone any more, but send a tweet to the CEO instead. That's a lot quicker and I can get more things done.' Unless intended as an explicit strategy, this is an ideal way to open a whole Pandora's box of problems.

Confronted with a self-feeding spiral of expectations, the poor community manager will eventually find himself swamped by social care demands, leaving him little or no time to carry out his core task: talking about the company's products.

This is usually the moment when the company decides to transfer responsibility for this self-created (and excessive) volume of social care tasks to… the contact center.

A logical choice?

Probably, but viewed from an operational perspective it is not exactly a gift from the gods for the contact center. Rather something of a poisoned chalice. Because almost every link in the 'normal' complaint chain becomes more complex when carried out in these new channels:

- Identifying the real problem among the background noise created by hundreds of conversations and the ventilation of raw emotions.
- Identifying the customer under his social alias. Keeping an accurate and up-to-date list of telephone numbers, addresses and e-mail addresses has been a nightmare for contact centers for years. Prepare to multiply this complexity by a factor of x.
- Estimating the value of the customer. Typically, this is done using criteria such as the number of online followers. But to what extent is this an accurate reflection of the importance of the customer? And how do you prevent this from rebounding back in your face like a boomerang? Everyone in Flemish and Dutch contact center land remembers what happened when Youp van 't Hek (a well-known Dutch *cabaretier* and journalist) was given preferential treatment that was denied to his less famous son…[22]

- The correct routing of the question based on very sketchy information.
- Contacting the customer to try and finally get enough details about the real nature of the problem, so that you can solve it in the right way. Twitter (the most frequently used medium to report this kind of complaint) is now limited to just 280 characters – pre-2017 it was 140 - which for most complaint cases is wholly inadequate. Think, for example, of the details that an organization like bpost needs to find a lost parcel. A damn sight more than 280 characters! As a result, the first response sets in motion a whole ping-pong of tweets backwards and forwards, until in the end you still need to contact the customer directly – usually by phone – to find out what you really need to know. Efficient? I hardly think so...
- Identifying a solution that meets the high expectations of the customer (and is therefore actually worth the bother of communicating). These expectations relate to both speed of response ('now!') and the perceived quality ('because I am going to make public whatever you tell me!'). This requires a delicate balancing act, which, as we have already seen, is different from other channels.

Taking all this into account and assessing the situation in an impartial manner, it becomes clear that social care is a sub-optimal process for everyone involved. To find a real solution you need more information than social care provides and you also need to search for the right moments to contact the customer again. This conflicts with the rhetoric reigning over contact center discussions, concerning the importance of making things easy and solving everything in one go. Or not?

Shut up and dance with me

Yet for all the wisdom of the past few pages, it is often too late to do anything about it. The die has already been cast! A company that is already active on social media can no longer ignore its service provision via that channel. You might like to turn the clock back, but you can't. So get over it and get on with it.

This is certainly the case for companies that do more than simply monitor the social platforms. If you engage with these platforms, the legitimacy of your presence will stand or fall with your care process. If your answers on social media simply say that the customer should get in touch with the company by phone, this flies in the face of the entire logic on which these media are based.

You just can't do it. And if you do, you will quickly be bombarded with negative feedback that will damage your digital reputation.

Believe me, I know. I tried. I failed.

Viewed in these terms, for most companies social care becomes a kind of unavoidable collateral damage, but one that you need to be aware of and plan for in advance. It must form part of the strategic decision-making process and the contact center manager must be able to make his voice heard when such matters are discussed. And if you don't want to provide customer care via social media, there is a very simple solution: stay off social media! This is a domain where there are no fifty shades of grey; only black and white.

So if you do find yourself on the dance floor, and if the music is playing and people are looking at you, there is only one piece of advice I can give you: shut up and dance!

For a contact center, this means the following:

- Make yourself thoroughly familiar with the social media strategy of your company. Make sure that your agents are familiar with it as well and can translate it into practice during their daily activities. In fact, extend this to cover your company strategy in general. It is always strange (or at least it is to me) when people talk about a 'digital strategy'. There is only one strategy – and that is the company's – and the digital channel is just one way of implementing it. If not, we could start talking about a telephone strategy, a mail strategy, etc. Do you get my drift?
- Claim social care right from the very beginning as a task for the contact center. This might seem counter-intuitive, but do it anyway. The normal 'survival reflex' of most contact center managers is to try and place as much distance as they can between themselves and this kind of 'tedious' standard process. In reality, this 'head-in-the-sand' approach seldom works. Sooner or later (as we have seen), the proverbial 'hot potato' will land in your lap anyway, so you might as well anticipate the inevitable by asking to be in on the social care game right from the very start. In that way, you can at least influence the basic direction and discussions. This is in keeping with our definition in the previous chapter: all virtual customer processes should be dealt with by the contact center.
- Develop the right processes and ensure above all that there is consistency between the different channels.

'You shouldn't be sending a different answer on Twitter to the one you give through your telephoned-based customer service.'

> Digital director Dieter Van Esch of RCA, a company that has managed a number of high-profile public accounts, such as NMBS (Belgian rail) and De Lijn (Flemish bus service), in *De Tijd* magazine on the 25th of October 2013.

In essence, the way you deal with a customer should not vary from (incoming) channel to channel. Of course, it goes without saying that the form will be different, but the content must be consistent. This inevitably means that you will need to ask critical questions about the procedures you follow on social media:
- Do we want to deal with this kind of question in the same way every time? If so, does this mean we will have a standard contact center answer for use in all cases?
- Is it acceptable for us that the solutions we offer are made public in the social media marketplace, where all our other customers can see them?
- How can we organize ourselves to give out-of-the-box answers time after time, but still manage to satisfy the first two criteria?

- Teach your personnel how to dance. Ensure that they are capable of conversing with customers in the right way. Social media have their own etiquette, so make certain your people are familiar with it and follow it. In practice, this means that you will probably need to select and train a dedicated group of operatives to take turns in dealing with this channel. Communicate openly about your availability. Otherwise a 24/7 channel might have expectations that you are wholly unable to meet. Give your agents: the details of the right people they can contact within the company, so that they always have someone they can consult at short notice to help them to answer the more philosophical questions.

In short, do all the things that you are supposed to do for each different channel. Clothe our naked emperor, using the fashions you already know.

And never forget – irrespective of what some people might tell you – that social media will never be more than just one of the various contact channels you need to deal with, and probably not even the most important one.

Make sure that your service provision via your primary channels is maintained at a level of quality that neither generates negative commentary nor creates a pull effect. Not too little, not too much.

SOUNDBITE

Social media as an integrated channel at Lampiris

In a closing panel discussion at the Contact Center Congress one of the speakers disagreed vehemently with the arguments I have just made above about social care. Tom Van de Cruys, the CEO of the Belgian energy company Lampiris, views social media as being the best way 'to bring the customer into the board room'. In his company, social media are integrated as a channel into both the strategy and the operational processes.

I can't remember exactly just how seriously we disagreed, but it was enough to let him have his say on the matter here. So off we go... (interview by Koen Delvaux, who was then the innovation manager at Lampiris and is now CMO at Joyn).

'Not every company looks at social media as a channel that should be dealt with separately. At Lampiris, we have opted for an integrated approach.'

Lampiris began on social media as a result of the engagement of its CEO, Tom Van de Cruys. Tom is personally active on Twitter and began to answer customers via this channel in 2011. This was later supported professionally by a community manager. In this way, Lampiris built up a presence on Twitter, Facebook, LinkedIn and YouTube. 'A large part of our product is the service we provide. Social media make it possible for us to demonstrate this service capacity to the public in conversations that we conduct openly online. In other words, it's a form of marketing,' says Van de Cruys.

In addition to reputation management and customer care, right from the very beginning Lampiris saw other valuable benefits in its strategy focus on social media. Tom Van de Cruys again: 'Of course, our reputation is important. But in addition we also learn a lot from these conversations with our customers. Thanks to our direct interaction with them on Twitter we discover much quicker where we need to improve our performance. Problems appear first on Twitter and only then on the other channels. If you actively support social media in your company, this effect is significantly enhanced.'

This social media learning effect was introduced in two phases in Lampiris. In the first phase, they created a virtual team: personnel from different departments who in addition to performing their normal duties also took care of social media matters. During this phase, the relevant processes for the future were designed and various roles on social media were defined.

In the second phase Lampiris decided to integrate social media into their contact center. The daily interaction with customers was carried out by the same operatives who manned the telephones and answered the e-mails.

These operatives were given training about the right way to react to different kinds of posts on Facebook and Twitter, but there is no script and no standard answers. Every conversation must be assessed on its own merits, with empathy as the main guideline. The final responsibility remains with the community manager, who reports to both marketing and customer care.

'We have started a feedback loop from within the social media team,' says Tom Van de Cruys.

'When our operatives discover an inefficiency in a process, they contact the community manager. He consults with the operational manager and then communicates what has been agreed on back to the operative, who in turn informs the customer. If the change is important enough, it will be incorporated by the marketing department into our charter of promises. In this way, we win in terms of innovation speed thanks to the visibility of our customer care on social media.

Many organizations give a "VIP" service on social media, often to protect their reputation. At Lampiris we look at this in a different light and justify the extra attention we give to social media by regarding it as a way to exert constructive pressure on our own organization. This can work well, but not every company is capable of doing it. And the question is also whether or not we are now in danger of spoiling the customer, so that he comes to expect too much.'

Still a little bit call center: the telephone is not dead yet

Even in the relatively short span of my career, I have heard the telephone pronounced 'dead and buried' on more than one occasion. The first time was in the 1980s, when it was argued that the irresistible rise of internet and e-mail would soon sound the death knell for the good old phone. Hundreds of companies were faced with the challenge, almost overnight, of finding people in their call centers who were also capable of writing e-mails. Looking back with the benefit of hindsight, the discussion then seems oddly similar to the arguments you hear nowadays about social media. But although e-mails do indeed form an important part of today's contact work, for most centers they still represent a minority of contacts. In many cases, the main source of contacts is still the telephone.

The second predicted demise of the phone came in the 1990s, with the spectacular arrival on the scene of text messages. It was then claimed that young people, the customers of tomorrow, were only interested in real time communication via their cell phones, without the 'old fashioned' need to dial and talk. At the time, I was working for Belgacom (the Belgian telephone provider) and I can still remember the lively discussions we had with our colleagues in Proximus, the company's mobile wing...

Text messages are often used today for proactive push notifications: 'your order has been received', 'you are now calling on a roaming tariff', 'our technician is on his way', 'we have sent you an invoice', etc. But if we are honest with ourselves, surely everyone will concede that for inbound traffic the text message has barely left the ground – and is unlikely ever to do so.

Next came video-conferencing, which, for a while – and certainly after the launch of Skype – was also seen as the next 'big thing' that would sweep the phone aside. But this too has faded away in recent years, certainly as a mass medium. It is now used typically as a high-end channel; for example, by the major banks to conduct their personal investment contacts. As such, it remains very much a niche.

Figure 11: the continuing popularity of the telephone

And now we have social media, which we have already looked at in this context. In the final chapter I will argue that chat, which is now being put forward as the next new communication messiah, will go the same way as all its predecessors.

And what will we be left with at the end of the day? Exactly. With the conclusion that the telephone is far from dead. In fact, for the average contact center the telephone will continue to be one of the most important – if not the most important – channel of communication for many years to come.

This prediction is based on solid foundations:

- The telephone continues to score well for most of the elements that are important for a customer contact. This is clear from the results shown in figure 11.

Channels and Customer Journey – The House of Contact Centers (April 2018)

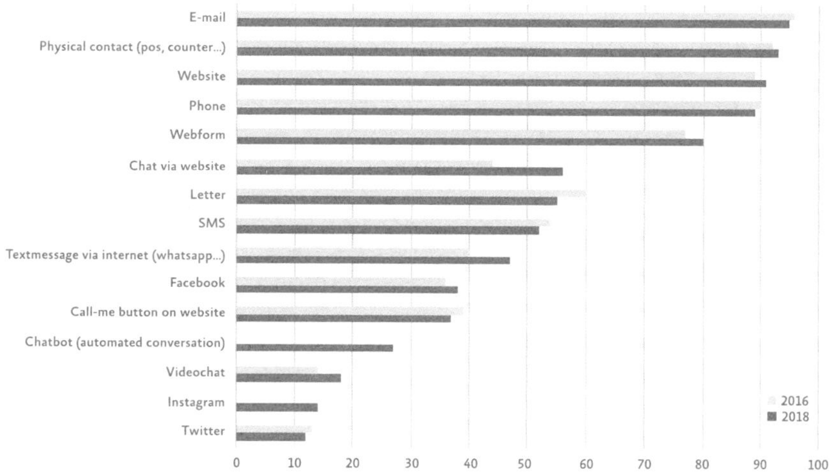

Figuur 12: channel preferences in Belgium

A representative sample of people aged between 16 and 75 years were interviewed on preferences and service expectations in March 2018. Results are shown in figure 12, including a comparison with similar research results from 2016. It is clear that the availability of a good information-based website can help most companies to eliminate contacts with a limited value. But when contact becomes unavoidable, the telephone continues to be an important channel. Of course, results of this kind are to some extent a self-fulfilling prophecy, influenced by the options that companies offer. People can only use the channels that are made available to them.

When asked about their 'trust'-level, the top three become 'all human': physical contact, e-mail and phone.

Channel preferences prove to be highly dependent on the nature of the contact. When customers are confronted with a service issue, phone jumps to first place as preferred channel, as is illustrated in figure 13.

When adding all of this up, and looking at the top two channel preferences, phone takes overall pole position (57%). This preference becomes even more extreme in emotionally charged or time-critical emergencies.

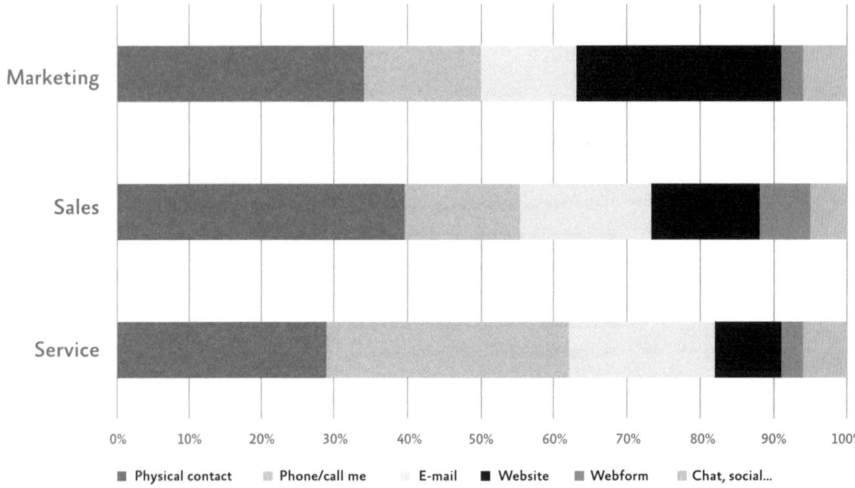

Figure 13: use of channels in specific customers journeys (THoCC research 2018)

Comparable results on an international level were published by Verint, in their 'Defining the Human Age' (2018). When dealing with an urgent request or complaint, phone becomes the most preferred channel.

The telephone is low threshold, always available and enables instant human dialogue, during which information can be freely exchanged, with all the emotional connotations this entails. Viewed from the perspective of the company, this is the easiest channel to integrate into the existing operational structure and the existing workforce. If we consider the way call centers came into existence and have developed over the years, the need for 'efficiency' will still favor the telephone for the foreseeable future.

- This is confirmed by the customers themselves. Recent research[23] has shown that the average Belgian citizen regards 'telephonic contact' as the most important channel for interaction. When you need to conduct a real dialogue, most people still reach for the phone.

And if any further proof were needed, research conducted by British Telecom and Avaya (2012[24], 2014[25]) into the channels that people think they will most use in future produced comparable results. With a score of more than 80% the telephone topped the poll by a mile. And social media? Down in thirteenth position...

The telephone of tomorrow is a smartphone

Of course, the telephone of tomorrow will almost certainly be a smartphone. Sales figures suggest that this trend is irreversible. On the face of it, this opens many interesting opportunities to introduce self-service via all different kinds of apps.

Think how much easier the exchange of information might become. For example, it is much simpler to check the status of a dispatched parcel by scanning a barcode with your smartphone than by having to type in a long code. Barcodes can be added to any physical carrier, allowing the smartphone to be used to reveal further information and explanation.

'Simple' consultation questions will move more and more into the domain of self-service. The (telephone) calls that the contact center continues to receive will be the more complex queries. The fact that this then increases the intrinsic value of these contacts is something that we will look at in more detail in a following chapter.

Choosing without losing

The decision about which channels of communication a contact center will support needs to be based on strategic considerations. This in turn will be based on the specific characteristics of the company and its customers. In other words,

		IVR	Agent	Mail	Web-form	Letter	Fax	Chat	Social	Website
Product information	price	N/A	M	L	M	L	L	N/A	L	H
	functions	N/A	M	L	M	L	L	N/A	L	H
	availability	H	M	L	M	L	L	N/A	L	H
Channel information	location	N/A	M	L	L	L	L	N/A	L	H
	opening hours	H	M	L	L	L	L	N/A	L	H
Orders		L	H	L	M	L	L	N/A	L	M
Help for starters		N/A	M	L	L	L	L	N/A	L	H
Invoicing	information	N/A	H	L	M	L	L	N/A	L	H
	credit note	N/A	H	L	L	L	L	N/A	L	N/A
	payment follow-up	N/A	M	L	L	L	L	N/A	L	H
Complaint		N/A	H	L	M	L	L	N/A	L	N/A
User support	use	N/A	M	L	L	L	L	N/A	L	H
	defects	H	M	L	L	L	L	N/A	L	H
Termination		N/A	N/A	L	N/A	H	M	N/A	N/A	N/A

yes
okay
no!

Figure 14: a channel preference matrix

there is no single 'one-size-fits-all' answer. The most important thing is that the contact center and the rest of the organization must be on the same wavelength. You might reasonably expect that the contact center should take the lead in this discussion. After all, it is the center that will be most affected by the decisions taken. Even so, this leading role is seldom granted to the center, as we saw all too clearly in the earlier example with social media.

To streamline this discussion, the use of a matrix as shown in figure 14 can be beneficial. It summarizes in a single table not only which type of channel strategy should be used for which type of interaction but also the eagerness with which interactions are considered.

A. The different rows are the possible stages in the life cycle of the customer, with particular attention to the stages which can be reasonably expected to result in interaction with the contact center.

B. The columns represent the different (possible) communication channels for which the contact center is responsible. Depending on the nature of the company, the matrix can be further supplemented with other options to create a multi-channel discussion and, for example, to plot the role of physical channels. The method of working remains the same.

Complaints as an illustration in the matrix

Because dealing with complaints will become a major topic in one of the following chapters, it may be useful to have a look at them within the context of the matrix exercise. Before we start, however, remember that the completion of the matrix in figure 14 is wholly fictitious – it is not intended to reflect the position of Belgacom or bpost. It is, however, fairly close to my own personal opinion on these matters.

The key question is, of course, which channels will the company use to support dealing with customer complaints? In other words, we need to find the 'complaints' row in the matrix and decide which channels we are going to fill in, and how. It has already been decided that the company is not prepared to offer a chat option; not only for complaints, but also for all other customer interactions. It is retained in the matrix simply to show that the option was considered (and dismissed) during the discussion process:

	IVR	Agent	Mail	Web-form	Letter	Fax	Chat	Social	Website
Complaints	?	?	?	?	?	?	not	?	?

Figure 15.1

- Complaints are a customer reaction we would prefer not to have. In essence, what we ideally want is to have nothing other than happy and satisfied customers, who never have a reason to complain. Research into causes and reasons for complaints must therefore seek to amend processes and communication in such a way that they generate as few complaints as possible. That is why this row is given a dark color. In all that follows, and even though we will always try to help the customer to the best of our ability, the whole organization needs to be aware that everything must be done to try and avoid this kind of contact.

	IVR	Agent	Mail	Web-form	Letter	Fax	Chat	Social	Website
Complaints	?	?	?	?	?	?	not	?	?

Figure 15.2

- Of course, when a customer does feel dissatisfied, we certainly want to know about it. And we cannot stop him from expressing his dissatisfaction in the manner of his own choosing.
- But we prefer him to do it by telephone. Human contact with a well-trained agent will at least ensure that the emotion inherent in the situation is toned down. In offline channels, it is too easy for the customer to give full vent to his anger and frustration, allowing his emotions to get the better of him in a spiral of furious invective. What's more, in a conversation it is possible to immediately ask for information about all the elements that will be needed to solve the problem. This prevents us from annoying the customer again later on by having to ask for additional information.
- For this reason, our telephone number will be explicitly mentioned in all communication as the company's channel for dealing with complaints (preference 'H'). 'Phone us' is the only published call to action.

	IVR	Agent	Mail	Web-form	Letter	Fax	Chat	Social	Website
Complaints	?	H	?	?	?	?	not	?	?

Figure 15.3

- For other channels, where the initiative rests with the customer, we will respect his choice, but with a degree of enthusiasm dictated by the needs of organizational efficiency (preferences 'M' and 'L'). Web-forms, if correctly filled in, at least allow us to guide the customer towards providing all the information we need in the right format. This is therefore the only other channel marked with an 'M'. All the others are channels that we 'have to' rather than 'want to' use. This is the same reasoning that we followed earlier in relation to social care:

	IVR	Agent	Mail	Web-form	Letter	Fax	Chat	Social	Website
Complaints	?	H	L	M	L	L	not	L	?

Figure 15.4

- The company will never take the initiative to offer a 'self-service' option for complaints via IVR (interactive voice response) or by providing a complaints page on the website. Instead, the customer will be referred to a telephone number or (assuming the website allows this kind of dynamic programming) asked to complete a web-form (only during the hours when the contact center is closed). These channels can also be used for other interactions.

	IVR	Agent	Mail	Web-form	Letter	Fax	Chat	Social	Website
Complaints	not	H	L	M	L	L	not	L	niet

Figure 15.5

C. A color code can be used to indicate the extent to which the company wants to encourage a particular kind of interaction. Complaints, for example, are something you wish to avoid (dark blue), but when they occur (and they will) the contact center needs to know how they should be dealt with. In contrast, sales orders are the kind of interaction (white) you want to encourage and actively pursue. In a following chapter we will look further at this process of estimating the 'desirability' of a contact, both from the perspective of the company and the customer.

D. The matrix can then be filled in by indicating for each type of contact which channels are provided and with what level of preference: H(igh), M(edium) or L(ow). 'No' means 'not to be accepted, supported or offered in any circumstances'. For instance, in the fictitious example shown in figure 14 a customer who wishes to chat about his query will find himself disappointed, since the company does not support this technically as an option. The customer will instead be offered the use of several other channels, but the H/M/L code is used to indicate which channels the company most and least prefers. An 'L' means that this channel should be avoided or its use by the customer discouraged, although the customer will always still be helped, even if he persists in using that channel. For example, if you want to discourage letters, you can bury your postal address deep in an obscure part of your website, while giving repeated prominence to your telephone number. But if the customer still insists on writing to you, his letter must be opened, read and responded to.

In figure 14, for example, the termination of a service is deliberately made relatively difficult for the customer by only offering the use of high-threshold channels. Within the context of customer retention, this may be a conscious choice, but it is certainly something that needs to be discussed in advance. Perhaps the marketeers do not want to go beyond a certain level of customer irritation in light of possible future win-back efforts?

Making considerations of this kind explicit and discussing them openly is the purpose of the matrix exercise. That is why the exercise is best initiated and conducted under the guidance of the contact center, although it must, of course, also be opened to all other departments.

The completion of the matrix forces contact centers to think specifically about the company's communication strategy but will ultimately provide it with a very clear 'why' for everything it does. It also stimulates general thought within the organization about the best way to achieve the desired channel funneling and makes it possible for the company to develop and publish consistently accurate 'calls to action'.

If one channel is preferred for a particular transaction, all communication relating to this transaction must be geared to reflect this. Think carefully about where and how you publish your telephone numbers, website references and e-mail addresses.

Experience suggests that channel funneling becomes easier when decisions are black and white. A channel is in or out.

Meet the real conversation manager[26]

The contact center agents are the real conversation managers and are therefore, with a nodding acknowledgement to the work of Steven Van Belleghem, the real human component in a business world that is becoming increasingly digital.

A telephone contact with an operative who wants to help and has the knowledge and possibilities to make things happen is a form of genuine conversation that contains everything that people find important.

Figure 16: what makes contacts human... (slide shown at the Contact Center Congress in 2012)

Because these conversations take place with real customers, their successful completion forms to a large extent the basis for the way in which contact centers are able to create 'value'.

We will look at this in much greater depth in the following section.

Always a value center

The fact that we now know to speak of a contact center rather than a call center is only a reflection of the different channels that are now available. It says nothing about the central dilemma relating to the positioning of the contact center within the organization. Irrespective of the modes of communication it uses, what should be the role of the center within the company, when viewed from a commercial perspective?

The answer is deceptively simple. Contact centers always contribute to the company's value creation. In other words, they are always a value center, in the literal sense of the term. And they should be treated as such.

Full stop.

New line.

No discussion.

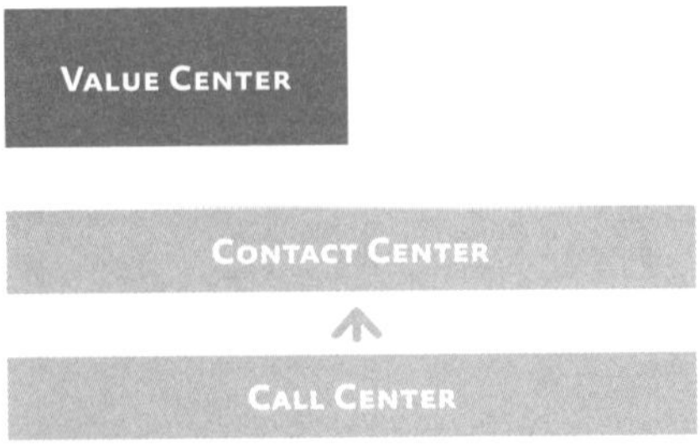

Figure 17: always a value center

By definition, contact centers are always engaging with customers. And marketing gurus like Peppers and Rogers[27] have been preaching for years that 'the customer' is the only true source of commercial income. It doesn't require a giant leap of thought to conclude that a part of the organization specifically set up to deal exclusively with large volumes of contacts with this source of income will therefore also be valuable per se. What's more, if this was not the case – if contact centers would yield no value – surely they would have been scrapped ages ago. You can regard it as a kind of organizational credo: 'I exist, therefore I have value'.

Even so, this simplistic but sound reasoning is often insufficient to convince many senior managers. This explains the endless discussions within companies about the return on investment from contact centers. It is remarkable, however, that a large part of this discussion is conducted from within the contact centers themselves. Whether this is because the centers feel a need to justify their existence or because they are plagued by some kind of organizational inferiority complex, the whole sector seems to feel obliged to take part in a struggle with other (marketing) departments to validate their right to survive, with the customer as the battleground and their ability to create added value as their battle cry. You will recall that this already complicated the simple task of defining the contact center concept.

The value of customer service

In their haste to prove the 'value' of the contact center, many of its champions are guilty of taking an intellectual short cut. They focus on the importance of "service" in general. The literature is full of impressive statistics that do indeed confirm the economic value of service.

This is logical. 'Service' is unquestionably an effective element within the organizational value chain and therefore forms part of the organization's strategic and competitive advantage.

Since the work of Michael Porter,[28] basic management 1:1 has looked like this:

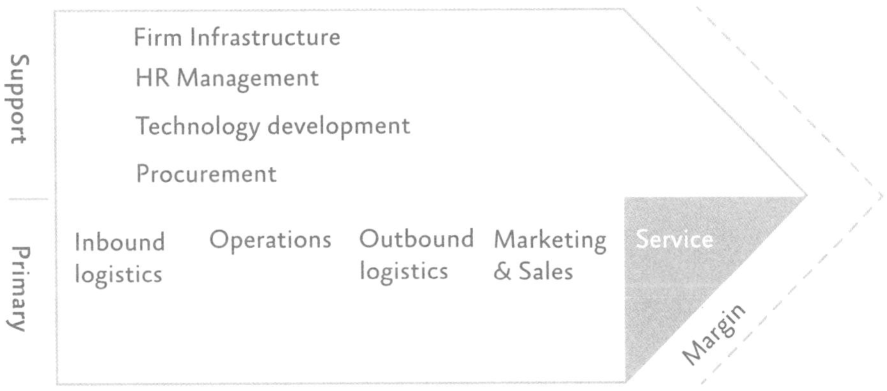

Figure 18: Porter's value chain

Again, there are libraries overflowing with books anxious to explain the importance of the 'customer experience'. Specific publications relating to the contact center's role in this experience also offer a generous sprinkling of laudatory and confirmatory figures in this respect.

This 'service' aspect is often positioned as the element of the value chain that is most difficult for others to copy. In time, every competitor can probably bring an equivalent offer to market, possibly even at a lower price. But the same is not true of (the experience of) service provision. This is an area where a real competitive advantage can be gained. Even in the sectors where government regulation plays a bigger role in the setting, for example, of sector-wide regulations for periodicity, conditions and other service parameters. After all, these regulations are only intended to serve as a kind of Olympic minimum, not as a differentiator. Differentiation occurs when companies (far) exceed the minimum in a unique way.

Viewed in these terms, it will surprise no one that outstanding service tops the hit parade of customer expectations. But automatically linking this to arguments in favor of the merits of contact centers is – sadly – taking things an enthusiastic step too far.

Customer service is not a department

Contact centers all tend to resemble each other. Most of them make use of the same kind of large call center platform, which means they end up implementing broadly the same operational processes.

Where they can make a difference is in the way the individual customer is helped; in other words, through the center's underlying processes and instructions. Do you remember Mrs Irlweg and her 'no' during the 'guitar' saga...?

This all goes much further than just the contact center itself.

Lee Cockerell, the former Executive Vice President of Walt Disney World, described the situation well when he said that 'customer service is not a department'.[29]

To begin with, he feels it necessary to make a distinction between 'service' and 'customer service'. Service is something, like products, for which the customer pays. In return for the price that you ask, the customer expects you to perform certain tasks on his behalf. The 'value' the customer derives from this arrangement is the ratio between what the service provides and what it costs.

In contrast, customer service embraces the customer's entire experience of your organization at all times and at all touchpoints. In other words, the totality of his experience, which will inevitably make a lasting and irrevocable impression in his mind about your company, product and/or brand.

This customer experience can therefore be described as 'the way a customer remembers and feels about a series of interactions with your company'.[30] In essence, it is about emotions; the emotions resulting from a whole series of different contacts with your organization. This is often also known as the 'customer journey', which is one of today's most popular buzz phrases in the business world.

This link with emotions becomes explicit during the so-called 'moments of truth'. These moments are based on content that is so emotionally charged that they have the potential to create a strong reaction – and therefore powerful memories – in the mind of the customer. The term came to prominence in a book of the same title by the Swedish author Jan Carlzon (SAS-Scandinavian Airlines), in which he wrote that 'SAS is created fifty million times a year, 15 seconds at a time. These 50 million moments of truth are the moments that ultimately decide whether SAS will succeed or fail as a company'.[31]

The value of service:
a short selection of facts, figures and opinions from contact center land.

With a score of 45%, customer service is by some distance the most important influencing factor in securing customer loyalty. It comfortably exceeds product quality (30%), price (19%) and brand (6%).

Genesys Telecommunication,
2007, *presentation for Belgacom – proximus.*

Some 85% of customers are prepared to pay more in return for the guarantee of an exceptional customer experience. Eight out of every ten customers will cease to do business with a company that gives them a bad customer experience, with 75% claiming that they will never return.

Customer Experience Rapport van Rightnow,
as detailed in Telecommerce 11/12 2010

85% of customers are happy to pay more for a better customer experience. 89% will take their business to a rival company if they suffer a bad customer experience.

'Fast, simple, flexible and proactive',
François Kroes, in Telecommerce 10/2013.

52% of the respondents stated that a good customer service experience would be a contributory factor to their repeat buying. 55% said that they had changed supplier after having a bad customer experience. 48% said that they would advise others not to use products or services from a company that had given them a bad customer experience.

ZenDesk study from 2013, cited in *The Effect of Poor Customer Service, and what to do about it*, Compare Business Products.

76% of consumers say that they would pay 5% more for a better customer experience. 55% would pay 10% more and 10% would pay 25% more. 66% of consumers said that an improved customer service would result in them placing more orders.

Accenture study,
mentioned in *Measure To Manage*, Syngro 2013.

69% of consumers have changed supplier at least once during the last 12 months as a result of poor customer service.

Accenture 2014 retail survey,
mentioned in *Why do customers tolerate bad service*, Syngro 2014.

Customer Experience remains an important driver when choosing a service provider, especially with the older generations

Verint, *Defining Human Age*, 2018

Since Jan Carlzon first developed the concept, it has been used as a kind of *passe-partout* in a whole variety of discussions.

All the many different touchpoints play a role, ranging from TV commercials and the 'look-and-feel' of your corporate website to the behavior of the receptionist at your front desk. Every member of staff can have an impact in his or her own way on moments of truth, either directly or indirectly.

Hence Cockerell's claim that customer service is much more about everyone in the company having the right attitude than about simply delegating tasks to people who – poor things – have to man the telephone all day.

From pure efficiency to emotional management

Does this then mean that we need to play down the role of the contact center, almost to the point of irrelevance?

No, it doesn't.

According to our earlier definition of the contact center, it is the most efficient way to deal with large volumes of (non-physical) customer contacts. As a result, the contact center almost automatically starts to generate a pull effect: numerous contacts with a high potential in emotional content are funneled towards it. As we saw in our discussion about channels in figure 14, this means that the contact center is one step ahead of the game in comparison with other departments. The majority of 'moments of truth', with all their emotional charging, are directed towards one of the center's various communication channels.

As a result, the contact center – more than simply creating value through efficiency – also plays a crucial role in shaping the customer's emotional experience of the brand, at precisely the moment when the customer most feels in need of a safety net.

Emotions make a lasting impression

Experiences create emotions and emotions, much more than facts, determine how we react to a specific brand or product. Our brain has the curious habit of transforming experiences into established facts.

My mother, for example, is convinced that a certain Dutch company consistently produces low-quality television sets, simply because she once – just once – had a bad experience with a repair carried out on her set. No amount of facts and figures in reputable studies can shake her from this conviction. Our emotional side dominates our rational side much more easily than the other way around.

To illustrate this point in the Expert Class, I always use an exercise that I first heard from Professor Christian Bluemelhuber of the Solvay Business School.[32]

I ask the participants if they have a partner and, if they do, I ask for a few facts about them. Usually, I am given things like name, date of birth, job, hobbies, color of hair, shoe size, etc. I usually stop before it gets awkward...

If the participants love their partners – and let us hope that they do – the reasons 'why' they love them will have nothing to do with these factual elements. Their affection is based on something much more important than a list of attributes.

In my case, for example, the reasons why I love Carla have little to do with the fact that she was born on the 3rd of October, works in a purchasing department, loves to cook and is the most beautiful blond on the planet.

Love is more a question of sharing a common history, its good times and bad times, its happiness and sorrow, its joyful births and tragic deaths. In other words, it is about experiences.

And if this applies in a human relationship, it applies equally in the relationship between a customer and a company or brand. Experiences create emotions. And emotions make lasting impressions.

By definition, the 'moments of truth' mentioned by Jan Carlzon contain this emotional aspect.

This has been perfectly expressed by Tony Hsieh, the CEO of Zappos, the e-commerce shoe company which has become impossible to avoid, Gangnam-style, whenever you want to talk about the creation of good service:

'As unsexy and low-tech as it may sound, our belief is that the telephone is one of the best branding devices out there. You have the customer's undivided attention for five to ten minutes, and if you get the interaction right, what we've found is that the customer remembers the experience for a very long time and tells his friends about it.

Moments of truth for a mobile phone operator: call the contact center!
When I was still working at Belgacom, our colleagues in the mobile phone wing Proximus once drew up a specific list of the moments they regarded as 'moments of truth'; in other words, the moments when the customer feels emotional or can react emotionally. Examples included the blocking of a phone number after theft, disputes over an unexpectedly high invoice, or even the cancellation of a subscription following the subscriber's death. In this way, their marketing department eventually arrived at a total of eleven explicitly defined moments of truth. For each of these eleven the explicit call to action was...' call the contact center'!

The Proximus communication strategy, which the company hoped its customers would follow, was therefore to allow all emotionally charged contacts to be processed by the contact center.

So what does this tell us about 'value'?

And what is the situation like in your organization...?

Too many companies think of their call centers as an expense to minimize. We believe that it's a huge untapped opportunity for most companies... ignoring its potential to increase the lifetime value of the customer.'[33]

In other words, Hsieh confirms the need for and the value of the contact center, as a place for interaction with customers that leaves behind a memory and thereby contributes to overall customer value, which in turn has a positive impact on the brand. Zappos goes to extreme lengths to give its contact center the necessary freedom of movement to deal with these interactions in the manner that seems most appropriate for all concerned. With this in mind, the company also allocates part of its marketing budget to the contact center.

We have already seen that the growing number of options for customers to find their own information has increased the complexity of interactions for contact center operatives. The future role of the contact center will be to focus on solving these more complex problems, as demonstrated in figure 19.

Figure 19: from transaction to solution

In this way, the 'value' that the contact center generates for the company also evolves. The pure cost management component (efficiency) is increasingly supplemented by the management of emotions and experiences.

This ability to solve problems or answer questions has a huge impact on the customer's total experience of the company, as illustrated in figure 20:[34]

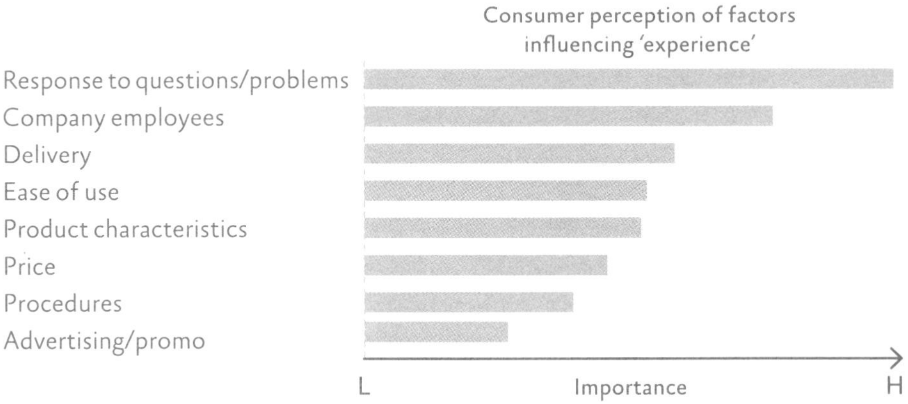

Figure 20: customer perception on 'experience'

Much more than product characteristics or marketing actions, it is the way his questions and problems are dealt with that will ultimately determine the customer's 'experience' of your company.

It is also worth noting how very different the graphic in figure 20 would have looked if the X-axis had represented the (marketing) budget expenditure. Not every company can or wants to be a Zappos...

'We bring relief'

The emotional contribution made by the contact center can perhaps best be described as: 'we bring relief!'

Of course, any contact center worth the name can easily draw up a more impressive-sounding mission statement than this, but it will only produce a text which – to paraphrase Dilbert – 'means everything to those who wrote it and nothing to those who have to read it'.

'We answer questions' might be a reasonable alternative, but this focuses more on the 'what' of the contact center, rather than on the all-important 'why'. No, 'we bring relief' sums it up best of all. The customer has a problem or a question. Perhaps he has already tried to find a solution or an answer, but was unable to do so at any other touchpoint. As a result, he has an unfulfilled need that persuades him to now get in touch with the contact center. When the customer discovers that this need can be satisfied by a friendly and empathic member of the contact center staff, this creates in him a sense of... relief, even if the final outcome of the contact is negative. Or as the old saying puts it: 'The certainty of misery is better than the misery of uncertainty'.

This feeling of relief, at the moment when the customer goes in search of it and urgently needs it, is much more difficult to create without human contact: 'It is very hard to have emotional loyalty without a human interaction'.[35]

Put simply, the contact center always writes a page in the emotional story of the customer's experience – and, hopefully, a positive one.

Value for the customer and the company in every phase of the life cycle

Whether for dealing with standard transactions or for more complex (emotional) problems, the contact center plays a role in each phase of the customer life cycle.

Phase in the customer life cycle	Value creation for the customer	Value creation for the company (optimizing income)	Value creation for the company (optimizing cost)
Informing	✓	✓	
Advising	✓	✓	✓
Buying	✓	✓	✓
Paying		✓	✓
Starting up	✓		✓
Using	✓		✓
Terminating	✓		

We have just seen how the emotional component in the contact leads to value creation. However, it is also possible to reason from a more mundane financial perspective. After all, we have said repeatedly that in origin the contact center is the most cost-effective way of dealing with large volumes of contacts.

As shown above, it is possible to summarize in a schedule the different ways that the contact center contributes to value in each phase of the customer life cycle. This value can be created for the customer and/or the company by the optimization of income or costs.

In this way, the contact center becomes the natural 'ally' of almost every other part of the organization.

Partner	Added value created by the contact center
Financial department:	• The contact center helps to follow up accounts receivable and bad debts and is allocated a package of tasks that forms an immediate and integral part of the financial process. • 'Invoicing' is often a moment of truth. The proper follow-up of customer reactions can ensure that future invoicing is more accurate and better implemented. The contact center is often the place where customer details are collected and corrected. • During the processing of an invoice complaint the collection of any outstanding sum is usually suspended. The efficient handling of complaints can therefore help to improve cash flow.
Marketing:	• The contact center functions as a source of real time customer information, with valuable feedback about the way campaigns, products and services are actually experienced by customers. • True to its origins, the contact center is one of the weapons used by the marketing department to give an added boost to commercial campaigns. • The contact center contributes actively towards different customer-related objectives (sales, loyalty, satisfaction).
Sales:	• The contact center can prepare the ground for sales by identifying real leads from amidst the general 'noise' of customer contacts and by making appointments with these prospects. The center can also contribute directly to sales figures (see further). • The contact center, of which the back office is an integral part, can ensure that 'sales' are effectively converted into 'orders' and, more importantly, 'payments'. • The contact center takes over 'difficult' customer contacts, so that the sales teams can concentrate on what they are best at: selling.

In a following chapter we will see that this picture of harmonious collaboration between departments is sadly not always reflected in practice. Though this is more a result of defective organizational structure rather than a fundamental misconception of the original starting point.

SOUNDBITE

The value of the contact center for energy company Eneco, according to Christophe Degrez, CEO

'Contact center? You mean value center!

At Eneco, we are convinced that, in addition to a good price and the guaranteed sustainable source of our electricity in Belgium, customer experience is the third main reason why people decide to change their energy supplier.

We have maintained this vision ever since we started to supply electricity on the consumer market and our operational organization has been geared accordingly. Not every company does that. If I need to phone the contact center of my telecom provider, it's like a nightmare: first I am talked at by a computerized voice; then I am played all the supplier's latest radio ads; next I am guided through a maze of menu options; and then finally, when 10 minutes later I at last get through to a real human being, having obediently entered my mobile number as requested, what is the first thing I hear? "Hello, caller. Can I please have your number again?" It's enough to drive you mad.

Customer expectations have evolved. And a good thing, too. The basic expectation of our customers is that their problem can be solved with a single telephone call or e-mail, so that they don't have to contact us a second time. In addition, they also want to be helped at double-quick speed by a competent operative. But above all, they want to feel that this operative is genuinely interested in helping them.

Because we at Eneco attach such great importance to customer experience, we decided right from the very beginning to organize our own customer service. In concrete terms, this means no IVR and no external personnel or managers. Instead, we have our own team of champions, who can answer all our customers' questions during every phase of the customer life cycle. We don't recruit these champions on the basis of how fast they can type an e-mail or deal with a telephone call, but based on how they match our value profile: sustainability, authenticity, togetherness, customer-friendliness. In other words, it's all about their attitude and their ambition to help our customers.

We also make all these things important inside the organization by taking daily measurements of customer satisfaction levels and the NPS,[36] based on the customers who have contacted us that day. What's more, we effectively use the results as coaching tools and guidance mechanisms throughout the entire organization, from the senior management target sheet to the regular appraisal reviews we hold with each champion.

Ensuring alignment around the vision is crucial, because in this way everyone knows exactly what they are contributing to the successful realization of our objectives.

The fruits of this policy are of real value to all concerned. Our customers can experience our genuine commitment firsthand on the telephone and, as a result, are happy to recommend Eneco to their family and friends. Our champions are super-motivated and happy in their work, and often move on to other functions in customer service or elsewhere in the organization. It's a win-win for everyone.

This is what I mean when I talk about the Eneco bath. In a few years' time, organizations that are lucky enough to employ one of our Eneco champions will be able to do so in full confidence, knowing that their new colleague has been 'steeped' in Eneco values. You can compare it with the way the style of some strategic consultancy agencies is easily recognizable. And that's something I am proud of.'

The contact center as the voice of the customer

'When you're sitting on oil... drill.'

This pearl of wisdom from the Texan oil industry applies equally to contact centers. In fact, it is perhaps the way that the centers can best make a valuable contribution to their companies. If the most emotional customer experiences continue to find their way to the company through the contact center, this provides them with unique real-time insights into what the customer is feeling, what moves him and what interests him.

If the contact center can succeed in supplementing its traditional (and largely figure-based) reporting of results (see further on) with this kind of relevant and revealing information, it can help to create a significant competitive advantage that rival organizations will not be able to match.

What's more, when the contact center is able to provide insights that specifically clarify the reason for a particular call or problem, this will springboard the center several links up the value chain.

'We, General Electric, only have two sources of competitive advantage:
- *the ability to learn more about our customers faster than competition;*
- *the ability to turn that learning into action faster than the competition.'*

Jack Welch

This role of the contact center as 'voice-of-the-customer' barometer is steadily increasing in importance. But first let's take another sly look at social media. The ease with which these media are able to spot new trending topics at Board level has so far not been equaled by the contact center. In one sense this is odd: the centers have a huge amount of information at their disposal, often from customers who form a more representative sample of the population. As a result, the centers should be better and more reliably able to assess which issues are of concern to the public and how these issues make them feel. What do they like and what do they hate? What makes them happy and what makes them sad?

To correct this situation, contact center managers will need to step more boldly out of their comfort zone. Traditionally, they approach the operation of their centers as though they were 'call factories', confining their reports to a limited and almost literal translation of input and output.

This is a yoke that the contact centers must learn to shake off as quickly as possible. Only then will they be able to better fulfill their role as 'a window into the world of the customer'. Only then will they be able to mine the gold that lies hidden in the content of those thousands and thousands of contacts and in the emotions (and their possible causes) that govern them.

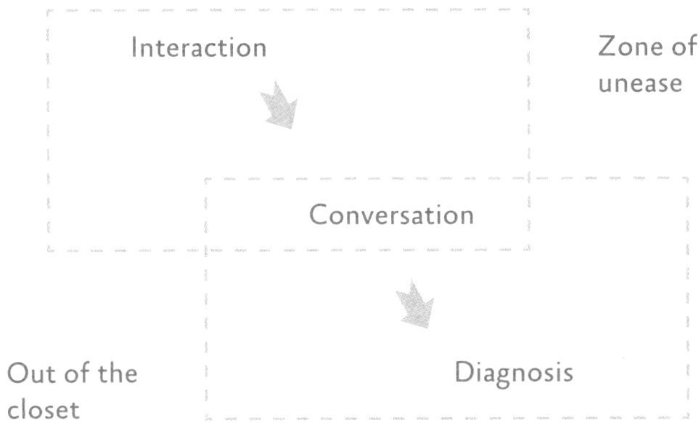

Figure 21: the contact center comes out of the closet!

From Doctor Doolittle to Doctor House

During my presentations I like to use a metaphor (*which also reveals my addiction to TV and film*) to demonstrate the evolution of contact centers in their role of diagnosing customer contacts.

In the past, it was often only the contact center - like Dr. Doolittle - that was capable of talking to those strange creatures, 'the customers'. It was necessary to understand the customer explaining in their own language what was wrong, so that their pain and anxiety could be relieved. 'Talk to the animals' as a strategic differentiator. However, this role was very reactive and always one-to-one. The rest of the world looked at it with a certain incomprehension (not to mention a good deal of suspicion), but was glad nonetheless that someone was there to do it.

But today's contact centers also have need of a Dr. House, someone who can use his cool analytical powers to look beyond the obvious symptoms and make the right diagnoses of very complex problems. In the hospital he is still a bit of an 'odd-one-out' and can sometimes be highly confrontational towards his colleagues, but he is recognized and accepted in his role. This forces the contact center and its surrounding entourage out of their comfort zone...

It has been clear for some time that contact centers need to evolve from the simple processing of interactions to the managing of emotions in real conversations with customers. They owe that much to their central role in the moments of truth.

But even greater added value can be gleaned from the proper diagnosis of those conversations, the discovery of causes and the sharing of insights. Notwithstanding how little this has been done in the past and irrespective of the discomfort it will cause to the managers who will be obliged to 'come out of the closet' to make this happen. They must have the courage to leave the safe haven of the operational and the transactional, voyaging instead through the stormier but more exciting – and more rewarding – waters of their customers' emotions.

When the contact center can point out to the other departments in the organization precisely where the main problems are located, as well as clarify their causes and their impact, its value to the company as a whole will become even greater than it already is.

The contact center is excellently placed to do this. It has structural insight into the 'quality' (as experienced by the customers) of the processes, the product and the related communication and commercial policy.

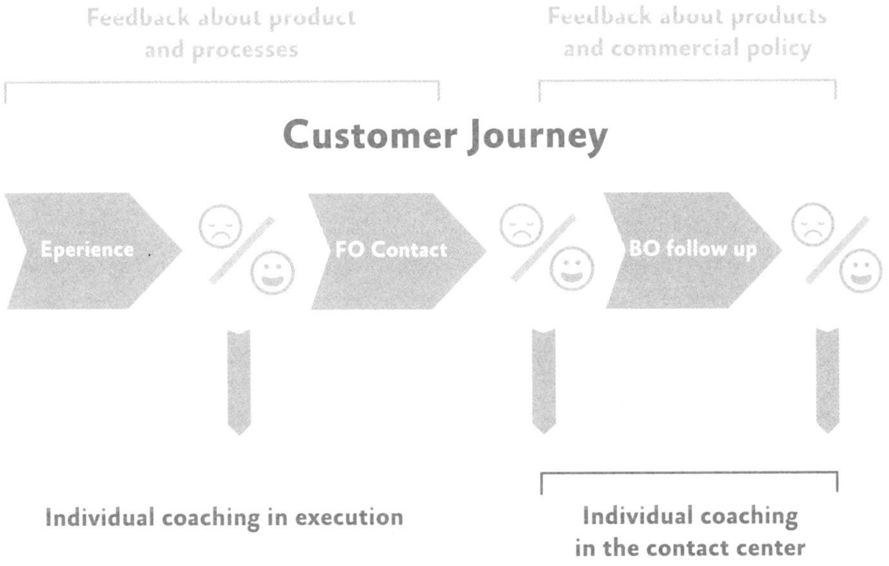

Figure 22: the feedback role of the contact center

Figure 22 sketches the moment when and the way in which the contact centers gets a privileged view of the emotions of the customer.

When the customer makes contact, he has already had a first experience of the company. The interaction with the contact center is a reaction to that experience. The extent to which this reaction is the one the company wanted, will depend on the context.

Be that as it may, the agent in the contact center is immediately in a position to witness the emotions of the customer relating to that experience. Using this as a basis for drawing up combined documentation detailing the content and the emotion of the contact makes it possible to identify useful connections and formulate structured improvement initiatives for the future. These are not limited to the coaching of the individual agent or the purely transactional handling of the contact. If a similar kind of incident repeatedly provokes a similar kind of reaction in the future, it is possible to make a conscious choice to do something (or nothing) to amend the relevant processes, the product and/or the implementation of the service.

At bpost, for example, distribution complaints are received and processed by the contact center, but are then systematically discussed elsewhere in the organization with individual postmen and women. At the same time, however, it is possible to sketch a consolidated image of the way in which our processes,

Why on earth?

At a Contact Center Excellence Congress,[37] Peter Sinden, the director of Sales & Service at the Liverpool Victoria insurance company, told how his organization had actively made use of their contact center to search for operational improvements. Personnel were encouraged to share their WOEs *(why-on-earth* reflexes) when they were expected by the company to give a particular answer to the customer, but couldn't for the life of them figure out why. Sinden's own experience suggests that if the operatives are unable to answer this question for themselves, there is probably something wrong with the underlying processes, procedures or products. Or perhaps the communication is not as effective as it should be.

But of one thing you can be certain: if the personnel are puzzled by something, the customers will be puzzled by it as well.

In the case of Liverpool Victoria this often relates (unsurprisingly) to the small print in their policies or the cumbersome administration that hinders them in their ambition to become 'Britain's best loved insurer'.

Do you know the WOEs in your organization? Or do you just hope there aren't any? Perhaps you should have a look at your contact center anyway. Just in case...

SOUNDBITE

Koen Van Gerven, CEO at bpost: the evolution of the contact center as the crucial mouthpiece of the customer

'For years, bpost has had a strong focus on customer-oriented thinking and functioning. Over time, the position of the contact center as the feedback channel for this focus has become ever more important.

Viewed historically, it has always had this role, by virtue of its responsibility for managing complaints. That is not illogical, given the very formal quality demands to which the distribution of mail is subjected, demands which are closely followed up by the supervisory bodies.

In all communication, the contact center is clearly positioned as the central point of contact for customers who want to express their dissatisfaction. It functions as a general barometer for complaints and has its finger constantly on the customer's pulse. In addition to the solution of individual problems, it also gives more structured feedback that makes it possible to amend our performance, both at the structural and the individual level. Complaints are used with success, not only for the individual coaching of our mailmen, but also for the improvement of processes.

An extensive analysis of complaints is a consistent item on the agenda of the executive committee. The challenge is to distill relevant management information out of the huge amount of available data. Senior management have actively assisted this process by looking beyond a straightforward detailed view of transactions to create a usable policy instrument.

This shows that attention to complaints remains an important issue at the executive level. Even so, we sometimes also get pushback from the contact center itself. At one point, the center – which has now been fully professionalized – made clear its view that the organization as a whole had too limited a view of customer interactions. By only focusing on negative perceptions, there was a risk that a distorted image of our operational reality would be created. Moreover, many opportunities for improvements would remain under the radar, because more than 80% of customer contacts remained unused. As a result, it was possible that shortcomings in communication and the inherent complexity of processes would be dealt with in a less structured manner than operational bottlenecks.

With a number of demo reports the contact center soon opened the eyes of the executive committee in this respect and showed us how much more was still possible.

All these insights are now included in a periodic 'voice-of-the-customer' report. This gives a global picture of customer experience, down to the process and product level. The report is available via the intranet, with as many details as are relevant and usable for internal stakeholders. For example, marketeers are encouraged to make proactive use of the feedback as a KPI for the clarity of our service concept. In addition, a top-down push on the various management committees continues to be given by monthly newsletters and quarterly reporting.

To make sure that this all works properly, it was also vital that the contact center should learn to think about things from the perspective of the process and product managers. Meaningless jargon needs to be eliminated. On the other side of the coin, the contact center has warned the rest of the organization to be on their guard against the excessively exhaustive documentation of all kind of exotic – and therefore unusable – exceptions.

For an organization like bpost customer orientation stands central. To ensure we remain on the right track, there is no more powerful instrument than the feedback of the customer himself. The contact center is in a unique position to capture this feedback. The entire organization would miss valuable opportunities if nothing was done with the information this unique position provides.'

products and related communication are experienced by the customer. This is particularly useful for our marketing colleagues.

Of course, the customer also has emotions relating to the interaction and the contact (center) itself. Later in the book we will look in more depth at the expectations of customers when they use the contact center to get in touch with a company. The resulting customer (dis)satisfaction is at the very least a powerful coaching tool. But again, it also allows a structured analysis that can boost the improvement of processes and commercial policy. Which solutions leave the customer feeling disappointed? What are the root causes?

It needs to be remembered, however, that the customer journey is by no means the exclusive preserve of the contact center. Many other touchpoints also play a role. But the contact center is perhaps uniquely placed to collect and share feedback about the entire trajectory.

This is a genuine goldmine of information. And it goes without saying that the extraction and processing of this gold creates 'value'.

But is there no quicker way to get to the bottom line? This is something we will look at in the next section.

Sometimes a profit center

I will admit it. At this point, the risk of ending up in a purely semantic discussion is real.

What in the name of all that's holy is the difference between 'value' and 'profit'?

If we have just so passionately defended the credo that a contact center always creates 'value', does this not automatically mean that it yields more than it costs?

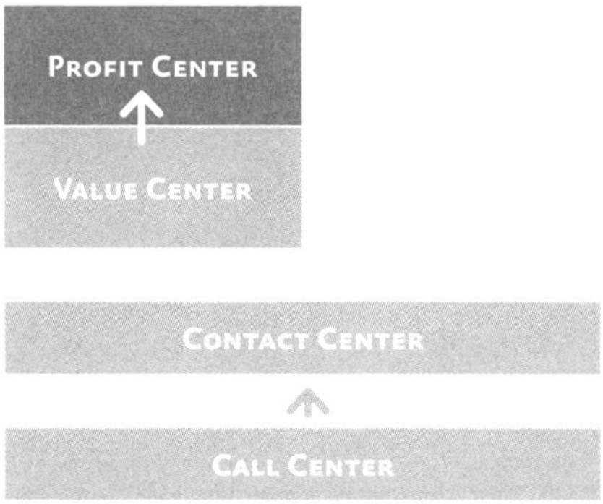

Figure 23: sometimes a profit center

Yes, it probably does. But the two concepts are being used here in a different context.

'Value' refers to the somewhat intangible, long-term contribution that contact centers make to the richness of the customer base. The notion of a profit center is more directly focused on the direct difference between attributable income and expenditure.

This is one of the few points in this book where the reasoning becomes easier when viewed from the perspective of an externally organized contact center. An outsourcing partner, who is paid to deal with contacts on behalf of a third-party organization, has directly attributable income as a result of its activities. To make this workable, the center's income must be sufficiently greater than its associated expenditure. In other words, there must be a profit.

In-house contact centers sometimes simulate this mechanism with a system of internal invoicing. Because other departments pay an internal invoice for its services, this gives the contact center a profit-and-loss profile within the organization and a bottom line. These mechanisms can be complex, using products and processes as a basis to quantify the workload – and therefore the costs.

It is easy to imagine how this might be an eye-opener for many other internal departments. If in the long-term these departments want to cut costs, they will need to be careful not to create too many unnecessary contacts. Of course, this does not create profit for the company as such. In accounting terms it is simply transferring money from one column to another. This perhaps explains why in this approach the concept of a value center is positioned as a higher form of development than a profit center.

The only way that a contact center can help to generate 'real' additional profit is when it is able to create 'real' additional income. And it can only do this if it is assigned a commercial function: in other words, sales.

So there. The 'S'-word has finally been mentioned.

To sell or not to sell...

The question of whether to give a sales role to the contact center is certainly an issue that seriously preoccupies thinking in the sector.

Use service as a sales channel or keep sales and service separate from each other: 40% of respondents in a research panel said that this was the biggest management dilemma they face.

Strategic Decisions Monitor, mentioned in Telecommerce 06 – 2013.

22% more organizations stimulated their contact center to make (more) sales than in the previous year.

Global Contact Center Benchmarking study by Dimension Data from 2009, mentioned in Telecommerce 04 – 2013.

75% of respondents said that it was highly desirable that service departments should promote sales through inbound calls.

National Contact Center Benchmark Platform study 2010.

Sales efforts must be a fixed element of service contacts, if sales are to be kept at the desired level, or so think 94% of the respondents.

Strategic Decisions Monitor, mentioned in Telecommerce 02 – 2013.

In matters relating to service conversations, 55% of callers report that they do not like it when sales offers are made during the conversation.

BRW research from 2009, mentioned in the Contact Center Magazine 7/8 – 2009.

Outbound telemarketing versus inbound bridging

The discussion of the sales role of contact centers is largely uncontentious in terms of outbound calls. Viewed historically, telemarketing – the proactive telephoning of potential customers with a commercial offer – partially drove the original creation of contact centers. In this role, the notion of a profit center is not controversial. Although there is sometimes fierce criticism about the way in which these commercial tasks are carried out, the actual role as such is not questioned, since this has automatically been associated with contact centers right from the very start. What's more, the profit contribution is by no means complex to calculate: it is the value of a successful sale, the level of conversion and the reach of the campaign divided by the cost for the campaign calls, preparation and processing. As simple as that.

This kind of activity is unlikely to result in existential discussions, not even when the contact center functions as an 'order channel', where (online or offline) orders can be dealt with in a highly reactive manner: the so-called 'call-now-order-now' approach.

No, the large philosophical discussions are more likely to concentrate on sales relating to the inbound traffic of the contact center. What if a customer takes the initiative to contact the center, but not in the first instance with the intention of buying anything?

Can and should a contact center, which was created first and foremost as an inbound service channel, seek to evolve in the direction of a profit center by taking on a proactive sales role in its interactions with customers?

To sell or not to sell, that is the question...

Let me immediately take the tension out of the situation. The answer is 'yes'...'usually'...'except'...

Hmm.

Elementary, my dear Watson

The position of Mary Lynn Ziemer, the former American customer service director at Belgacom, if perhaps a little extreme, was always very clear on this: 'Every call is a sales opportunity. Always.' Her Ameritech-inspired vision was unambiguous. No matter what the reason for the customer's call, the end of the conversation will always offer an opportunity to bridge to a product offer, which the customer can either accept or decline. She consistently refused to see the contact center as anything other than a potential sales channel.

Naturally – and even for her – the first priority remains making sure that the initial question gets answered properly. This is the primary task of the contact center and must never be subordinated to other considerations, unless you are willing to risk value destruction. Or to paraphrase Vidal Sassoon: only in the dictionary does 'sales' comes before 'service', not in a contact center.

But after the customer has been helped – especially if he has been helped successfully – the conversation is indeed ripe for a commercial twist. This is by no means illogical, since this moment contains all the success criteria that marketeers look for in a commercial contact:

- There is interaction. A real dialogue is taking place between the contact center and the customer.
- There is consent. By virtue of the fact that the customer took the initiative to call the center, he has automatically given you permission to talk to him. In our present age of 'don't-call-me' registers, Robinson lists and other GDPR frenzy, an invitation from the customer to talk to him is an opportunity not to be missed. This is Seth Godin's *Permission-based marketing* in its most elementary form.
- There is emotion. In all probability, the customer has just experienced a moment of truth and therefore – let us at least assume – currently has a positive feeling towards the brand.

In these circumstances, it requires little effort to suggest an extension of the conversation to the customer to look briefly at the range of products or services from which he already buys. This extension can either be in the breadth (cross-selling) or in the depth (upselling). Alternatively, it might simply be an adjustment to the customer's existing price and contract conditions.

The commercial exploitation of incoming calls is increasingly being seen as the best way to interact actively with existing customers. Many companies have discovered that working exclusively on acquisition has its limits. In general, attracting new customers is perceived as being more expensive than holding on to your existing ones. What's more, incoming service calls are perhaps also an ideal moment for the customer himself to be approached. Given all these factors, is this a chance that any company can afford to let slip by? Of course not.

Sales is also rendering a real service.

Or at least it is if we assume that the customer is no worse off after the sale than he was before or has not been deliberately 'tricked' in any way. The above arguments do not support, for example, the sale of a whole pallet of toilet paper to a 90-year-old pensioner or any of the other dubious practices of the minority that have given the entire sector such a bad reputation in recent years.

In the book *Knock Your Socks Off Service*[38] the authors pursue this line of reasoning to its logical conclusion by identifying just three circumstances in which a service conversation cannot form the basis for a possible sale, with sales in their opinion being regarded as the ultimate form of service:

- The operative has no room to maneuver. For example, the customer belongs to a particular customer segment for which telephone sales are not permitted (for example, bad debtors) or the product itself is not suitable for offer by phone.
- The operative has no appropriate solution for the customer need with which he is confronted.

Sales is service

The most striking example (*in my personal experience at least*) of this bold statement was the launch by Belgacom of ADSL, the provision of fast internet via the telephone line.

Contact center operatives considered offering a faster and cheaper alternative to surfing with a modem as providing a real service to customers. Even though in reality... they were selling.

It was also interesting to note that the most 'ripe' conversations turned out to be the ones where people had called up to complain about the high cost of their most recent invoice, often as a result of the activities of dubious sites having made connections to various exotic locations, without them knowing or approving it. Initially, the most difficult aspect for the operative was to explain to the customer that this was probably a consequence of some saucy surfing by their partner or children, but this actually turned out to be a good moment to make a pitch for a safer, better and cheaper form of internet connection.

Even today, it is recognized that the ADSL story helped to bring about a fundamental mentality change in Belgacom contact centers, the start of a process that saw them gradually transformed into the company's most important sales channel in the residential market.

Much the same effect was created when the switch to a new tariff plan was also treated as a 'sale'. Personnel and customers both regard it as an example of good service, when it is possible to offer tariff reductions as part of the company's loyalty policy.

- The emotional state of the customer makes clear that a sales pitch would serve no purpose. A customer who has just completely lost it is probably in no mood to stay open to any kind of offer.

According to the authors, all other contact center calls are by definition a commercial opportunity. Mary Lynn Ziemer revisited...

Not black and white, but many shades of gray

Notwithstanding the arguments put forward by Mary Lynn and other authors of her ilk, in my opinion the idea that every conversation must be a sales opportunity cannot be universally applied in all contact centers in all sectors.

We must be open to thinking in nuances of gray.

For example, the bpost service center gets most of its volumes from the receivers of parcels and letters, whereas the actual customer relationship exists in the first instance with the sender who paid the postage. In a slightly different vein, a financial contact center needs to take account of a whole batch of rules and regulations, so that the telephone sales process become cumbersome and difficult. And if you are the contact center for the tax administration office... You see where I am heading...

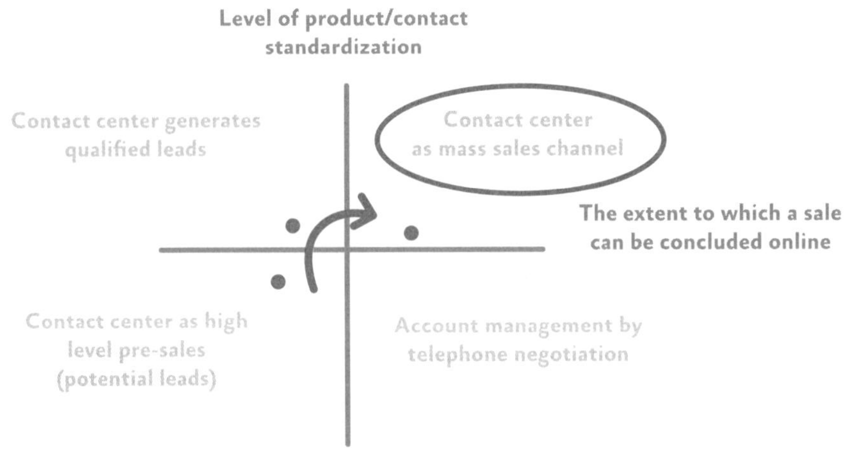

Figure 24: the contact center as an efficient sales machine

Making use of the contact center as a genuine sales channel must therefore be both a strategic choice (what do we want) and an operational one (what can we already do and what things do we still need to develop/improve?).

In this respect, there are essentially two parameters that determine how efficient a contact center can be in a sales role:

- How *standardized* are the products and services being offered? The more individualized the offer becomes, the more necessary it is to resort to a form of negotiation on the phone, which is difficult to 'industrialize' on the scale of a contact center.
- Can the sale be effectively *concluded online*? Can the operative immediately activate the service, product, tariff plan, contract that has just been agreed over the phone. Is it possible, to use the terminology of Jan-Roel Van Rhee, to proceed from 'service rescue' to 'sales deal'?[39] Every additional step that is necessary after completion of the conversation reduces the efficiency of the process.

Based on these two parameters, it is possible to depict the commercial role of a contact center as shown in figure 24:

- When products are not standardized and the sale cannot be concluded in full online, the contact center is at best a preparatory step towards a sale. The basic interest of the customer can be identified and documented, but the following steps need to be taken by other departments.
- When the products have a degree of standardization, contact centers can book physical appointments (at offices or with account managers) and can help to separate the wheat from the chaff. This kind of telephonic 'prequalification' is still most efficiently carried out by the contact center and not by using the more expensive time of other channels.
- When it is possible to conclude the sale of a non-standardized product online, the conversation will typically have the characteristics of a negotiation. This occurs almost 'accidentally' on the phone, but is cheaper than arranging a physical meeting. Having said that, this kind of telephonic account management does not have the bulk volume of calls that typically plays to the efficiency strengths of a contact center. Their specific nature and their (over-)long duration make these negotiation calls difficult to match with the operational philosophy of an inbound center.
- The greater the level of standardization, the easier the industrialization of the process. When activation is possible online, the contact center becomes

a powerful sales machine. If activation is not possible, it remains a powerful instrument for generating real qualified leads, but this requires a further follow-up process outside the center.

Sales via the contact center – the product perspective: bpost case study

To establish the possible positioning of the contact center as a sales channel – albeit in a B2B context – a few years ago an internal work group within bpost used the matrix in figure 25 (products are not detailed, for reasons of confidentiality). In essence, the operational feasibility of making the sale via the contact center was tested against the characteristics of the product and/or the sales process.

Making sure products are fit for phone sales

	Contract/ Offer Acceptance	Inclusive Solvability Check	Offline Activation Process	Pricing Variable	Pre-payment	Formal Customer Authentica-tion	
Product A					✓		→ Favor web
Product B	✓		✓	✓	✓		→ Favor web
Product C	✓	✓	✓				→ Re-engineer?
Product D	To be determined (in development)						→ TBD
Product E	To be determined (product in pilot phase)						→ TBD
Product F	✓		✓				→ Web? Re-engineer
Product G	To be determined (new product)						→ TBD
Product H							→ Likely candidate
Product I			✓		✓	✓	→ Favor office?
Product J	✓	✓	✓	✓			→ Re-engineer?
Product K	✓	✓	✓	✓			→ Re-engineer?
Product L	✓	✓					→ Re-engineer?

Figure 25: Are products suitable for sale by telephone (internal slide)?

All the product characteristics were listed and analyzed for likelihood to hinder sales efficiency.

This kind of summary makes it possible to streamline the channel discussion. Can the idea of selling via the contact center be justified? To what extent will this require the adjustment of products and the related support processes? Or are other channels better placed for sales?

- For example, the need for pre-payment (products A, B and I) complicates matters for the contact center. It implies either a relatively cumbersome payment process during the telephone contact or else an interruption of the conversational flow, so that the operative can check whether the payment has been made, before moving on to activation. For these products, the internet is a much more efficient channel, since secure online payment can immediately be built into the process.
- For a large part of the population, a formal customer authentication (for example, the necessary identity card check for product I) is still much easier to arrange via physical contact. This is certainly the case when an actual signature on a document is needed.

It is recommended to initiate this kind of exercise from within the contact center, since it has the best knowledge of the processes involved. At the very least, the results of the exercise will make clear to everyone just how much and precisely what 'homework' they will need to do before taking on a possible sales role.

In many respects, 'sales' is not so very different from all the other content a contact center deals with. The more exotic and fragmented the content, the more challenging it becomes to organize its processing efficiently.

Not an island: the contact center in a multi-channel approach

Figure 24 positions the contact center as a potential lead generator for other sales channels. This is a reality for many in-house contact centers and a perfectly logical approach in a multi-channel environment.

That being said, traditional multi-channel reasoning tends to be dogmatic in ways that do not work to the advantage of the contact center.

One of my first public engagements as someone responsible for a contact center was at the Contact Center Café of The House of Contact Centers. Based on my practical experience at Belgacom, I was asked to talk about the role of the contact center in an organization that also had other strong sales points, retail partners, an in-house sales team and a well-developed website, which were all clear evidence of a multi-channel sales approach.

As 'inspiration', I was given an article from the 1990 *Harvard Business Review* about what was then known as (to use a fancy jargon term) 'hybrid marketing'. This suggested a sales process as illustrated in figure 26.

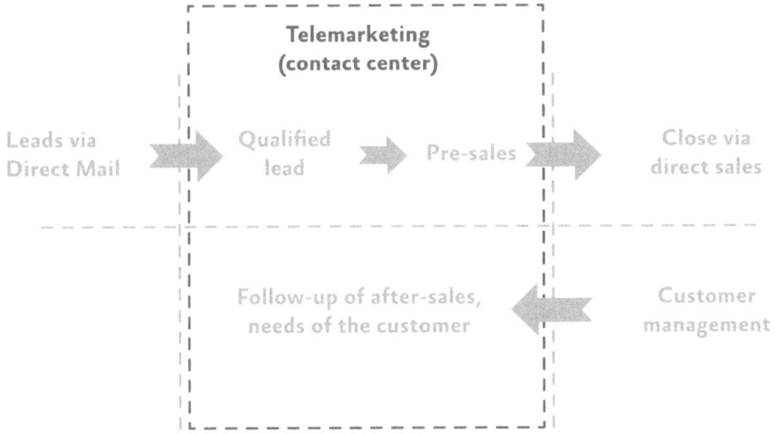

Figure 26: the sales process according to HBR

Nowadays, both the article and the process have become somewhat dated. Though you would be surprised how 'current' the basic ideas remain for the way traditional marketing circles view contact centers. Even today, these centers are still seen primarily as an instrument for generating pre-sales; or to use a sporting metaphor, crossing the ball so that the 'real' sales people can score the goal. Throughout this approach, no one ever stops to ask whether or not it might be possible to conclude the deal by telephone.

In essence, this reasoning is derived in its entirety from channel economics, a cost-oriented approach in which the return per channel is central.

According to this theory, 'expensive' channels can best be used for the more valuable transactions. In this way, you arrive at a linear progression, as illustrated in figure 27.[40] In one sense, it is hard to argue with the logic that costly channels should not be 'wasted' on 'small tickets'. The tragedy is, however, that this logic is also often incorrectly used in the opposite direction.

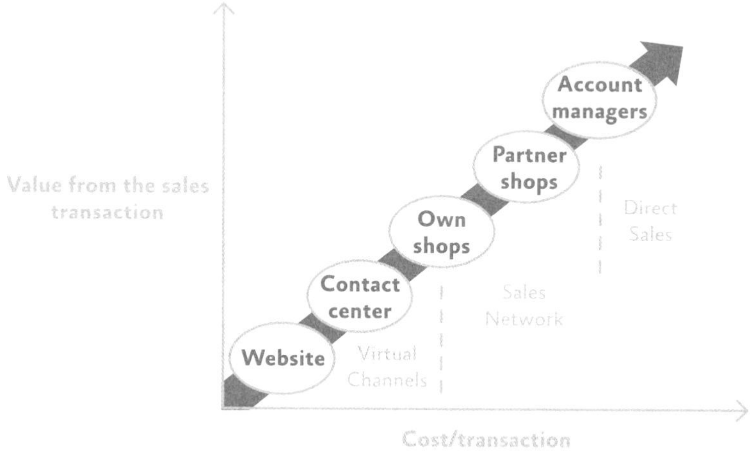

Figure 27: the relationship between cost – value/transaction, based on *The Channel Advantage*

High-value transactions become the exclusive preserve of the expensive channels. The wings of the 'cheaper' channels (web, telephone) are artificially clipped, because the return per transaction is overlooked. Instead of product and process, transaction value becomes the deciding factor. 'The contact center can conclude the deal if the value does not exceed xx euro.'

In this manner, the potential profit-making character of the contact center is deliberately held in check. Equally bizarre, also for the customers, is the fact that the sales process is broken off and transferred elsewhere once the amount under discussion exceeds a certain amount! This is a kind of commercial coitus interruptus, which is seldom appreciated by customers and is difficult to explain, particularly when they pass from one threshold to another for different transactions. In terms of customer experience, this is hardly ideal. Quite the reverse.

Multichannel in all facets

We have just looked at the potential sales role a contact center can play in a multi-channel context. That is logical, since we are still in the section on profit centers. However, multi-channel discussions must be about more than the simple dividing up of the sales arena. It is necessary to think about the positioning of all channels in all kinds of customer interaction.

In what ways are the channels promoted, not just for sales but also for service? To answer this, you could draw up a matrix similar to the one in figure 14, in which the different forms of communication available to the contact

***Leads:* contact center and branch offices in synergy for bpost bank**

bpost, which organizes the commercial customer contact for bpost bank, plays very much to the strengths of its different channels.

Rudy Moens (former Retail network director) and Hans Tops (sales development manager) explain:

'The focus of the contact center for bpost bank goes much further than simply answering questions and making sure the customers are kept happy.

Of course, this is still the main task, but the commercial reflex of the agents is also becoming increasingly important. Each day we are called by people who have never set foot in one of our offices. Calls are therefore a great opportunity to turn those contact moments into qualitative leads. The contact center sees or hears the possibilities, but is not always equipped to follow them up. However, it can stimulate the customer's interest and arrange a meeting with a financial sales expert.

To do this efficiently, we have made it possible for the contact center to directly book appointments with the financial experts in the network. In this way, hundreds of leads are generated each month. This not only contributes to the subsequent generation of additional income, but we have also noted that it has had a positive effect on the mutual understanding between the two channels.

The offices are encouraged to give as much feedback as possible about the results of the various appointments. The aim is not only to support the motivation of the people working in the contact center, but also to help management give more targeted coaching related to the quality leads.'

center were linked to different types of calls. Now the question becomes which transactions would we like to see happen through which channel and with what preference. And which combinations do we explicitly want to exclude?

Rather than thinking exclusively in terms of products or processes, it is better to take the specific needs of the customer in each transaction as the starting point. This means that the question then becomes: 'in which ways can we draw upon the specific strengths of each channel to best respond to those needs?' In this way, you arrive more quickly at the 'why' of the transaction, rather than the 'what' and the 'how'.

Figure 28, loosely based on *The Channel Advantage*, links the choice of channel to the purpose of the purchase. Someone who wants to take a gift along to an important meeting will perhaps seek a different channel from someone who impulsively decides to buy something for himself.

CHANNEL	CHANNEL STRENGTH	SALES CRITERIA	
Internet	• simplicity • availability • delivery	• price • ease to order	**Impulse buy**
Contact Center	• simplicity • availability • delivery	• ease to order	
Shop	• expert guidance • tangible/testable • product stock	• customization • expert advice • immediate availability	**(Emotional) Important**

Figure 28: channel choice as a function of buyer need

Every organization must be capable of translating this to reflect its own products and services. And every contact center manager must be capable of completing it for his scope.

Benedikte Paulissen, CCO Telenet: the sales role of the contact center perfectly matches putting the customer central

For Benedikte Paulissen (Chief Customer Officer at Telenet) the sales role of the contact center is a logical consequence of the freedom the Telenet operatives have to think and act in a customer-oriented way.

'Putting the customer central... You really have to mean it.'
Today's contact centers are continuing to evolve into real customer centers, the place that can really make the difference, starting of course with the provision of information and the solving of problems, but increasingly through the creation of customer experiences. That is the real added value.

'Everything from the customer's perspective' or 'the customer central' must be much more than just a buzz phrase. It needs to be a philosophy, a culture that must be shared by the entire organization at every level. At Telenet we expect all our operatives to think of the customer at every moment and in every situation – and not just in the contact center.

Good and genuine customer service makes customers happy and happy customers stay longer and buy more.

You need to listen to and get to know the 'person' on the other end of the line in an honest, open and interested manner.

Really listening to what people are saying is the key to success in a contact center. The customer has changed and he wants you to know that he has changed. He also expects that you will behave accordingly. The greatest challenge is to centralize all the important information about the customer and to use it in your conversations with him. A contact center has at its disposal a huge and valuable store of knowledge about each individual customer. That is why the contact center is so important and why it will continue to grow in importance as a sales center.

Sales from the customer's perspective

More than any other channel, the contact center must approach sales from the perspective of the customer.

This is where we need to encourage an evolution in the sales process: from product-based selling to customer-based selling. This means that you always need to focus on the customer, not on the product. It also means that you need to discover what each individual customer wants and what is important to him. And that is not just a task for the sales department. Close collaboration with the marketing or CRM department is vital. We are talking about a personal approach based on customer data that you already have, now combined with new data that you obtain during the sales conversation. This necessitates a new kind of training and the development of more personalized offers. Contact center management has an important role to play in this respect: the focus must no longer be on technology and products; from now on, it is your customers and your operatives who must be central.

Without passion there is nothing

Selling is making people happy. Happy people make other people happy. This is why it is important to entrust sales to enthusiastic members of staff, staff who love selling and have a warm heart for the customer. When we are recruiting, we look for two qualities in particular: passion and perseverance. Passion gives energy, perseverance demands energy. Take care of your people and make them happy.

If you can do that, the rest will follow!'

What makes your contact center attractive to customers, when compared to the other channels within your organization?

Reality check 1: no fields of dreams

The risk of organizational navel-gazing becomes very real when the channel discussion only takes the needs and wishes of the company as its starting point. Irrespective of the reasoning you decide to adopt, you should be under no illusion about the degree of spontaneity with which your customers will be willing to follow you in that reasoning.

A simple 'build-it-and-they-will-come' approach[41] seldom works in the real world.

Just because from an organizational perspective you want to see so-called 'low value add' transactions carried out via the web and your contact center, this does not necessarily mean that the customers will automatically agree with you! They will need to be carefully guided to your preferred channels by clearly communicated calls to action. The more black-white you can make your thinking, the easier it is to get your message across.

Whatever your strategy, you need to remember that it will require a serious communications effort from within your organization to make it work. Customers must be made aware of the available channels and must be able to see the benefits for them of picking the channels you want. Only then can you persuade them to move in the right direction.

Reality check 2: the customer's willingness to accept

How happy are customers with the fact that 'every contact is a possible sales opportunity'?

It would be (too) easy to avoid the potentially worrying implication in this question by trying to rationalize it out of existence, based on arguments like the following:

- Because the customer always has the last word, he decides the final outcome of the sales element of the conversation. He decides what will make him happy. If he wants to buy, he buys. If he doesn't want to buy, he doesn't.
- Because so many companies have successfully attached sales to their inbound calls, this must mean that the concept is popular with customers.
- If customers complain about *teleselling*, this usually has more to do with the way it is done rather than the fact that it is done at all. Complaints tend to focus on a bad approach (ignoring the customer's original question), bad preparation (pointless and/or repeated offers), bad scripts (reading from a menu), bad implementation (not listening to the customer) and bad ethics (forced sales).
- A research study published in 2009 in the *Contact Center Magazine*[42] offered a more nuanced perspective on this last point. It reported that 55% of customers do indeed have a problem if an attempt is made to sell them something during a service call. Having said that, the article then went on to promote a commercial approach by suggesting that the concept of 'sales' should be replaced by cross-selling and upselling, based on an analysis of the individual customer's needs.

Conclusion? One sale is clearly not the same as another... In my opinion, this reflects the difference between, on the one hand, a bad script with unrelated and irrelevant offers (which, according to the above survey, an amazing 45% of people are willing to tolerate!) and, on the other hand, a correct approach to building commercial bridges. Customers do not mind being persuaded to buy something, as long as it is done in the right manner.

Of course, these are all no more than theoretical projections. The surest and safest way to guarantee that your sales approach is not harming your customer relations is to test it against your own customer base. You can do this by monitoring your customers' actual behavior (for example, by in-depth analysis of customer satisfaction in different scenarios) or, more directly, by simply asking them in a carefully prepared survey.

It is perhaps no real surprise that customers are open to commercial offers during service conversations, provided they feel that have been helped in the first place. In part, this is possibly a consequence of the context of positive emotion that we referred to earlier, maybe even a form of psychological gratitude on the part of the customer.

At the same time, of course, the process is also very user-friendly. The customer is approached at a moment he himself has chosen and he retains full control over the transaction, which also takes up very little of his valuable time. And if the transaction can be completed online, he is required to do nothing further. What could be easier? In an era when companies are trying explicitly to make things as simple and convenient as possible for their customers (known in the jargon as 'customer effort' – a concept we will return to later), this can really make a difference.

To sell or not to sell… ask the customer

The best way to be certain about your customers' willingness to accept anything - in this case, their willingness to accept commercial approaches during service conversations - is to ask them.

This is what we did at Belgacom, back in 2007. A representative sample of customers was asked if they had had a commercial discussion at the end of a service conversation and, if so, how satisfied were they with the way this discussion was conducted.

The answers to the first question were useful for management to check to what extent the 'every-call-is-a-sales-call' claim was reflected in actual practice, with the aim being to see if any remaining potential for growth was still not being used. The answers to the second question gave an indication whether or not an attempt to further push the 'sales-during-service' policy might be self-destructive.

The results showed that the level of satisfaction with the commercial approach far outweighed the level of dissatisfaction. Hopefully, this had something to do with the nature of the offers and the qualitative manner in which our agents proposed these offers. Or that's what I'd like to think…

Reality check 3: talent or technique?

Sooner or later in the thinking process, you will surely hear that 'selling' requires a special kind of person and that the service-oriented operatives in contact centers perhaps do not have the right profile to fulfill this sales role.

According to this argument, selling is a talent, a passion that you can only do with your full heart and soul, which demands a kind of drive and determination that is diametrically opposed to the typical service attitude of a contact center employee. This is a line of reasoning that can lead to heated discussion, with each side fanatically defending its own point of view. Philosophizing about the nature of man...

But perhaps this is not the right discussion.

Perhaps we should be talking less about how a contact center operative can be turned into a salesperson and more about the basic question of whether something can be sold at the end of a service call. This might sound like trying to weasel out of the more philosophical debate, but there is a meaningful difference between the two.

Asking a service operative to 'sell something' at the end of a conversation is more a question of technique than of talent. It is essentially about:

- learning how to ask the right questions, so that the bridge can be made between the customer's initial service query and the commercial opportunity;
- learning how to describe the characteristics of a product or service as something beneficial for the customer;
- learning how to counter objections;
- learning how to conclude the sale.

At first glance, none of these things require any more (or more complex) knowledge than is already necessary to answer service questions. What's more, in many contact centers the operative can rely on the technical support of CRM applications, which are capable of predicting and scripting the 'next best offer' based on the customer's profile.

In other words, nothing seems to really prevent a contact center agent from conducting online sales if they've been taught a few key questions and answers. Turning them into 'real' salespeople, with all that implies, is, of course, a very different matter. In that case, talent and desire do indeed play a much bigger role. And it is certainly open to question whether contact center operatives, with their service-minded attitude, could deal effectively with hard outbound calls or conduct a proper in-depth sales discussion.

But in the meantime, contact center operatives will continue to generate significant revenue by adding a sales element to their processing of inbound service questions. Sales which otherwise would never have been realized.

Technique, not talent

'Anxiety is the price to pay for an unprepared mind'

That is the basic philosophy behind *Breakthrough Service Performance®*, a long-term change program that bpost is implementing in collaboration with the Cohen Brown company. It's a variation of a known theme. 'By failing to prepare you are preparing to fail' (Benjamin Franklin),or 'Preparation is the key to success' (Alexander Graham Bell).

This philosophy assumes that you can prepare conversations with customers so thoroughly, through role-paying and scenario scripts, that you will only rarely have to improvise during the conversation itself. And this applies both to service and sales.

Bpost's post office network, which is indispensable as the company's primary sales channel, makes full use of sales bridges and has learnt to deal with the questions and complaints of customers. In what is called an 'objections clinic', counter clerks are trained by asking them to think up for themselves all the possible complaints, queries and objections that the public might throw at them, following which they are challenged to think up all the answers, which they then practice, either individually or in group.

Many of the same techniques are used in bpost contact centers to prepare service conversations in which the operatives need to 'sell' certain important steps in the service process to customers who may, initially, not be all that interested or co-operative. Likewise, where the contact center generates sales leads, the same methods are used. In other words, it is about technique, not talent. And technique can be learnt, studied and practiced. As a result, you can prepare your conversations in such a way that 'anxiety' will never trouble you again.

Reality check 4: 'It's the people, stupid': the operative's willingness to accept

Especially if the commercial role of a contact center needs to be introduced from scratch, by far the biggest challenge for the contact center management will be overcoming the resistance of the center's workforce and, in particular, the objections put forward by their team leaders and representatives.

'Happy people sell.
Miserable bastards don't.'

Nev, from the BBC3 series
The Call Center

Much of this concern is connected to the fact that in many organizations 'sales people' are managed in a way that is different from other personnel, with tough sales objectives and rigorous performance-based assessments. These elements create a perception that extra pressure will be added to any new sales environment – in this case, the contact center – where in most cases there is already pressure enough as it is. Little wonder, perhaps, that the initial response might be so wary.

Not that this is specific for contact centers: most departments feel under pressure and most of them are resistant to change. It does, however, show that contact center managers, like their colleagues elsewhere, will also need a good dose of change management knowledge.

Nathalie Werbrouck (now communication & change manager in the Consumer Business Unit/Sales at Proximus): Belgacom helps the team leaders at the contact center

'Overcoming the resistance of agents often begins with overcoming the resistance of their line managers and coaches.

With this in mind, a few years ago we started writing "Yes... but" guidelines to help facilitate the implementation of important changes. In this document we listed all the possible objections that people in change situations might be expected to raise and also formulated answers to counter those objections.

We first used the "Yes... but" exercise for the introduction of sales into the front office for Mobile. In this case, we only involved the project members.

Later, we did the same for two other projects, but this time we extended involvement to the line managers. As a result, the experience was even more positive: it enriched the project as a whole and above all created a positive feeling among all the participants, both the project leaders and the line managers.

It was a great help to think together as a project team about the objections that people frightened by the prospect of change might put forward. There are two ways you can do this:

- You can search together for answers to the agents' reactions, so that you try to think of things from their perspective (as far as you are able – the greater the distance between you as a project leader and the agents, the harder it becomes). This teaches you to better understand each other's suggested arguments and points of view, which creates greater alignment between the members of the project team;
- You can proactively defuse many objections by making small adjustments to the project (mainly for matters that you had not thought about before).

The whole process becomes even more interesting if you can involve the line management (managers and coaches) and persuade them to formulate their own list of objections, for which they can then develop answers, either on their own or together with other members of the project team. In this way:

- They suggest objections that the project team would never have thought of;
- They also learn things from the exercise, which helps them to prepare for their future task of "selling" the project to their agents. Thinking together and jointly formulating answers to expected objections puts them in a better position to face the possible storm of reactions from their teams. It can also help to overcome their own resistance to the project, which is often as serious as that of their agents;
- They become partners in the project. The project is now also "their" project: they are more fully in the picture, feel jointly responsible and can no longer hide behind claims like "I didn't know" or "If only you had told us this before..."

In our experience, this approach results in interesting and enjoyable meetings, during which all the participants work constructively to build something together, with the process itself being just as important as the resulting "Yes... but" document. What's more, it also becomes clear which members of the line management are not "on board" with the change project, which is something you might not otherwise notice.'

In annex 1 you can find part of the 'Yes... but' document that was used for the introduction of sales in Mobile. Sensitive or commercially confidential content has been removed. Even so, it still reads like an extract from a 'objection clinic', but from a time before we had ever heard of the concept.

'It's the end of the world as we know it'

It is a strategic choice to make 'sales' one of the basic tasks of the contact center. The decisive factors in making this choice are: the wider strategic choices of the organization, the nature of the products and services, the underlying processes and, to a degree, the willingness of the center organization to adjust to the sales requirement.

The importance of this final factor should not be underestimated.

As soon as 'sales' becomes a part of the center's operations, this opens a whole new range of challenges for the management team.

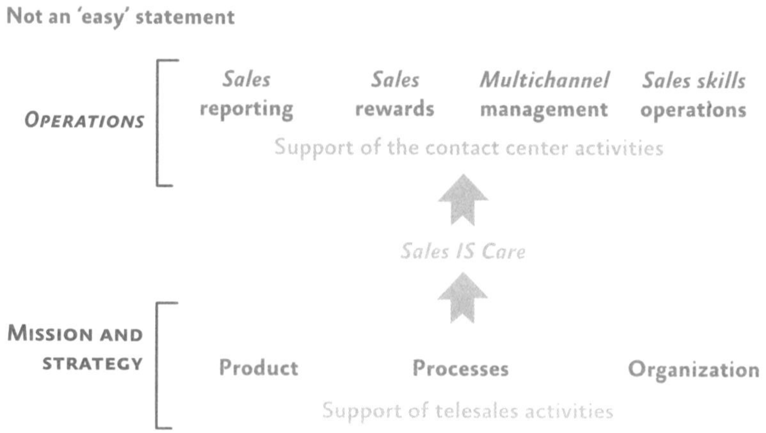

Figure 29: easier said than done...

Figure 29 shows a number of the most crucial aspects where things have the potential to go wrong. Many of these aspects are not specific to contact centers, but apply in every sales environment. However, the contact center environment does give them a special 'twist'.

Sales reporting

One of the things that makes the contact center such a special management environment is the fact that results and performance can be followed in almost real time. In terms of sales figures, staff and management will expect no different. But for some order systems this can be a step too far. For this reason, the centers often fall back on a kind of self-reporting, with all the challenges this involves, from the retrospective reconciliation of information to the need to manage perceived differences between reporting schemes.

Moreover, to accurately assess the performance of operatives, a link will need to be made with other contact center data (for example, between sales and the number of answered service calls). The data complexity of such linkages is self-evident.

But there are other complications as well. With distance selling the customer usually has a legal entitlement to a waiting period during which he can cancel his purchase free of charge. Should the sales figures for the contact center therefore give a kind of net result, which can also be used to assess the 'quality' of the sales? If so, must these results be linked back to individual sales figures? Once again, this quickly becomes highly complex. Trying to correct this in advance by building a margin into objectives runs the risk of giving too strong an impression that it is acceptable to generate sales that in the final analysis will never be realized.

Sales rewards

In order to stimulate operatives to generate more sales, it is usual to set objectives for commercial results, either in absolute terms (xx euros) or in relative terms (yy sales/100 calls). To make this tangible, an element of variable remuneration is attached to the successful realization of the objectives. Alternatively, incentives can be offered for intermediary or very specific results.

This is not so very different from what happens in most sales environments. In this respect at least, a sales function in a contact center is not so very different from a sales function elsewhere.

- The frequency and scale of the incentive must have a continuous motivating effect.

- The possible fiscal consequences of the reward system must not be overlooked. In view of the otherwise modest salaries paid to agents working in contact centers, this might lead to unexpected and unwelcome surprises.
- Incentives do not necessarily need to be money-related, but can sometimes have a more frivolous and playful nature. However, make sure in advance that your personnel also see things in this light. It would not be the first time that unions have intervened because employees feel as though they are being treated as children. For this reason, it is a good idea to let this kind of reward be worked out at local level, with a part of the incentive budget being allocated decentrally for this purpose.
- For the motivational aspect to work, it is important that everyone has the feeling that he or she can win. Instead of always expressing objectives in absolute terms, express them occasionally in relative terms (for example, the operative who makes the most progress in a given period).

The specific context of the contact center, however, means that some aspects of the reward system are a little more challenging and complex.

- If you expect to operate with a 'sales-after-service' mindset, this must be anchored in your management and control mechanisms. For example, variable bonuses, awarded simply on the basis of sales realized, send out the wrong signal. You must make clear at a psychological level that 'customer service' remains the center's primary task. But how can you do this? One way is to have a very clearly defined performance management system, which leaves no room for discussion. Failure to provide correct service = failure to do your job properly, with all the consequences this entails. Although this sounds really good, in many companies this remains an HR illusion. A possible alternative is to make bonuses also dependent on reaching a certain level of service or on the realization of certain service results (for example, customer satisfaction ratings). These objectives can be included in your variable targets.
  Whichever system you choose, it must:
  - send the right message;
  - be adequately followed up;
  - direct the actions of the operatives in the desired manner.
- In a contact center, ensuring good levels of customer retention is a key task, particularly as dissatisfied customers or customers planning to terminate are often automatically routed to the center. The ability to persuade a customer to stay is a valuable contribution to any company, made possible by the

contact center and the individual operative. But unless this happens via an active switch to a different subscription or price schedule, it is very difficult to effectively include it in the reporting, which makes it even more difficult to include it in meaningful objectives.

- Making sales an element of all incoming calls is a reflex you hope to encourage in all your operatives. It needs to become an integral part of their call handling, their standard manner of dealing with any call. But once this mentality has been introduced, it is an illusion to think that it can be turned off again at the press of a button.

  Some companies believe that this can be made depending on the service results of the moment. For example, the systems technology will block the next best offer if the level of service falls below a certain point or will send a message to operatives along the lines of 'no sales now'.

  Although this is theoretically correct in terms of the contact center's priorities, it is difficult to reconcile with the implementation of the concept of a real sales machine. You cannot expect your operatives to turn their reflexes on and off to suit your convenience. What's more, you can expect some serious discussions if people risk losing their bonuses simply because the management has (temporarily) 'changed its mind' about sales. Developing emergency scenarios for the moments when service seems to be suffering as a result of sales therefore requires very careful planning and communication in advance.

Whichever policy, methods and system you adopt, the management and stimulation of sales remains a very special – and additional – task.

Sales skills operations

Similarly, your operational management will never be the same again. The routing of calls to operatives, which in the past was based solely on the combination 'nature of call/skill of operative', suddenly becomes less straightforward. Do all your personnel have the same sales potential? Will some operatives be advantaged or disadvantaged because they must deal with a particular type of call, even though they have the same sales objectives as their colleagues? How do you decide who to take offline during calmer moments, so that (in their perception at least) they 'miss out' on sales opportunities?

Of course, you can try to take account of all these things when setting objectives, but in practice it often comes down to having to readjust the situation after the fact.

In short, every decision relating to staffing and routing suddenly becomes more complex – and less innocent.

Moreover, when you want to take account of likely conversion rates in your route programming, it is important not only to estimate the sales potential of a call, but also the sales skills of the different operatives. Hello, complexity...

Multi-channel management

In many companies the contact center will not be the only sales channel. In an ideal world multiple channels lead to complementarity, so that every customer can be reached, irrespective of the channel they choose. In reality, however, the different channels often have the feeling that they are competing against each other, which leads to the mutual suspicion that sales might be cannibalized. It is certainly true that when the sales objectives are ambitious (in other words, always) there is a temptation to see 'the others' as a missed opportunity to generate more sales in your own channel rather than as a way to make more sales for the organization as a whole.

This is also something extra that the contact center managers will need to (help) monitor and control. For the reasons just given, some figures are deliberately counted twice: once for the contact center itself and a second time for the portfolio holders (account manager, geographical office, etc.). This kind of 'oversight' drives financial managers to despair, but it is at least more customer friendly than devious behavior to try and poach each other's sales.

One thing is certain: no matter how logical or justifiable the sales role of the contact center is, it always means an extra challenge – or rather several challenges – for the center's management. The number of plates you need to keep spinning in the air has just increased – so you had better make sure you are well prepared to make the additional effort this will require!

SOUNDBITE

'You are born a seller – or you aren't' – Geoffrey Peyttier (The House of Contact Centers and ex-footballer for KV Mechelen)

'Everyone (who wants to) can (learn what is needed to) sell.' In one sense, this is true, in the same sense that it is also true that everyone can play football. When my wife and ten other fellow mums got together a team to play against my son's under-10 team, most people watching the game regarded this as "football". But if you ask a football trainer what he thinks about this kind of game, he will be more likely to label it as "amusement".

That being said, all the necessary ingredients for a football game were present: a ball, two goals, two teams, a referee, a shot that occasionally went in the right direction and (not to be overlooked!) an awful lot of enthusiasm. Perhaps this final element didn't last for long, but even so... However, for a football trainer – a professional – a few things are still missing to make this a "proper" game of football. Having the right skills and strategy will help to move you in the right direction. Add a dollop of passion and the determination to give 110% during every training session and match, and before you know it you will have a game played by real footballers and not by people pretending to be footballers.

And it is just the same with selling.

Selling, like football, is a sport! It demands a set of the right skills, the right attitude, a good strategic approach and a whole lot of determination. Some of those things can be learnt; others cannot.

You can teach people how to read off a clever and amusing sentence from a script that is designed to lead in to your upselling or cross-selling story, but do they have the drive and the fire to put that sentence across in the right way and then follow it up in the right manner? That is less obvious.

Of course, it is always possible that just by reading off the sentence any old how the customer will still be prepared to make a purchase. At that moment, the operative will genuinely believe that he has sold something. But he hasn't. In such cases, there is a strong likelihood that the customer was already planning to buy something anyway. The operative just proactively exploited this intention with perfect timing. Good work, but you can hardly call it selling. The difference with real sales is made after you get the first "no".

A number of concepts that everyone associates with sales only come into play after this first "no": persuasion, persistence, influencing perception, etc. You won't often come across these things in a conversation where a customer does not raise one of the classic "no sale" objections like "I think it's too expensive". In order to sell, you need sales signals. You can teach people this as well, but some of them will continue to interpret the customer's first "no" as a clear, definitive and not to be ignored refusal. That is the way it feels to some agents, and once they get this idea into their heads, it is almost impossible to get it out again.

Real 'sellers' are rare. You will find plenty of people who are keen to learn all the necessary tips and tricks, which will help them to reach their targets. But I often notice that these people lack the emotional and social intelligence that makes a good sales person. Someone who possesses a good dose of this intelligence will find it easier to build up a relationship with the customer, which is the basis of every sales conversation. Selling begins by creating a bond between you and the person you are trying to sell to.

The extent to which you succeed in creating this bond will also determine the extent to which the customer is prepared to let you do the things that are necessary to convince him to make a purchase for you, whereas other sellers might fail. And what are these things?

Persuade, influence, argue and close!

If, as a company, you want to remain true to the ideas of "the right product for the right customer" and you do not wish per se to try and sell everything to everyone, even then you should not worry about putting a born salesman or woman on the end of your telephone or behind your counter. They will not only ensure that you have more customers and that your average income per customer increases, but because they always sell with the customer rather than the product in mind, they will also bring you more positive customers, who are more satisfied and stay for longer.

Long live the pure seller! Selling is a job apart.

But selling has also become something a little bit "dirty".

"Hard selling" is a term that is now widely used as a term of shame...

Shame! What is so shameful about it?

And a number of the competencies possessed by hard sellers are now seen as being wrong... Wrong! What is so wrong about them,

Selling is about binding: first binding the customer to you as a person and then binding him to the product. Your success in creating these bonds will determine how far the customer will let you go to persuade him to accept your offer: discuss, argue, give advice and, yes, sometimes even contradict.

Defenders are also footballers, but everyone knows that it is better to play a Christiano Ronaldo in the striker's role, rather than a Vincent Kompany!

Sellers are often more competitive than other people. Chasing figures, meeting targets and the urge to perform are all in their blood. This is what makes them so good at what they do. Managing this competitive environment and ensuring a good balance between quality and maximum conversion is a task that requires inspirational and motivating leaders.

A true seller is not afraid of a "no". He sees it as the starting shot in the race to make a "real" sale. Less efficient sellers will try to dodge this "no". As a result, they need more contacts before getting a reasoned answer that might be either a "yes" or a "no", so that their level of conversion is much lower.'

But always a cost center

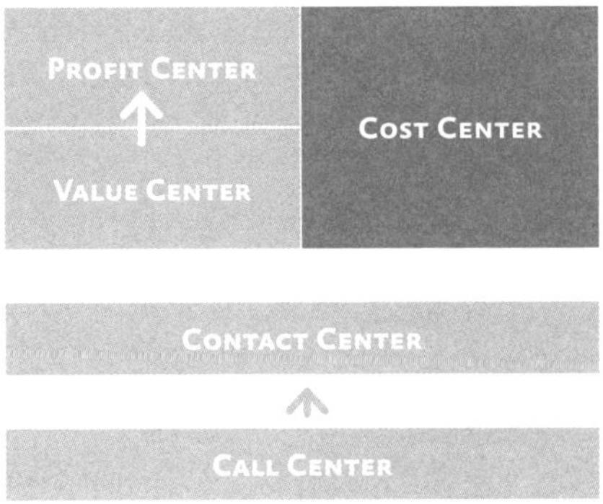

Figure 30: always a cost center

The contact center always creates value. It also has the potential, as a sales channel, to develop into a major profit center.

But this doesn't mean that contact center managers should get upset when people describe their centers as cost centers.

Because that's what they are – always.

It will always be the contact center managers' responsibility to create that value and profit in the most efficient way possible.

The contact center will always remain a cost center, even if only in the accounting sense to the word.

Like all other echelons of the organization, the contact center must do everything it can to keep costs low. In fact, perhaps it needs to try even harder than other departments, given its very specific origins. If we agree that part of its reason for existence lies in being 'the most efficient way to deal with contacts', this implies that efficiency – including cost management – must automatically – and unconditionally – be in its DNA.

So why can't contact center managers stop moaning about this issue (which is what most of them do)? Or stop feeling as though they are being unduly targeted?

Cutting costs = cutting personnel?

In practice, any discussion about cost management in contact centers tends to revolve around the way personnel are used. This inevitably means that these discussions can sometimes be emotional.

In her book *Implementatie en optimalisatie van het contact center* (Implementation and optimization of the contact center),[44] Marion Van den Brink estimates

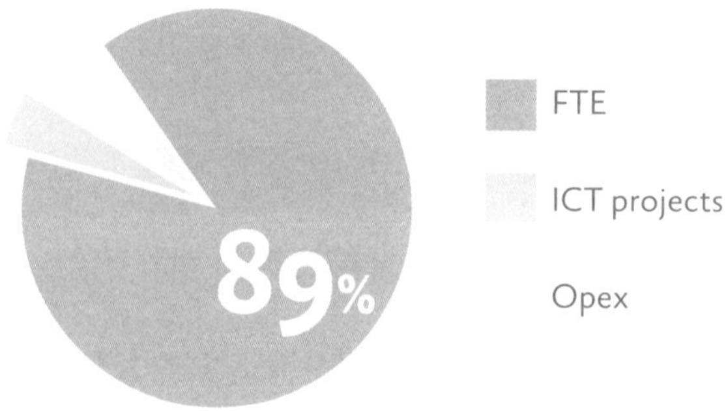

Figure 31: personnel costs: by far the biggest share

that 70% of the costs of a contact center are linked to its staffing. IT (20%) and telecommunications (10%) account for the remaining expenditure.

Of course, the exact proportions will vary from center to center, but there is little doubt that personnel will be by far the biggest element in every case.

'Personnel' is also the cost factor over which the contact center manager has the most direct influence. In many companies, the ICT and telecom budgets are managed centrally in a different silo. True, there is often close collaboration and even perhaps a degree of internal invoicing, but the impact on the contact center remains essentially indirect.

This is certainly the case for in-house contact centers if they form a relatively small part of the organization as a whole.

In this respect, figure 31 is reasonably representative of the budget over which I currently have direct responsibility, in the knowledge that part of the costs will be managed by other colleagues.

Reaction and action

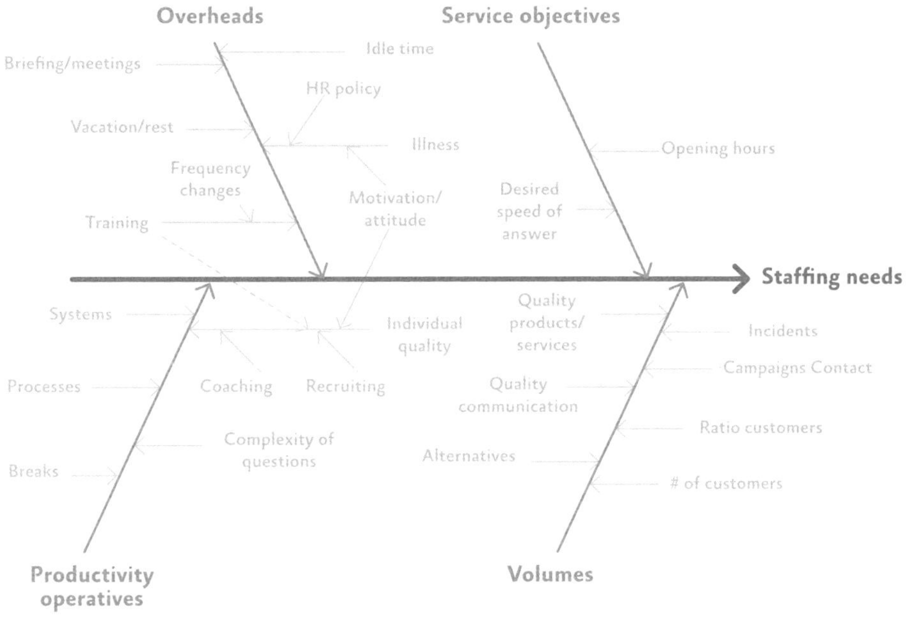

Figure 32: the drivers of staffing needs – and therefore costs – in the contact center

Cost related to telecom: a paying number or not?

A question that is raised time and again in the discussion about contact center telecom costs is the choice between whether to use a toll free number (which in Belgium is an 0800 number) or a paying number.

In Belgium, legislation forbids the over-pricing of help desk numbers (for example, they cannot be priced 0900 numbers). Companies are not allowed to make excessive profits from the incoming traffic it attracts to its contact center. That is deemed to be improper – and rightly so.

But should the call number for customers be entirely free, as the Customer-friendliness Charter[45] so warmly recommended in 2012?

Of course, 'free' in this context only means free for the customer. If someone calls an 0800 number, it is the receiver not the caller who pays the charge. When you are dealing with large volumes and with inter-connection tariffs for fixed and mobile phones, these costs can quickly become quite substantial.

In the final analysis, the question is more a strategic/philosophical one. There is no evidence in the literature (or anywhere else) that a toll free number has an influence on the perception of customer-friendliness. This is something we will see later, when we look at the drivers of customer satisfaction in chapter 6.[46]

The choice must be inspired by the general positioning of the contact center as part of the customer experience. Is the offering of free access something that the company wants to use to differentiate itself? Does the company think that free calls form part of the general customer experience and, therefore, have an impact on customer perception?

In many companies, a distinction is made between a (free) campaign number designed to attract new customer and a (paying) service number to help existing ones. This is based on a certain reluctance to give new prospects the impression that they need to pay for the 'privilege' of becoming a customer. Which is fine if you are a new customer – but can seem a bit odd if you are already on the company's books!

Whichever choice you a make, once it is made it is difficult to change your mind. This is certainly the case if you want to go from free to paying. Because no matter how rational the idea that you want to keep costs per customer as low as possible, replacing a free number with a paying one will always bring you bad publicity.

The emotionality of this subject is no doubt intensified by the fact that managers of an inbound, service-oriented contact center feel as if they have few discretionary powers when it comes to costs. In their experience, volumes – and therefore costs – are caused by factors outside their direct sphere of influence. Is it then right that they should then be held accountable for these costs? 'How unfair can the world be?' you will often hear them ask, when they are in their most self-pitying Calimero mode.

Mentally, costs are seen as something to which one is subjected, not as something that can be autonomously managed and controlled. In this context, personnel costs are seen as a consequence, the corollary of linking workload volumes to the correct handling of all incoming calls

And indeed, many of the drivers in figure 32 are not under the immediate control of the contact center manager.

Even so, the discussions on this subject quickly become too defensive too fast. As often as not contact center managers forget to do their own homework thoroughly enough or fail to liaise clearly enough with their own superiors in the organization. As a result, they also fail to see that insight into the levers in figure 32 and the proactive influencing of the different underlying mechanisms are ways in which they can still influence staffing needs.

The balance between volume, resources and results

We have already come across the volume-resources-results triangle earlier in the book, where we discussed how contact center managers need to find a balance between these three inextricably linked elements (see figure 3 on page 28). And nowhere is this truer than when discussing the cost component.

Of course, the first duty of the contact center management is to optimize the relationship between volumes and resources. This is the non-negotiable basic task of the contact center and therefore something for which the management can and must be held accountable.

In turn, striking this optimal balance is closely related to the productivity of the individual agents in combination with the best possible planning of resources. This implies a need to invest in systems and tools, which can help to improve the performance of the agents.

Of course.

The desired result in terms of quality of service is a strategic choice made by the company. What is the required speed of answer for incoming calls? What is an acceptable level of lost contacts? How thoroughly do questions need to be investigated before giving a standard answer? What are the hours of service? These are all questions that have an impact on staffing (and therefore on costs) and they must be facilitated from within the contact center.

Of course.

But results will never be earth-shattering if the volume component is not brought into play.

The key to cost management in a contact center lies in the accurate control of the inflow of calls, rather than just their processing.

Reducing costs = reducing volumes

If you wish to maintain an equivalent result, and after you have optimized the means to achieve it, the only balanced way to reduce your use of resources (read: costs) is to reduce your volume of incoming work. In other words, cost management in a contact center actually begins outside the contact center.

The logical approach to follow is shown in figure 33.

It is worth noting that the earlier the step in the chain,

- the better it is for the customer, from the perspective of effort (see further),
- the greater the impact, and
- the lesser the direct influence of the contact center.

Let this once again serve as a warm appeal to step outside the comforting cocoon of the contact center environment and engage with the rest of the organization to take concrete action based on the center's customer insights.

The various steps in the process are as follows.

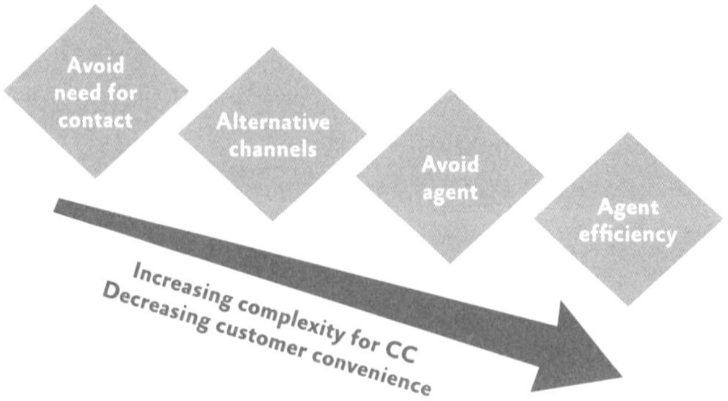

Figure 33: avoiding the use of contact time in a contact center

Avoid the need for a contact

The first way to reduce costs is to remove the need for a customer to make a call. The best service is no service. [47] In an ideal world, there is no such thing as unclear communication, complex products, imperfect processes, imperfect implementation and human error. And all the customers are super-intelligent as well. In an ideal world, the size of a helpdesk is... 0.

Unfortunately, the real world is not ideal. Far from it. This means that there is plenty of room for improvements, which can make the life of both the customer and the organization that much easier.

Although the contact center is not always in a position to push through initiatives, it is still the best placed location within the organization to receive signals about where improvements are necessary.

Figure 34: customer journey insights as a source of inspiration for volume reduction

That the contact center can and must take on this role was already made clear in the section on value. But in comparison with figure 22, the emphasis in figure 34 is now on the lessons that can be learned from global feedback.

In other words, this role now acquires a degree of clear self-interest.

A possible guide for identifying potential reductions in contacts is the value-irritation matrix,[48] as illustrated in figure 35.

The matrix is based on the premise that not all questions, although they might carry similar emotional weights, will be experienced as equally 'valuable', neither from the perspective of the customer, nor from the perspective of the organization. The examples in the table are by no means exhaustive, but they illustrate the kind of thinking involved. They also give an immediate indication of the kind of strategy that can be followed for each category of call.

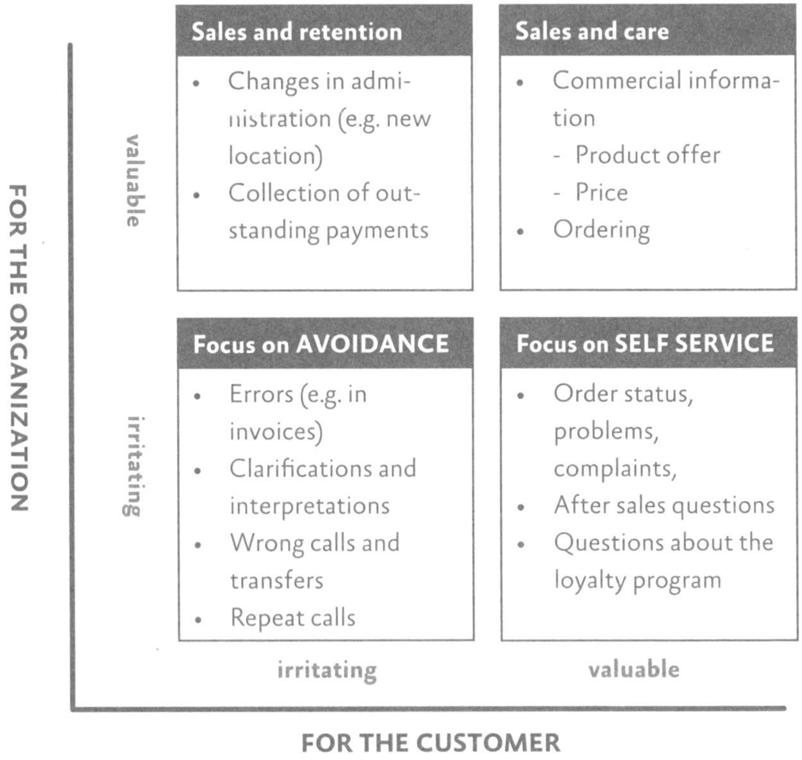

Figure 35: an illustration of the value-irritation matrix

At this point in our story, it is primarily the bottom left quadrant that interests us. Questions that are irritating for both parties fall indisputably into the category 'to be avoided' and offer significant potential for cost reduction. Remember, however, that this does not alter the contact center's 'we-bring-relief' task for all possible calls and questions. There is a value component attached to every contact. This remains a constant from which we must never seek to pull back. Whenever a call is made, in whichever quadrant of the matrix, it always has a potential for value creation or value destruction. In other words, the story we told in the section on the contact center as a value center remains – happily – valid in every respect.

Here, however, we remove ourselves somewhat further from the contact itself, and look at the stage in the customer journey that precedes the decision to call.

Lose-lose scenario: transfer

A special category in the 'irritating-irritating' group of contacts are the transfers, calls that need to be put through from one operative to another.

Studies[49] have shown that transfers have a limited negative effect on final customer satisfaction. But qualitative feedback suggests that in terms of perception they are a major source of frustration.[50]

Leaving aside the question of customer emotion, transfers are also operationally irritating for the contact center. In essence, it means that one call occupies the attention and time of more than one operative, sometimes even at the same moment.

Avoiding transfers therefore has considerable potential for savings. In addition, it is also better for the customer.

In practice, it is possible to distinguish two types of transfer, as illustrated in figure 36:

- an operative transfers the call to another operative with different skills;
- an operative transfers the call to another operative with the same skills.

TRANSFER

	Skill A	**Skill B**
Skill A	• Training? • Accesses in system? • Individual behavior?	• Clarity of IVR? • Routing strategy? • Instructions?
	Operatives!	**IVR and routing?**

Figure 36: two kinds of call transfer

Transferring calls to someone with the same skill is highly inefficient. These transfers indicate that the customer – according to him – has made the right choices in the IVR and has been connected initially with an operative who – according to the system – has the right skills to answer his call, only to then be transferred to a colleague with exactly the same profile.

Possible 'innocent' explanations for this situation are a lack of training in the first operative or a lack of access to the right resources. In less innocent scenarios, an operative might simply pass on the kind of calls he doesn't like to deal with. In all these instances, individual coaching is the solution.

When calls arrive at operatives who clearly have the wrong skills, you need to examine whether this can be avoided by making the questions in the answer menu clearer or by the better routing of calls.

In these cases management also needs to look at the instructions they give to their operatives about what to do when they are confronted with a question they cannot answer. Is it better to make a transfer, or to promise that someone will call him back with the answer, or to give him a ticket to the back office?

Which of these options is best for the customer? Which is the most efficient for your internal organization? How compatible are the answers to both these questions?

Viewed in terms of profit and cost, the simple conclusion is that not all calls are equal. Material errors, unclear communication, badly managed expectations, etc. create unease in the customer and have no interesting potential for the organization. Rather than having to deal with the emotion in the contact, it is much better... not to have to deal with it at all.

If, for example, customers have to call because they fail to see the difference between an 'O' (the letter) and a '0' (the figure) in the activation code of a credit card, that is obviously irritating for them. But it is also irritating for the contact center, because it needs to handle a very emotional call, but for a matter that offers little in terms of added value. However, once the contact center discovers that there is a pattern in such calls, the product management team can ensure that the offending characters in the codes are removed. In this way, a double source of irritation is eliminated.

Cost control meets value creation. Hell yeah...

Offer an alternative: promote self-service

Static information or after-sales questions on 'how to use' the product or service are valuable for the customer. In one way or another, they help him. In contrast, they offer very little added value to the organization. As a result, these are not the kinds of contact that the organization actively wishes to promote.

SOUNDBITE

Gert Linthout, Möbius, prefers to avoid 'irritating' contacts

'There is a fierce discussion about whether customer service in an organization should be seen exclusively as a cost center or whether it can also be a source of additional income. For me, this last point is self-evident: customer service agents are in contact with customers day after day, and are therefore ideally placed to do upselling or ensure retention. However, the debate is often reduced to the single issue of the contact center's rate of conversion. And this while the agents are fully aware that not every contact need be a sales opportunity: often they deal with complaint calls, and at that moment value is created by offering a listening ear and sensitively dealing with the problem. As always, the answer is segmented: some contacts are valuable for the organization and/or the customer, others aren't. Some are even an irritation. This is depicted graphically in the value-irritation matrix.

But how can you deal with this in concrete terms?

What exactly is the customer asking?

This might seem a simple question, but it isn't. Contact logging categories in CRM systems are often too general, too focused on suggested solutions or are not accurately filled in. Likewise, IVR data only give a vague direction. Without an accurate version of the question, investigation of the root cause is superficial or even impossible. Our example is based on listening in to 500 calls, stratified on the basis of IVR data. Where the question or background was unclear, the customer was called back.

The sample was also linked to the costing details of the contact, so that value could be weighed against cost.

What does 'value' mean for your organization and the customer?

This is not an exact science, but the debate about it is nevertheless an important part of the process. In our example, we brought together staff and management from sales, marketing, customer service and logistics in a world cafe and asked them to answer this question: what is valuable for the company and what do you think is valuable for the customer? Their answers to the second part of the question were then checked with customers in focus groups and one-to-one interviews. The categorization was made in part on the basis of a previously defined scale, so that simple "yes-no" answers could be avoided, but this was supplemented using clear questions and criteria: "Was there an earlier moment when we could have dealt with this contact?" "Is there a possibility to act preventatively?" "Does this apply to all customers?" Sending a detailed statement of an invoice as standard often leads to more calls than when you don't send it, but for customers who want a statement it must be made easy for them to request it.

Getting to the root cause

The categorization gives a first indication; then begins the hard work. Each contact category needs to be examined by a work group (preferably cross-functional).

Because the starting point is value for the customer and the organization, lean management techniques are a handy frame of reference. This might involve, for example, an end-to-end analysis of the process for that contact type, with the aim of eliminating the causes of a complaint. But it might also mean the adjustment of the invoice layout (to avoid generating additional questions) or the reformulation of the category choices in the IVR or on the website.

Test it!

It is utopian (and can also have an obstructive effect) to think that you can find the ideal solution at the first attempt.

It is crucial to think about your initial solution from a cross-functional perspective and then to improve it in stages by repeating the exercise. For the improved self-service options we wanted to offer on the website we first asked customers to read through the different scenarios, to see if any further improvements could be made based on their feedback. This is often a matter of details: on the website, customers want to search for the word "contact", and not "support". The result of this change was a hit rate that was two-and-a-half to three times higher.

A wise lesson: always test your gut feeling with the customer.'

We are now in the bottom right quadrant of the value-irritation matrix in figure 35.

In this quadrant self-service is the best tactic. Let customers find their own answers to the questions that are important to them. At this point, the previously discussed communication matrix from figure 14 can be an important aid. It can help you to determine the kind of questions that you would prefer to push to the self-service channel. In this respect, the organization's website is the natural 'ally' of the contact center.

Help a stranger on your website

For anyone who wants to transform their website into a better service transaction channel, *The Stranger's Long Neck* by Gerry McGovern is a must-read.[51] It describes how visitors to your website, most of whom you do not know (and are therefore 'strangers'), are largely searching for answers to a limited number of exactly the same questions. These are the so-called 'top tasks'. The website must facilitate these searches and make them easy to find, rather than hiding them in a complex structure that largely reflects internal organizational needs. The book also offers a number of tips and examples to help you on your way.

At bpost we were able in part to validate our list of top tasks by... listening to the contact center.

To begin with, a team of agents was asked to question customers on ways that could convince them to use the website instead of calling. There was great consternation when it became clear that... customers already consulted the website first. The majority had already made such searches and, when they didn't find what they wanted, had called the contact center. Talk about having areas for improvement. And the categories of the resulting calls matched our list of top tasks.

This was later further confirmed by customer surveys.

Via the contact center additional insights were gathered about the 'why'; in other words, about the point at which the website failed in its primary function as a transactional service channel.

This immediately formed the basis for a project to increase self-service via the website, with the aim of reducing the workload on the contact center, but without influencing the initial customer reflex.

Here again, the contact center can play an important feedback role. Does the center know why customers call, when it is clear they have already looked at the website? Or if they haven't already looked at the website, what stopped them from doing so? Is it possible during the call to refer the customer back to the website for eventual future questions?

Avoid using an agent during a call

When it is not possible to avoid a call, the next best thing is to try and provide the customer with an answer to his question over the telephone, but without the need for him to talk with an operative.

Purely static information, which is relatively context-independent, can be provided perfectly well through the automatic answer menu (IVR – Interactive Voice Response). The customer gets the reassurance he was looking for and the contact center is spared the need to deal with additional volume of a low value nature.

Some managers think that this is 'not done', seeing it as an unfriendly way of brushing off customers the organization does not want to talk to. Hopefully, the following concrete examples from practice will show that this is not the case:

- For a technical malfunction already known to the organization, callers to the repairs service automatically hear that the organization is aware of the problem and is working to fix it, preferably with an estimated time-to-fix. Customers in regions not affected by the malfunction do not get to hear this message.
- For calls to notify the non-delivery of a newspaper, bpost always automatically gives the reference of the publisher by IVR. Simply because the customer always ends up having to contact the publisher, in any scenario (for example, to extend the length of their subscription as compensation for non-delivery). If the customer was actually able to speak to an agent, all he would be told is... the details of the publisher's reference.
- Customers who want to know the status of their bank account are immediately notified that it is not possible to give this information over the telephone for security reasons. They are referred to an alternative channel. Again this is identical to what the agent would have said in a live call.
- The notifications issued to customers that the call center is extremely busy, so that waiting times are increasing, is actually a form of proactive communication, which on the one hand can help to relieve the frustration the caller probably feels and on the other hand can serve as a filter for less urgent enquiries.

In contrast to the commercial reflex of contact center personnel, the IVR self-service option can be turned on or off at short notice, depending on how busy the center is. In other words, a contact center manager can use it as an active aid to control volume in response to the pressure of the moment.

Of course, this means that your IVR must be capable of being operated flexibly, but that is a purely technical question.

The IVR is just one of the existing alternatives. But it is often a very popular one, as it is often under direct influence of the contact center, is quite agile, and has immediate effect.

"In 2030 consumers will not be able to distinguish between machine and human dialogue in online interactions and machine voices will have more engaging personalization. As a result, the majority of customers will place higher value on services delivered by real people".

Prof. James Woudhuysen, in Verint *Defining the Human Age* (2018)

In deciding between the above propositions, the need for emotion is an important guiding factor. If the contact, for whatever reason, requires the injection of some emotion, it is better to have the call transferred to a human operative. We saw this same reasoning in the section on dealing with complaints and it is also consistent with the 'moments of truth' principle.

People always generate emotions. But if you don't need them, automatic alternatives are an interesting option. Research indicates that this is how people tend to think as well:

63% Is OK with being helped by a chatbot, if the possibility exists to call for human help	**72%** wants human contact to remain part of the service-offering

Verint, Defining the Human Age, 2018

Cherish what you have, but optimize!

The call types that contain a positive aspect for both parties (help for the customer, value for the organization) should be cherished and stimulated. If the contact center has a sales role, these are the real commercial opportunities!

Man versus machine

Machine	Man
Personalizes	Makes it personal
Delivers	Overdelivers
Confirms	Smiles

Benedikte Paulissen at *Genesys User day*, 24/09/2015

But even these types of call need to be dealt with in the most efficient way possible. Improving productivity is always a part of the solution. Agents must be helped and coached to answer questions as quickly and as satisfactorily as possible. The right technical aids to assist in this task must be made available to them.

'Satisfactorily' means avoiding an inaccurate or incomplete answer that leads to a repeat call. In addition to customer-friendliness, this is the main (and also slightly selfish) reason behind the idea of 'first time right' (about which we will see more later on, in the section on 'measurements').

'Quickly' implies keeping control over the conversation and not spending more time on it than is necessary, which, in its way, is also customer-friendly. This is largely a matter of correctly applying the right processes and good conversation techniques, not keeping the customer hanging on the line when the solution requires more research than originally thought, correctly judging when to offer a call-back, and achieving a good balance between front office and back office.

In 2007, Belgacom wins the first Belgian Contact Center Award.

At first glance, the efficient and effective management of incoming volumes doesn't sound like a particularly 'sexy' task. Even so, it was a project involving precisely this kind of challenge that was recognized – and rightly so – by the sector in 2007 with the granting of the first ever Belgian Contact center Award to Belgacom.

Gerry Cools (now wholesale service & operations manager at Proximus) tells the story:

'Contact centers are faced with performing a difficult balancing act between sometimes contradictory expectations. On the one hand, efficiency needs to be improved by assisting customers more and more through self-service. On the other hand, customer loyalty needs to be maintained or even increased. At the same time, contact centers are also expected to be profit centers, with ever growing income.

In 2006, the Customer Care division of Belgacom was asked to take this triple challenge to the extreme. A project was launched with the aim of reducing the number of incoming calls by one million (1,000,000... some 20% of total volume at the time) without creating a negative perception among customers, without a negative impact on sales figures and with an increase in customer satisfaction.

The decision to launch the project was taken by the then Management Committee (BMC), the most senior management body in the company. The significance of the project was underlined by announcing it in advance to financial analysts as one of the most important objectives for Belgacom that year. This announcement meant that the contact center could suddenly have an impact on the stock price of the company, an impact it had never had before.

I hardly need to say that the challenges were huge, not only in terms of scope and impact, but also because of its several different dimensions. It wasn't possible to find the solution in a series of one shots. Instead, it required a change of mindset throughout the entire organization. In other words, it evolved from a project into a new philosophy. Every element that could influence our contact centers was critically examined. It was an end-to-end challenge with an impact on different processes and different departments.

To reach these objectives, a special program – dubbed EVOII – was set up, which combined different sub-projects in various strategic fields (IT/technology, E2E processes, etc.). It is worth noting that no use was made of external consultants. The whole project was run internally by our own people.

Right from the very start, we made sure that there was a clear project structure, with a member of the BMC as sponsor. This structure highlighted the need for the involvement of different departments (IT, marketing, sales, strategy, finance, HR, processes, etc.) and clarified their impact on the organization of the contact centers.

The project strategy was founded on four main pillars:

1° The avoidance of contacts (without added value): this was tackled at both the product level and the strategic level. A program of far-reaching product simplification was undertaken and policy in matters such as payment reminders was changed.

2° The offering of other channels for customer care contacts: here the focus was on providing alternatives via the internet, as well as making available specific applications that would allow the customer to manage his own account and transactions.

3° The avoidance of agent interventions: various interactions were automated via IVR and the proactive provision of information to customers.

4° An increase in the efficiency and the quality of call handling: here we concentrated on the correct routing of calls and on quality in general. For this second aspect, we introduced more thorough training and coaching to increase 'first time right' and decrease the average call time.

The involvement of IT in all this was self-evident. The automation of certain calls required advanced IVR. This investment made it possible to automate a number of calls with a limited added value (for example, requests for a duplicate invoice). This in turn made it possible to reduce the total number of calls by 300,000. In addition, the new architecture made it feasible to develop more customer-friendly IVR menus and to make use of basic applications with a text-to-speech functionality. This facilitated both the introduction of highly flexible IVR applications and the more proactive informing of customers, and all under the full control of the business (for example, the request for duplicates, the automatic processing of customer complaints, customized menus, straight-through ordering, etc.).

The importance of "people" in this kind of project is obvious. It needed the involvement of everyone. That was why one of our first actions was to launch an awareness campaign throughout the entire company.

Via a series of workshops and internal communications, people were sensitized to the needs of the project and were motivated to contribute actively towards its success. In this way, the staff were prepared for change and given the opportunity to put forward their own ideas.

At the end of the road, the project was a great success. Within a year, the number of inbound calls was reduced by 1.1 million and customer satisfaction increased by 5%. At the same time, sales figures also improved, with a rise of 3% overall and an impressive 13% in the average income per call. This was made possible thanks to the fact that more non-sales calls were dealt with via self-service. The capacity that this released in the contact centers allowed an extra focus to be placed on sales.'

What costs are we really talking about?

Now that we have been talking at some length about the contact center as a cost center, perhaps the moment has come – better late than never – to think about what the term 'cost' actually involves. As we have already seen, the macro-cost of the contact center – its budget – is relatively simple and only covers a few large cost factors.

However, it is much more complex to distill the so-called 'cost-to-serve' from these macro-costs; in other words, to define the cost per call, case or customer. If we can succeed in reducing volume, how is this reflected in a reduction in costs? Or in the case of growth, what costs need to be included in the business case for the additional tasks of the contact center?

The more homogenous the scope of the contact center's functions, the easier it becomes to calculate the cost of each 'unit' of production. Simply dividing the total cost of the center by the total production is enough to give a sufficiently accurate impression. Done and dusted.

When, however, there is much more heterogeneity – for example, a mix of front and back office or a mix of different types of calls and cases, each with a very different average handling time – this simple method of calculation lacks the granularity to paint a realistic picture.

If there is a need for this more intricate approach, much depends on the level of detail in the internal reporting.

If there is no documentation relating to the different categories of calls and cases and if there is no registration of the way in which time is spent, all you can do is revert to using overall averages. One can reasonably expect however that this crude approach will be the exception rather than norm. The (almost exaggerated) measurability of contact center operations has the advantage of almost guaranteeing that there will be plenty of data to work with.

Of course, it is then a question of ensuring a correct use of the information available.

The way in which the outside world typically calculates the cost of a call is almost a simple rule of three.

Figure 37: the wrong way to make a cost calculation

Wrong!

It is a mistake to just multiply the average handling time by the hourly salary cost of the operative.

Unfortunately, the simplicity of the reasoning in figure 37 is both inaccurate and, from the financial perspective of a contact center, relatively dangerous. Not only does it ignore all non-salary costs, but it also fails to take any overhead into account. To make matters worse, it likewise ignores all non-productive time (training, illness, vacation leave) and the waiting time between calls. In short, contact centers that allow themselves to be reimbursed on this basis will soon find themselves with a financial headache. A project that calculates its costs in

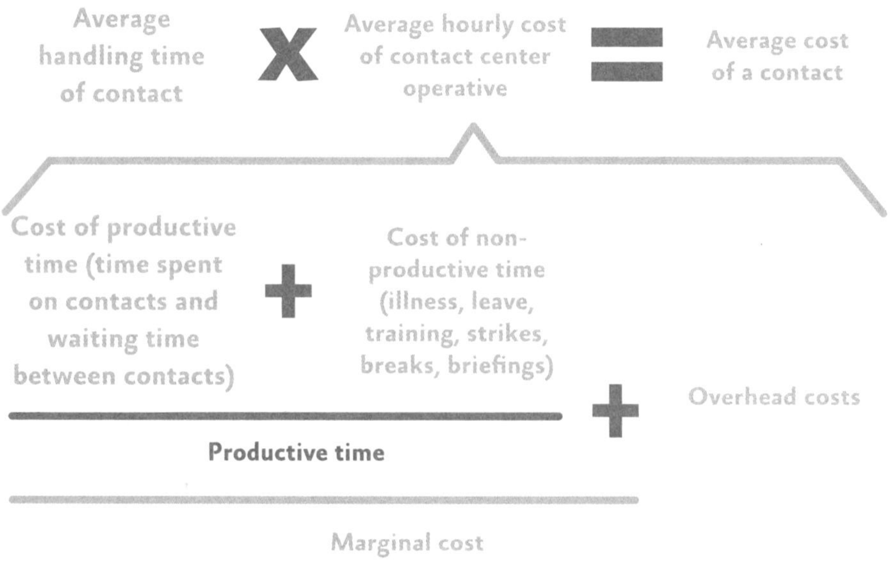

Figure 38: the right way to make a cost calculation

this manner will not find much of its original business plan left when it gets to the end of the road (if it ever gets that far).

A better method of calculation is presented in figure 38.

Right!

All non-direct costs associated with production are now factored into the hourly cost of production.

- The total cost of the contact center is first translated into a 'cost per productive time unit', in which all non-productive time is also included. In this way, for example, higher levels of sickness absence will result in a relatively higher cost for the hours actually worked.
- In addition, the various overhead costs are now added to the direct costs, in layers that match the organizational structure of the company.
- This resulting cost is then multiplied by the handling time of the calls or cases. For calls, this is the actual time that the call took plus a pro-rata element to take account of so-called 'idle time', the time when logged-in operatives are waiting to receive their next call. This time is inherently linked to providing the necessary service results and should therefore be counted as productive time.

Based on this calculation and bearing in mind any internal agreements, it is then necessary to decide how these cost figures should be used. Their use for business cases or cross-charging are relatively straightforward matters. For (FTE) cost budgeting an extra step is first needed to translate the figures into a total number of necessary operatives. For example, the calculation of the necessary FTEs for a contact center that provides a night service will be completely different from a simple cost per (scarce) call.

The same applies for savings. Volume reduction only yields significant cost reduction when the number of personnel can also be reduced.

It applies equally when process analyses are translated into savings.

Cost price insights give a good indication of the points in the process that can perhaps be better redesigned.

In some cases, this can lead to fairly radical proposals.

If, for example, the cost price of an investigation is higher than the level of compensation eventually given to the customer, it is tempting just to pay the compensation in the first place and close the matter.

If, however, this does not result in any real saving (in other words, a reduction in staff numbers), all this proposal does is to increase the organization's 'out-of-pocket' expenses.

Cost calculation at bpost

In a fairly recent exercise, carried out by the bpost contact center in collaboration with the business control unit, the different layers of cost for the calculation of a cost per call or cost per case were identified as follows:

Op. agents
- Salary costs
- Internal cost drivers (ICT, HR, etc...)
- Direct operative-related opex costs

CC overhead
- Direct overheads contact center
- Management and local support
- Project costs pro rata

Customer Care
- Overheads Customer Care department
- Central support teams
- Pro rata ifo FTE share

HQ MRS
- Divisional overheads
- Divisional support teams
- Pro rata ifo FTE share

HQ bpost
- Global overheads
- Fixed % on costs (cf. costing assumptions)

Figure 39: contact center cost at bpost

The outcome of this exercise gives a detailed insight into the cost of front office calls and back office cases, both in terms of products and underlying processes. Above all, the figures serve as an eye-opener for various managers within the organization, particularly in the Marketing and Operations departments.

The same figures were also agreed on as the basis for an in-house convention relating to the inclusion of costs and savings in investment dossiers.

Last but not least, the reporting was also made to the very highest executive level within the company, in Euros. A language that, in the end, is understood by all.

Redirect: when everything comes together

When channel and communication management meet cost management, you get strategic choices and projects. One of these projects at bpost was 'Redirect', the aim of which was to divert telephone calls away from post offices and towards the contact center. This was one of the most important bpost projects in the period 2008-2009. It is however not a postal specialty. Since then, I know first-hand about similar projects in banks, insurance and interim agencies.

The reasoning is simple. Telephone calls in a physical office interrupt the normal flow of work. They frequently come at an inconvenient moment and force a choice to be made between keeping a customer waiting on the phone or keeping a customer waiting at your service counter. An office is not equipped to manage and process call volumes efficiently, whereas that is precisely the purpose of a contact center. The center's organization and resources allow it to carry out this task with a consistent quality through the training of a group of specialist operatives concentrated in a single location, rather than by using a multiplicity of geographically dispersed counter staff.

Of course, the customer remains free to contact the organization in the manner he pleases. A 'redirect' approach does nothing to restrict this freedom of choice. However, if the customer opts to use the medium 'telephone', it is only normal that the organization will organize itself in the best possible way in terms of customer satisfaction.

Or to put it another way: channel choice meets value meets cost efficiency.

The bpost experience allows for some generic lessons to be drawn:

- Regarding such projects as a purely budgetary exercise often leads to disappointment. If the extra staff necessary to deal with the extra calls in the contact centers can only be financed by making savings in the office network, this needs to be realistically achievable in practice. For example, 9 FTE is 'cheaper' than 110 times 0.1 FTE, but the net gain of 2 FTE will only materialize if it is possible to free up all the 0.1 FTE units in 110 different offices.
- The estimation of volumes received in offices is difficult. The options for reporting on classic telephone calls are limited and assessing the levels of accessibility and repeat traffic is far from easy. Pilot schemes need to be used to validate estimates and to determine the objective

drivers (for example, the scale of the customer base, the number of letterboxes serviced in the region, etc.) on which the staffing levels of the contact center can be based. Even so, it is important to retain a degree of operational flexibility, in case the reality turns out to be different from your estimates.

- Pilot projects also make it possible to closely monitor customer satisfaction. They enable the certainty that the large majority of questions can indeed be answered effectively at distance. If this is not the case, all you succeed in doing is creating transfers that you would much rather avoid.
- Sometimes, customers can react with surprise to the new changes and hang up. Expecting to be connected to an office and suddenly finding yourself connected to a series of IVR messages is not to everyone's liking. In some cases, this can lead to negative emotions and repeat traffic. Good communication, choosing the right texts and making use of smart applications in the IVR can all help to ease this problem. Even so, it remains very much a trial-and-error process; it may take a while before you find the best way to do things. But you need to find this way before the large volumes start coming in...
- Not all telephone numbers will need to be redirected. Think, for example, of emergency numbers, staff who always need direct contact with their superiors, certain clients, headquarters, etc.
- Change management of the (office) personnel is crucial. When office staff see redirected traffic as a threat to their sales potential (and the related bonuses), they may quickly be tempted to offer the customer alternative direct call options. If this happens, the benefits of your planned changes will soon be lost. All of them. This is something you need to monitor closely, from your pilot projects onwards. You can check if you are moving in the right direction by measuring internal satisfaction levels. If a sample group says, for example, that they are experiencing a positive effect in terms of workload, this might help to convince their other colleagues to adopt a similarly positive approach.

A comparable change of mindset among contact center staff is also needed. A customer who asks to be transferred to an office must not immediately be given what he asks. With a simple 'how-can-I-help-

you' question it is possible to keep the call in the contact center, which is where it belongs.
- 'Begin with the end in mind':[52] how will you scrap lines and reprogram your switchboards once all the offices have changed to the new system?

In summary: remember that this is not exclusively a contact center project, but is a multi-channel project that requires significant ITC support and should be treated as such. But with the contact center in the lead, it will eventually become a fantastic showcase, in which all aspects of the contact center story can be placed well and truly in the spotlight.

4

THE FAIRY TALE GOES BAD

It all sounds so good, doesn't it? The contact center functioning as a value and profit center, closely allied to all the organization's other departments. The contact center as the internal voice of the customer that helps to improve future products and processes. And all in a stream-lined, multi-channeled environment, in which the different components are attuned to each other to create beneficial synergies.

The model stands. But the endless discussions and the Calimero reflexes of too many of those involved were perhaps already the writing on the wall... In practice, things don't always turn out the way you hoped.

Ask any organization to what extent the idyllic plans went as envisioned and more often than not you will get a disappointed response.

Ask the same to contact center managers and you will most definitely get a disappointed response!

Your dream in ruins?

It is painfully easy to find dozens of counter-examples. I will bet that most contact center people will more easily recognize these stories than the fairy tale. What to think, for example, about the following:

- the promotion campaign that was never notified to the call center, so that the agents were informed by the customers, rather than the other way around;
- an important communication that was sent to the entire customer base at the same moment without a spreading over time, so that a massive peak of incoming calls was generated that overwhelmed the contact center;
- the new documentation that was so unclear that it gave rise to more questions than answers, questions that (not untypically) had not been included in the contact center briefing;
- the evacuation exercise that the building manager had planned exactly at the busiest moment of the contact center's day;
- the maintenance work to existing systems and applications carried out 'outside normal office hours', but forgetting that the contact center, unlike other departments, was supposed to be available during those hours;
- the loyalty program that led to a huge avalanche of complaints because there was an insufficient supply of the gifts that had been promised;

- the special prices and terms that were offered to customers, but were impossible to program into the existing system;
- the product launch for which no extra personnel for the contact center was foreseen, even though the launch communication encouraged people to contact the center for interactions that required manual processing;
- the price offer for a total solution, with a contact center component that was not validated in advance by the contact center, resulting in structural understaffing right from the very start and producing predictably poor results. Leaving it to the contact center to find solutions in crisis-mode;
- the candidate that HR really wanted to employ in the contact center, only to realize later on that the person in question had a serious hearing problem.

Under these circumstances, it is very easy for the situation to deteriorate into a polarized 'us-and-them' story.

L'enfer c'est les autres ('Hell is other people' – Sartre)

The self-doubting, world-on-my-shoulders mindset that is typical of the contact center manager fits perfectly into this polarized situation:

- 'Do those jokers in Marketing really think that in a four-minute conversation our agents will put right everything they've messed up? Why didn't they think about the consequences in advance?';
- 'Are we supposed to do all the dirty work for Sales, while they pick up a nice fat bonus and we don't?';
- 'Do HR honestly expect us to be an employment safety net for all the hopeless cases in the organization? Don't they realize that working in a contact center requires professional skills?';
- 'ICT can't continue to expect us to use all those "work-arounds" on systems that aren't performing the way they should.'

And how does this leave the rest of the organization to think about the contact center? For many of their colleagues, the center seems to be the department that is always complaining about everyone else because their incomprehensible KPIs are (still) in the red.

'Customer service as an appendix.
Without any other function than keeping customers away from that part of the organization which is busy creating revenue, profit and prosperity.
Nearly like (...) office cleaning.'

N. Kjellerup

In short, the contact center is generally seen as a worry rather than as a real support for reaching objectives and realizing new income. And it is expensive and inflexible as well. Isn't it perhaps time to consider outsourcing whatever it is they do...?

The dream of synergy has been well and truly shattered. Instead, it has been replaced by the less than complimentary view of contact center work put forward in the quote by Niels Kjellerup.

How on earth did this happen?

It is just a little bit too easy for contact center managers to claim that these strained relations are always the fault of others. What is the image that the center projects of itself within the organization? And what internal feedback does it receive?

Let's blame Adam Smith...

In 1776, Adam Smith wrote *The Wealth of Nations,* in which, amongst other things, he praised the division of labor as the productivity motor behind the Industrial Revolution. He introduced thinking in terms of tasks instead of thinking in terms of processes, leading to the introduction of the production line and many other organizational structures.

Some 240 years later, this kind of silo thinking still dominates many organizations.

In organizational terms, contact centers often find themselves in 'another' department. Internal communication and coordination are hampered by thick silo walls and by the isolated pursuit of 'local' objectives, which are seldom properly attuned to each other or to the objectives of the organization as a whole.

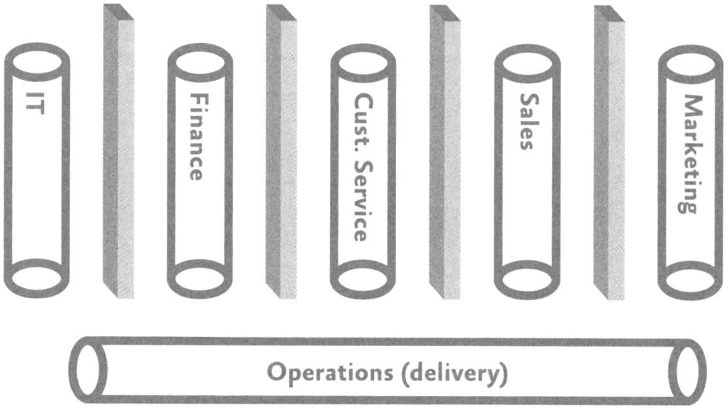

Figure 40: the silo organization

This also explains why the different departments in the organization look at customer contacts in fundamentally different ways. The perception of the finality of the contact varies significantly, depending on the angle of vision.

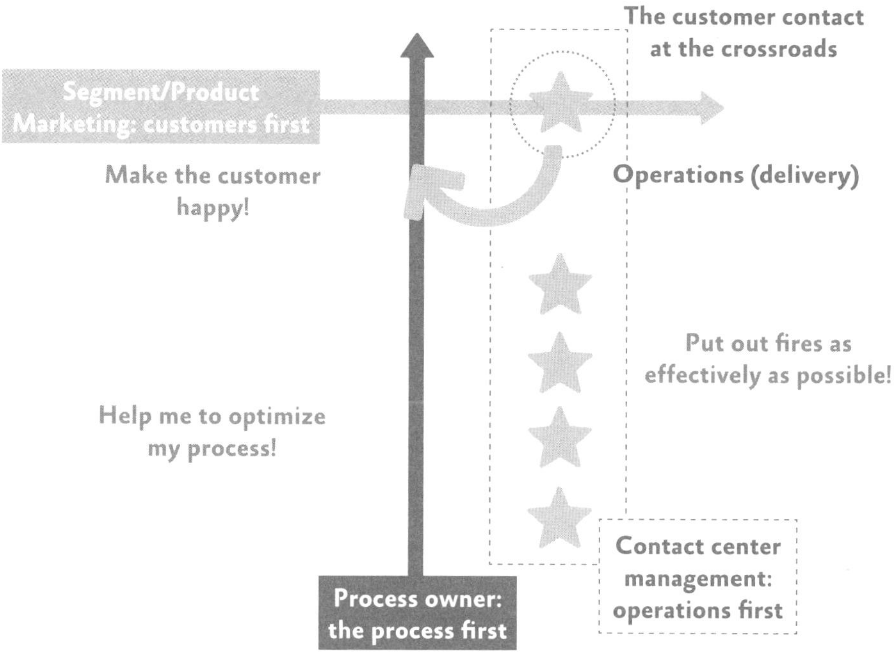

Figure 41: silo thinking about customer contact

This can range from seeing it as 'the possibility for creating a positive experience for the customer in the here and now' – a typical marketing point of view – to 'a learning moment to improve my process for the future' – a typical process holder's perspective.

Inevitably, the contact center manager finds himself in the middle, trying to deal with a multiplicity of different contacts in the most efficient manner possible.

This creates a potential source of tension, which in a silo-based organization is not so easy to clarify or put right. Who is the actual 'owner' of the customer contact? This is one of the reasons why a certain professional literature pleads to introduce a transversal function for a chief customer officer.

Existing structures mean that reconciling the different visions of customer contact in one and the same process will always be a difficult balancing act, with the customer on the receiving end, hopefully blissfully unaware of all the complexity surrounding the 'simple' fulfillment of his needs and wishes.

How do you view complaints?

The difference in perspective on customer contact can easily be illustrated by sketching how the different parties look at the different steps in our favorite example: the 'customer complaint' process.

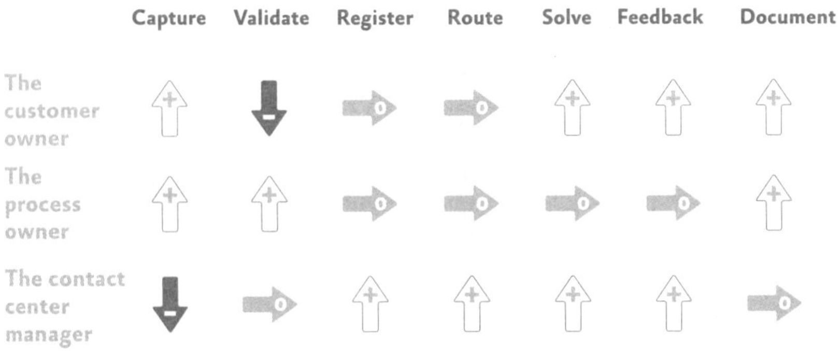

Figure 42: the importance of the different processes in dealing with customer complaints

- The contact center manager has a clear - operational - interest in limiting the incoming flow of calls. Blocking calls on known problems (for example, a technical defect) is therefore a logical reflex. We saw this earlier during our discussion of the possibility to give static information via an answer menu. But this reasoning is obviously less valid if the contact is seen as a possibility to create a positive emotional experience or to create input for analysis that can be used to improve a process. Viewed from these last two perspectives, the aim must be to try and capture as many contacts as possible.

- Validating if a complaint is justified or not is usually not advisable, when viewed from the customer perspective. Soothing the customer's feeling of dissatisfaction is not likely to benefit from first questioning whether he has the right to complain at all. For the contact center manager, this makes very little difference in terms of workload. In contrast, the owner of the process will hammer repeatedly on the need for validation, so that he can be sure that corrective measures do need to be taken to improve the process and that the 'fault' does not lie elsewhere within the organization or with the customer.
- From this point on, the further handling of the complaint is less relevant from a process perspective. The solution of this single case is less important than the lessons it can teach for the future. This is why the correct documentation of the case is crucial. The other functions are more concerned with the correct handling of the isolated incident.
- The internal processes, which in the contact center are so important to ensuring that the complaint is dealt with as quickly and as efficiently as possible by the right operative, are of no interest to the rest of the world.

However, perhaps the most important question has not yet been asked at all. Who is responsible for defining the service concept for which the company stands? Can the complaint rely on a sympathetic response? Or will the small print in the contract or conditions of sale be used to brush off the complaint as the customer's own responsibility?

This is the fundamental question that arises at the point where all three perspectives meet. And the answer will ultimately determine the task, operations and reputation of the contact center.

What has the contact center ever done for us?

With a nod of acknowledgement to Monty Python's *What have the Romans ever done for us?*, a similar question can also be asked about the contact center. In a hilarious scene from the film *Life of Brian*, a group of Palestinian rebels ask the question: 'What have the Romans ever done for us?', with the clear implication that the answer is probably 'not very much'. However, after talking about things for a few minutes, the scene ends with a very different restating of the question: 'Apart from the sanitation, the medicine, education, wine, public order, irrigation, roads, aqua ducts, and public health, what have the Romans ever done for us?'

So, what has the contact center ever done for the organization of which it is a part? Like in the film scene, most colleagues will probably need a little help before they can see all the useful achievements.

We kind of come back to the point about communicating the role as value center. This might have also complicated defending the cost component, by the way, as we were so inadequate in explaining the return.

Nevertheless, maybe the question needs to be asked with some modesty and humility. 'What has the contact center ever done for us?'

It is not because the center contributes in an important way to the emotional customer experience that it can immediately be regarded as a differentiating competitive weapon. Especially when making the distinction (as previously mentioned) between 'service' and 'customer service via the contact center', the center should not claim an exclusivity it does not merit.

When the literature refers to typically iconic customer brands, names like Apple, Starbucks, Harley Davidson, Amazon, Disney, etc. are usually top of the list. But when you think about these companies and what they stand for, how often do your thoughts spontaneously turn to... their contact center?

And while we are in this mood of intellectual honesty, let's be equally frank when assessing how their contact center would contribute to the brand experience.

Some of you might immediately throw Zappos onto the table. But to what extent is the contact center at Zappos more an emanation of an obsessively driven service mentality, for which the channel is almost an incidental?

The contact center as... the toilet of the organization?

I was able to note a great - but slightly risqué - metaphor at a Contact Center Café.[53] Sensitive souls might want to skip this paragraph.

Inge Vissers, managing partner at The House of Contact Centers, compares the contact center with... the toilet in a top-class restaurant.

The decision to eat at the restaurant is based on various considerations, such as the chef, the reputation of the kitchen, the atmosphere, the service... but not the toilet. When customers need to visit the toilet in the course of the evening, they do, however, expect it to be a positive rather than a negative experience, on par with the rest of their evening. If it isn't, this might be a significant factor in deciding to dine somewhere else in future.

No one will question the need for a hygienic, practical toilet in a top-class restaurant. At the same time, no one will regard it as a competitive advantage.

To what extent does the contact center play a comparable role in your organization?

The predictable experience

When marketeers talk about the so-called 'branded experience', what they hope to achieve is a consistent, deliberately created experience, which is valued as such by the customer and helps to differentiate the organization/brand from its competitors.

The evolution of this experience, as shown in figure 43,[54] also immediately sketches a challenging trajectory for the contact center.

In what way can a contact that lasts for an average of just a few minutes give concrete shape and expression to the branded experience?

This is by no means easy, especially in sectors where best practices, both in terms of processes and technology, are regularly shared and copied.

The consistent/intentional part of the comparison calls to mind the notion of scripts, previously written 'conversations' that need to be repeated parrot-fashion by the contact center operative. This is supposed to guarantee that similar questions are always given a similar answer, validated in advance by all the relevant internal partners.

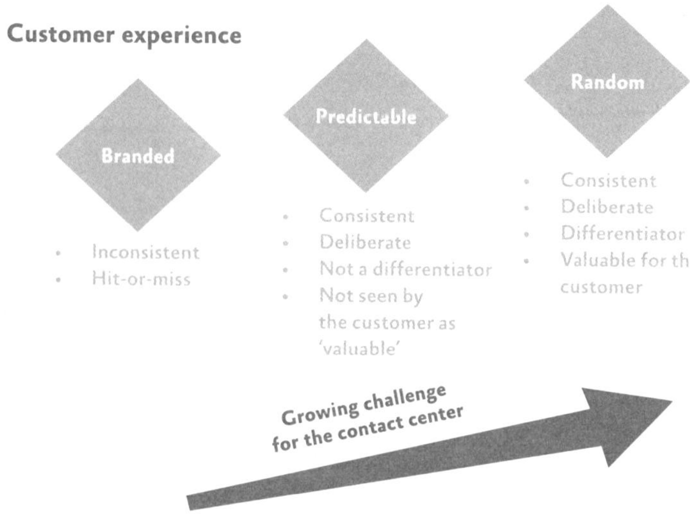

Figure 43: characteristics of a branded customer experience

Leaving aside the highly impersonal nature of such a 'conversation' – something that customers generally don't like – this reasoning contradicts the previously sketched evolution in which calls become increasingly more complex and deal with problems that are increasingly 'out of the ordinary'. It is almost impossible to write an exhaustive library of scripts to deal with this type of non-standard problem. But if, alternatively, contact center agents are empowered to use their own insight to determine what is the 'right' solution in any given circumstances, the challenge then becomes one of ensuring consistency.

'Differentiated' means that you do something in a fundamentally different way from everyone else in a domain that is valued by the customer and for which, if necessary, he is willing to pay more.

But is this differentiation situated at the level of the contact center or is it part of the underlying processes that need to be followed? And what exactly is this 'difference'? Mrs Irlweg probably knows the answer to that question. And so too, I imagine, does Zappos.

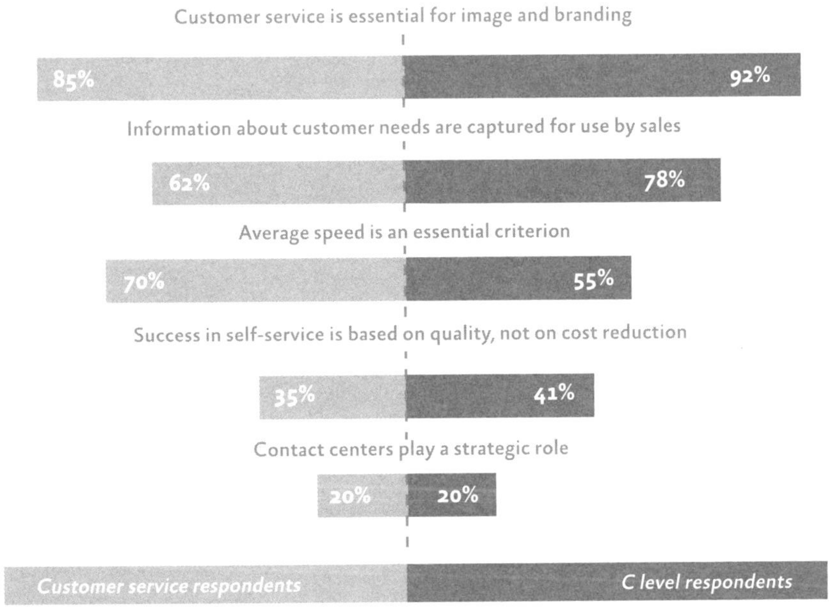

Figure 44: estimation of the contact center from different perspectives

The predictable disappointment

The end result of all these environmental factors is often as disappointing as it is predictable. The often high levels of expectation that people have of the contact center, as the spearhead of service-offering, are seldom met in practice or not perceived as such by those involved in the practical implementation.

Research[55] shows that executive management often has a more optimistic view about the service provision of contact centers than the centers themselves.

The only point about which both sides seem to be in full agreement is the center's lack of strategic importance. Please note how this is in contrast with how customer service is judged as being essential.

Ouch.

Our fairy tale seems to be in urgent need of repair.

Before we look at some of the possible remedies, let's first look at the way that contact centers talk about themselves or have others talk about them. We'll see that this is not always that innocent, and might even increase the 'executive discontent'.

Or how we tend to be quite proficient in digging our own graves even deeper...

5

REPORTING THE CONTACT CENTER PERFORMANCE

Reporting on the functioning of the contact center is not straightforward. Sometimes it even creates additional problems, when the parties involved do not even understand each other. As a result, the fairy tale becomes ever more like a horror story.

Even so, reporting is necessary, if only to justify the costs that are incurred. And if done well, the organization as a whole can benefit from it.

It's all your fault!

The cries of the contact center often reach no further than the walls of the silos.

But let's not put all the blame for this on the silos. We saw earlier how contact center managers are inclined to succumb to the temptation to concentrate exclusively on internally-focused feedback, which largely bemoans the way the rest of the world treats the center with a negative impact on its operations.

In many cases, the response to this is then an indifferent – and not wholly unjustified – 'who cares?' In a previous chapter, I broke a lance in favor of doing exactly the opposite; namely giving contact center reporting a more outward-looking approach as the 'voice of the customer' within the process of value creation.

This does not alter the fact that the contact center still needs to report on its operational performance. Whatever the center's position and role within the organization, nothing relieves it from the obligation to account for its results.

But even within this operational aspect it is easy to lose sight of relevance and meaning. The technical platforms spew out a dazzling quantity of largely specialized standard indicators. Either from laziness (or perhaps from a kind of 'if-its-standard-it-must-be-okay' reasoning), the end result is that contact center reports often consist of a large collection of difficult – and therefore easily misunderstood – 'things'.

Are these 'things' the important message that the contact center really wants to tell, or are they simply the things that are conveniently available in the center's different systems?

Whatever the answer, there is a risk that reporting that is not properly understood will push the different islands in the organization even further apart. And once again, the contact center must accept part of the blame.

One size does not fit all

The question of how contact center reporting should be compiled is highly dependent on the person(s) or the department(s) for whom the report is intended.

This is easier said than done. Contact center managers typically need to satisfy a number of different needs. Their metrics and KPIs must:

- give a correct impression of performance at the different levels of the organization;
- support taking correct management decisions;
- allow guiding individual operative behavior in the right direction.

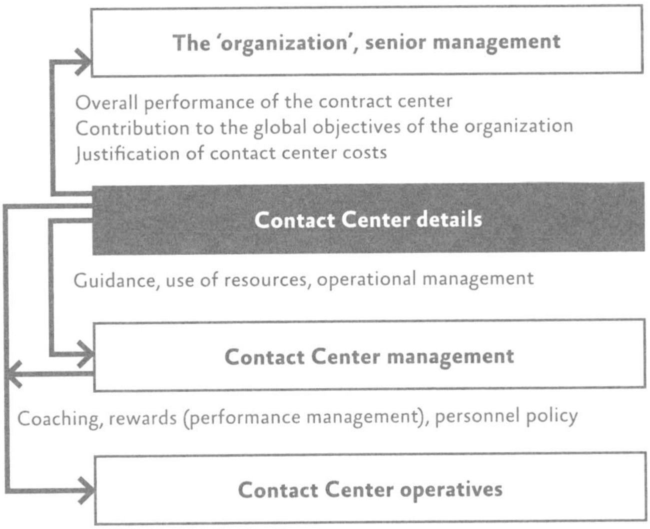

Figure 45: reporting in the contact center: one size does not fit all

In the first instance, the contact center management has a need for concrete guidance indicators that can assist the adjustment and improvement of operational matters, support decisions relating to the use of resources, and help manage the volume-resources-results balance.

In addition, it also has a need for objective data that allows it to monitor, coach and evaluate the individual contact center employee.

Finally, the contact center also has a reporting obligation in respect of senior management and the rest of the organization. These reports must not only highlight the center's wider contribution to the global objectives of the organization as a whole, but also (since everyone regards them as a cost center) provide some justification for the costs they have incurred.

It is on this last element (the top part of figure 45) that the rest of this chapter will concentrate.

This is far from being an unnecessary luxury.

As we shall see, in today's world the risk is (too) great that the corporate dashboards and senior scorecards will be contaminated beyond meaningful use by too many, too operational indicators. All too often, the contact center manager, so often plagued by his Calimero-like inferiority complex, suddenly displays an excess of misplaced arrogance by assuming that the whole world will not only understand what he's saying, but will also – automatically – care.

This is not a good basis for making reports...

Martin Luther King in the contact center?

In the chapter *How do I tell my boss*, Brad Cleveland[56] outlines (amongst other topics) a list of ten things that senior management must know about contact centers. These ten things are summarized in figure 46.

I do not doubt the sensibility of this list. But in my lessons I tend to refer to it – tongue-in-cheek – as the Martin Luther King list.

'I have a dream.'

In essence, the list is a contact center equivalent of advanced mathematics. I would not like to have to feed all contact center managers incapable of understanding the finesse of the list, as accurate as it might be. I would soon be bankrupt. And if there aren't many contact center managers who can understand it, how much hope is there for the rest of the organization? Consequently, it is fair to question how realistic it is for the author to expect that senior management will have sufficiently deep insight into a part of the organization that almost no one regards as core business.

It is perhaps wiser for contact centers to follow the advice of the legendary cowboy actor John Wayne, also quoted in the same book. Wayne said that the secret of playing cowboy roles was to 'talk low, talk slow, and don't say too much...' It might get you further.

When centers need to report to higher management, there is always a danger that top-down expectations and bottom-up concerns will fail to match.

Ten things that senior management should know:

1. Calls pile up.
2. There is a direct correlation between resources and results.
3. Saving on staff is expensive.
4. There is no industry standard for service levels.
5. When the service level increases, productivity decreases.
6. You need to schedule more operatives than the center's basic staff requirement.
7. Budgets for personnel and telecommunications must be integrated.
8. Buy the best systems you can afford.
9. Telecom and IT specialists should support contact centers, not run them.
10. A limited ACD summary report does not paint a realistic picture of the true situation.

Figure 46: contact center reporting 'by the book' (Source: Brad Cleveland)

Your financial colleagues will love points 2, 3, 6 and 8.

Not.

Points 4 and 5 risk coming across as a purely defensive reaction - certainly with regard to the results you are currently announcing. As for point 2... perhaps the least said about that, the better.

Points 7 and 9 are food for an 'interesting' discussion between silos. Point 10 might be the coup de grace that seals your fate...

Worlds that... don't meet

The organization is primarily interested in global insights and sees the contact center as a barometer, without necessarily being too concerned about the levers for its operational improvement.

There is certainly little or no interest for local organizational details.

It is perfectly possible that senior management and other departments are searching for insights for which the contact center does not have the necessary measuring instruments. After all, there are limits to what you can learn about the psychology of customers from a conversation lasting just minutes.

These top-down expectations are then confronted with a veritable diarrhea of technical indicators, often at the lowest level of operational detail and liberally sprinkled with terminology that presupposes a far-reaching technical expertise.

Top-down expectations of the organization

- External focus on customer insights
- Long-term view
- Supporting strategic policy
- Limited set of data
- Ad hoc questions
- 'The big picture'
- Philosophical/strategic questions translated into metrics

Confusion

Bottom-up response of the contact center

- Internal focus on operations
- Short-term view (real time)
- Supporting operational improvements
- Expert jargon
- Extensive mass of indicators
- Inflexible set of ICT or BI solutions
- Details
- Use available metrics correctly

Figure 47: the typical problem with dashboards

These two different angles of approach – two different worlds, if you like – will never meet. This is clearly illustrated in figure 47, which is loosely based on a report by the Executive Board of the Customer Contact Council.[57]

To make matters worse, the relative inflexibility of contact center reporting means that this problem cannot be solved easily. Precisely because so much of contact center practice is conducted based on standard technical platforms, even a minor adjustment means a long and expensive ICT process.

In these circumstances – to paraphrase Dilbert[58] – what the contact center reports to senior management is not what they want to hear, must hear or should hear. It is more likely something they simply don't understand.

Lessons from research in practice

The Expert Class in Contact Center Management[59] allows to draw lessons from the practical use of executive reporting, by 138 contact center managers from 47 companies. The most relevant points in this domain can therefore by illustrated with very concrete facts.

As such, it offers a unique insight into how contact center reporting is viewed in Belgium today, based on findings from the contact centers themselves.

Field research from the Expert Class Contact Center Management

'Measurements' is a standard module in the Expert Class Contact Center Management. The participants are given 'homework'[60] to do in advance, in which they are asked to list five indicators that they think should be included in the corporate scorecard of their company (see annex 2).

What follows is based on the answers of 138 participants in 11 editions of the Expert Class between 2007 and 2018. The companies/organizations represented are (in alphabetical order):

- 24Plus
- Argenta
- b-bridge (a Randstad company)
- Belfius
- BNP Paribas Fortis
- bpost
- Call Excell
- Call-it
- CallMetrics
- Carglass
- Colruyt
- EDF Luminus
- Eneco
- ENI
- Essent
- Euphony
- Floyd
- FOD Economie
- Ikea
- Infrax
- ING
- Ingenico
- IPG
- Job At – outbound
- Lampiris (as contracting client)
- Luminus
- Mediahuis
- Mifratel
- N-Allo
- Nextel
- Partena
- Pidpa
- PWC
- Rabobank
- Santander
- Sitel
- Smals
- Taxipost
- Telenet
- Tennant
- THOCC
- THOCC NL
- TNT
- Touring
- Unamic
- Vanad
- Z-staffing

Treating the answers of these diverse companies as one whole creates something slightly artificial. Important to note however, is that a similar exercise conducted with 14 managers of the same utility company... produced very comparable results. It is therefore quite reasonable to assume that these combined results, notwithstanding the 'potpourri' manner in which they were obtained, are genuinely representative. In the section that follows, the consolidated results will therefore be used as a unique illustration to make certain issues clearer. For details and a full summary of the research, please see the various annexes at the end of the book. Of course, you will understand that every effort has been taken to ensure that these do not contain any company-specific sensitive details.

Please do the practical exercise for yourself while reading this chapter. Which five indicators would you give? And which five would you expect others to mention for your contact center?

One, two, three, four... five

Although the participants in the exercise were given an explicit top-down task to limit themselves to five indicators, practice shows how difficult this is to respect. Even if feedback was mostly given as five bullet points, the actual number of indicators included in those points frequently exceeded our requested total. In fact, roughly half of the participants came up with more than five.

This in itself is an illustration of what is known in the jargon as 'metric bloat', the continual expansion of the universe of reporting indicators. This becomes a bit more painful when follow-up discussions made clear that some of the suggested indicators were not available or even measurable. In other words, the participants' own input had immediately created expectations that were clearly impossible to satisfy. Talk about setting yourself up for failure...

The exercise also illustrates a number of other universal contact center phenomena:

- The correct management of a contact center demands much more than the monitoring of five higher-level figures. Of course, it does.
- Apparently, it is not easy for a manager to limit himself in his reporting to a total of five metrics, especially if he fails to remove his operational spectacles beforehand.

Results of the field research: the relativity of the figure 'five'

In the first instance, only 51% of the answers complied precisely with the instructions to give five indicators.

58% gave five or less. This means that over 40% of the participants submitted more than the 'ordered' five indicators.

The average number of indicators was 5.94, a figure distorted to some extent by a number of extreme scores (the top input list contained no less than 23 indicators).

These extreme scores are often the result of a wish to apply the same set of indicators to all the different channels of communication (telephone, fax, e-mail, etc.) or for different types of contact (order, invoice, etc.).

Challenging the inputs, and in particular the way in which they could be delivered in concrete terms, reduced the net total number of indicators in the exercise by roughly 2%. Things that could not be delivered/measured were filtered out at this stage.

The average number of indicators for use in the remainder of the analysis was therefore reduced slightly to 5.8. This was still higher than the original task requested, but it was clear that the impact of the extreme scores had at least been moderated. But with the corrections, the number of inputs complying precisely with the assignment (exactly five) decreased slightly from 51% to 49%.

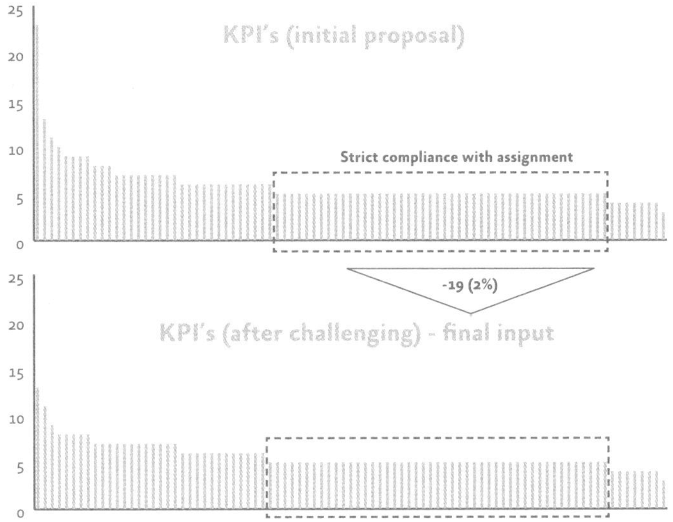

Figure 48: the number of KPIs on the scorecards of the participants

- It seems to be far from evident for a manager to know which indicators remain relevant and pertinent at a level that goes beyond the operational.
- The fact that several of the indicators originally suggested were later discounted shows that many managers know what they want to report or what they should report (viewed from a politically correct perspective), but that in practice this is not always possible. How do you set yourself up when suggesting to the CEO an indicator that you will not be able to provide?

The right number?

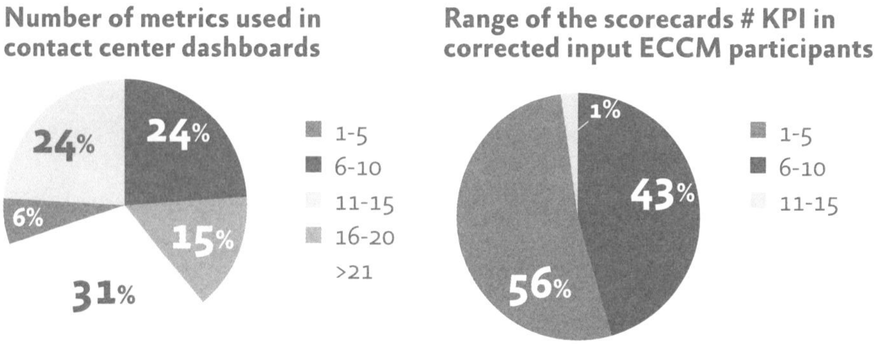

Figure 49: the number of dashboard indicators in relation to the benchmark
Source: Effectively monitoring and communicating the health of the contact center function (2007, Executive Board – Customer Contact Council)

As far as I am aware, there is no ideal figure for the total number of indicators to be included in a 'good' contact center scorecard. This is largely dependent on the center's scope and the particular points that the management wants to/must follow up.

A 2007 study by the Executive Board of the Customer Contact Council[61] indicated how scorecards could be divided up in terms of the size of their indicator range, based on the data they had collected during their research.

In our Expert Class series of lessons, these ranges are used as a kind of mental benchmark.

The comparison with the input of the participants in the Expert Class might be slightly forced, since the task attempted a priori to limit them to five indicators.

Be that as it may, if senior managers ask contact centers to provide a particular number of metrics, it is never a bad idea to make sure that you stick to that number.

Proof that it is possible: three indicators suffice
At the Frost & Sullivan Customer Contact Exchange in 2014, Nicolas Lenoir, director of European operations and supply chain at Belron (Carglass), told how he wished to simplify things for his company's otherwise excellently organized contact center. For processes and KPIs, he aimed to use just three indicators:

- Net Promoter Score;
- conversion;
- productivity.

At his level, these three indicators are enough for him to follow an organization with more than 3,000 agents, spread over more than 30 contact centers.

And how exactly do you choose the 'best' indicators? We will be looking at that a little later on.

'Seek first to understand, then to be understood'[62]

The task in the Expert Class stated that the answer should be formulated as though it was being reported directly to the C level.

Within the context of the exercise, I assume that the receiver of the report has a perfect knowledge of the organization and its activities/sector. As far as contact centers mechanics are concerned however – forgive the arrogance – I assume that the CEO is not more knowledgeable than myself. In many cases (more than a third) even an 'expert' still needed additional information from the participants before I could understand what they were trying to say.

'Houston, we have a problem.'

The what and how of the proposed indicators were often insufficiently given, so that even someone with close to twenty years of experience in the profession couldn't fathom what they meant.

In this respect, contact center managers often seem to suffer from the 'curse of knowledge', which prompts them to talk in a specialized (and often incomprehensible) jargon of their own. They assume that the rest of the organization speaks the same language and shares the same level of expertise, which, almost

Results of the field research: the inadequate manner of communicating the inputs

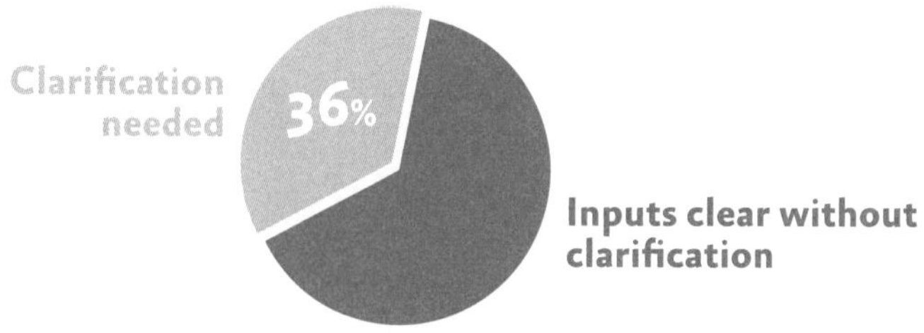

Figure 50: the need for clarification

Follow-up questions were necessary for more than a third of the inputs, simply to be able to understand the context of the indicator(s). These additional questions had nothing to do with company or sector-specific matters, but related to:

- the way abbreviations were used;
- what exactly was being measured;
- the way a concept was measured.

self-evidently, is not the case. This gulf in communication serves only to create an ever-greater distance between the contact center and everyone else.

Curiously enough, an explanation for why a particular indicator was chosen for inclusion in the top five was even more frequently lacking. The reasons for picking the individual indicators are crucial. Without these reasons, you increase the risk that the person reading the report will not be able to interpret it correctly, and this even before the first scorecard has been filled in!

Looking at the most recent editions, participants only provided a 'why' in 16% of the cases. The 'how' is provided in less than half (47%). And in still 20% of the cases, even the 'what' is not that obvious.

The components of the ideal input are graphically depicted in figure 51, with, the most frequent errors and omissions.

The results of the Expert Class confirm these errors conclusively.

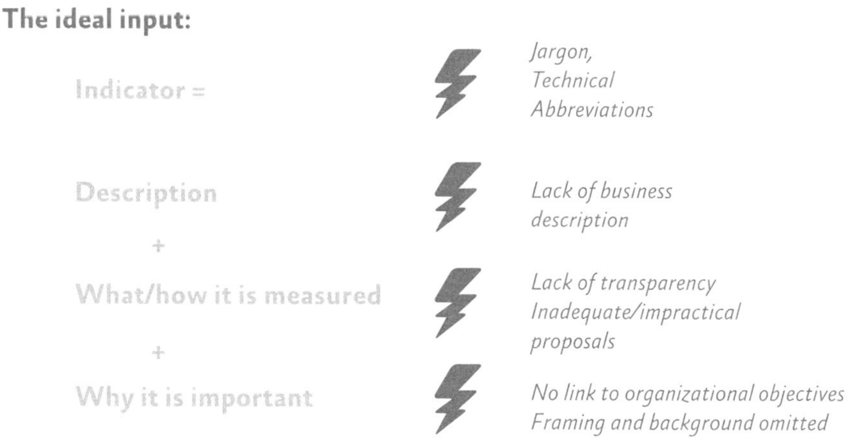

Figure 51: the problems with KPIs

Quality of inputs: service level as example

Further in the book it will become clear that I am not a big fan of 'service level' as a determining KPI for contact centers. But let's put that aside for the moment.

Because at this point, it does serve as a perfect example of how the quality – and above all the comprehensibility! – of the inputs can vary.

Figure 52 illustrates this with actual examples from the exercise: totally different ways in which the exact same proposed KPI was submitted

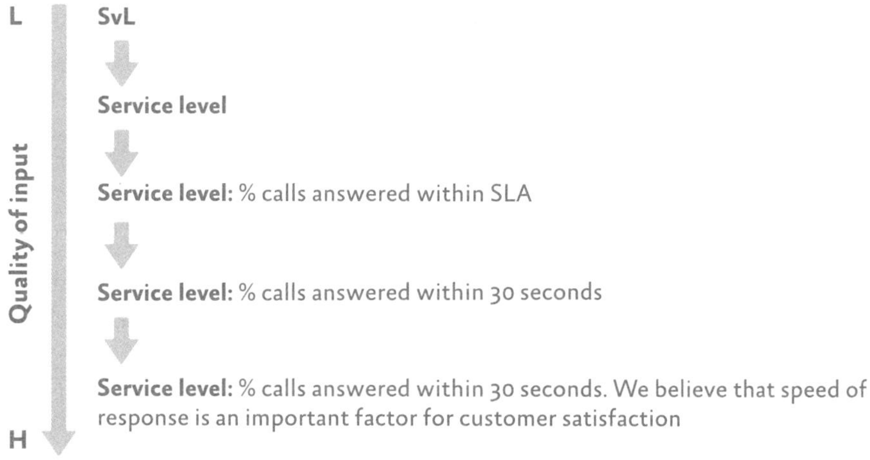

Figure 52: the quality of input for 'service level'

Well, which one would you prefer to read in your report?

A large heterogeneity of indicators, with a very long tail

In a perfectly homogenous world and with perfectly disciplined participants, the number of different indicators would theoretically be equal to five. All contact centers would then choose exactly the same five parameters as being the most relevant at the corporate level.

It would be the ultimate proof of the existence of a universal truth about contact center reporting.

In reality, the opposite is true.

The 138 participants gave a total of 166 different indicators. The full list of the inputs and their relative frequency are given in annex 3.

This heterogeneity can only partly be explained by differences between the various contact centers. It goes without saying, for example, that sales-related indicators will be lacking for centers that only have a service role. Likewise, a center that follows up on outstanding payments will have a number of invoice-related indicators that are irrelevant elsewhere. And, occasionally, some distinctions will also be made between external and in-house contact centers.

Even so, these functional differences cannot explain why more than thirty times the theoretical number of indicators was given.[63]

What's more, the heterogeneity is wide ranging. It was not as if the choices were concentrated around a limited number of popular indicators, with a whole batch of 'own' inputs typical for each different type of contact center banished to the periphery. The list does indeed clearly show a 'long tail' profile, with a long extension of many indicators that are only seldom mentioned. The long neck is also relatively modest.

Again, some generic conclusions can be drawn:

- We are far from approaching a universal truth.
  - The top ten indicators represent roughly half of the inputs. However, this popularity is relative. Only one indicator succeeded in being mentioned by half of the participants (50.7%). Only 2% of the submitted KPIs was mentioned in 10% or more of the participants' answers.
- There continues to be a very strong focus on the 'call' aspect.
  - In the full list, 39 of the 166 indicators are specifically linked to the 'telephone' channel, and seven of the top ten indicators are similarly linked to it.

Field research: a limited concentration around 'popular' indicators, but with a long and heavy tail

The list shows a clear 'long tail' profile, with a long extension of indicators that are only seldom mentioned: 99 of the 166 indicators (60%) are only mentioned once. At the other extreme, there is a small concentration around 'popular' indicators mentioned by various participants, but this concentration is only of modest proportions.

Figure 53: the long tail of KPI inputs

The top ten indicators represent 50% of all inputs. Thirty-eight of the 166 indicators cover 79% of all inputs. The remaining 21% therefore includes 128 indicators.

The first five indicators in popularity were mentioned by at least a quarter of the participants. However, only one indicator succeeded in breaking the 50% barrier, be it only by just. In other words, only one of the more than 160 indicators was included by half of the contact center managers in their proposed scorecard.

The best scoring indicator (customer satisfaction based on surveys) was mentioned by 50.7% of the participants.

The top ten indicators and their relative frequency are illustrated in figure 54.

Indicator	Frequency	Relative frequency
Customer satisfaction (via survey)	70	50,7%
Service level calls (% calls answered within an agreed number of seconds)	61	44,2%
Accessibility/abandon rate (% calls answered or not answered)	58	42,0%
First Call Resolution (First Time Right, measured through transfer/repeat contacts)	43	31,2%
Quality Monitoring Score (calls)	42	30,4%
Gross conversion (sales on calls)	34	24,6%
Net Promotor Score	29	21,0%
Service level non-call transactions (% non-call contacts answered within given delay)	24	17,4%
Inbound call volume	21	15,2%
Average Waiting Time calls/Average Speed of Answer	20	14,5%
Employee Satisfaction	20	14,5%

Figure 54: the top ten indicators of the participants in the Expert Class

This indicates a surprisingly wide difference of opinion about what is fundamentally important to include in contact center reporting. It also reveals an evolution. In the Dutch version of the book (published early 2016, with research results from the Expert Class until 2014) the top ten was slightly different. The top six remained unchanged, but Net Promoter Score (rank seven) and Employee Satisfaction (rank ten) make a chart entry, at the expense of 'Income' as KPI.

- This is no doubt related to the dominance that this channel (as we saw earlier) still enjoys in customer contacts. It is fairly obvious that the phenomenon also reflects the greater ease of availability of this kind of indicator. Many of them are standard in the technical platform. Availability automatically creates focus. And bias.

- The results show that in strict mathematical terms there is a much smaller concentration of non-call indicators. There are lots of them, but their frequency is low.

• The very long tail of indicators reflects a great attention to detail for the constituent aspects of certain contact center phenomena, for which other more 'general' indicators were sometimes already included elsewhere in the list. To some extent, this was a consequence of the way the exercise was set up. Many of these detailed indicators would not have survived a consolidation process if we had really done this for one organization. This applies equally to the indicators that are very similar in nature, which were nonetheless retained in our exercise because of slight differences in the 'what' and the 'how'. Consolidation would certainly result in limitation. It would however also slightly falsify the results as a function of the exercise. In what follows, the spontaneous inputs of the participants therefore remain what they are.

Only healthy branches can be pruned

It seems, then, that there is a real risk that contact center scorecards will contain too many indicators. Some pruning is clearly needed. It is preferable that the contact center takes the initiative to do this, rather than waiting for senior management to do it for them. It certainly benefits credibility more.

But be careful how you proceed. A proposal to carve out an indicator, when its results are far from the acclaimed target will be met with some logical disbelief. Questioning the (non)sense of an indicator becomes a lot easier when you're performing well on it.

The typology of indicators

When we look at the 'nature' of the suggested indicators, it is possible – thanks to the research by the Executive Board – to broadly divide them into the following categories, each with the definition to which they are linked in the Expert Class in Contact Center Management.[64] Annex 4 lists the individual categorization of each indicator suggested by participants.

Typology of indicator, as per the Executive Board	Definition consistently used in the different editions of the Expert Class
Channel Monitoring	Indicators that observe incoming volumes in the different communication channels.
IT Systems	Indicators relating to the availability/performance of the information technology used by the contact center.
Productivity and cost	Indicators that reflect individual or collective cost components or relate to the internal productivity of the contact center.
Quality	Indicators that offer insight into the (perceived) quality of interaction, both from the perspective of the customer and the organization.
Sales and order management	Indicators relating to the commercial sales role of the contact center. They reflect sales results (expressed in Euros or transactions) or give insights into the processing of orders.
Service levels	Indicators that relate to the extent to which and the speed with which contacts are handled.
Other	Indicators that cannot be included under any of the other headings/definitions.

If we look at the inputs at the level of scorecard (the proposed set of five or more indicators) figure 55 shows how well the different categories were represented:

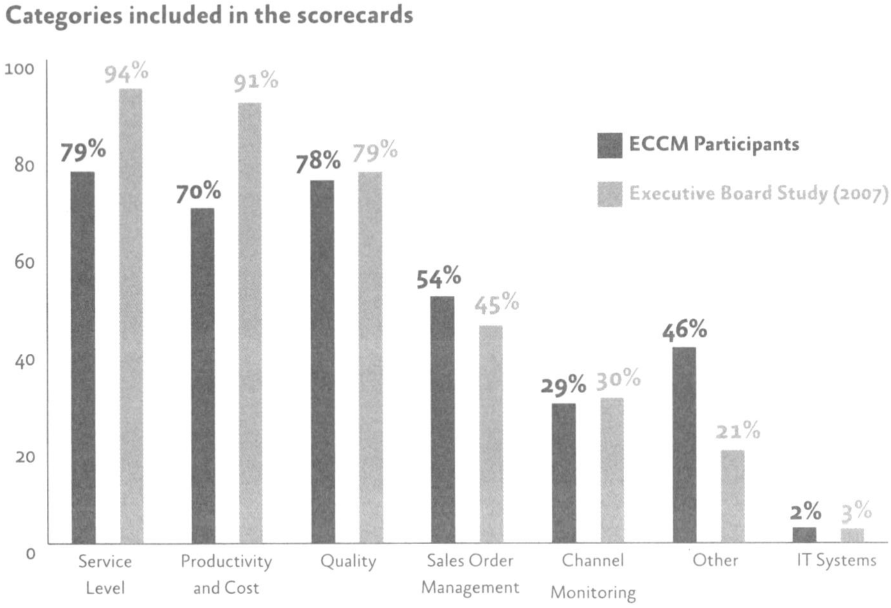

Figure 55: the composition of the scorecards

I can't exclude the possibility that the forced limitation of indicators may have restricted the range of choices. This might explain some of the variances as compared to the benchmark.

Field research: the evolution of scorecard composition over time

It is an interesting exercise to compare how the distribution of the different types of indicator has varied over the years, bearing in mind that the number of participants is not the same each time and that the weight of a single strongly divergent scorecard will not always be uniform.

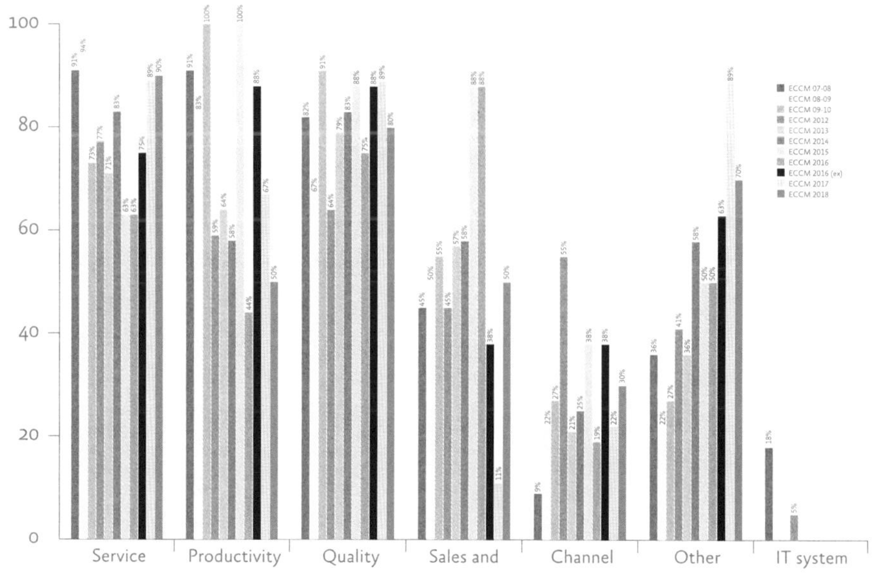

Figure 56: the evolution in the composition of scorecards over time

Two parallel evolutions jump out. The traditional dominance of the 'service level' category weakened during a few years, but has regained full force. Is a 'back-to-basics' approach at the heart of this? A similar evolution occurred for the 'cost' category. Did the economic reality gradually reinforce a new reality upon participants? The steep rise of the 'sales' category on the other hand might be too linked to the profile of participants as to draw heavy conclusions.

On the other hand, this graph might also reflect a sensitivity of indicators to fashions and trends. There are always certain moments when it is bon ton to include something different in the scorecard, often inspired by the role the center wishes to emphasize at that particular time. In this respect, it is the rise to prominence of the Net Promoter Score, one of the big hypes in recent years, which accounts for the increase in the 'other' category.

Even so, there are a number of things still worth noting:

- 'Service level' indicators occur most frequently in both the research exercise and the benchmark. Some 79% of the proposed scorecards contain one or more indicators related to service level. This is logical: the category contains 'accessibility', which is after all one of the basics of contact center performance. Viewed in these terms, it is perhaps more surprising that one in five managers in the Expert Class proposed submitting scorecards to their CEO that did not contain a single service level indicator. This phenomenon is far less pronounced in the benchmark study.
- 'Quality' comes in as a close second. Reporting how 'well' the contact center is performing seems fairly common practice. Productivity & Cost still appears quite frequently. Although it has dropped a few points since the Dutch version in 2016, it still reflects a primary objective of the contact center.
- The figures for the 'sales/order management' category suggest that only half the participating companies allocate their contact center a sales role. It is certainly my experience that if a contact center is given this kind of role, it is always reflected in the scorecard in one way or another.
- The relatively high percentage of 'other' can largely be attributed to staff-related and customer loyalty indicators (including the Net Promoter Score, about which more later). This category is clearly on the move. In the 2016 Dutch version, it stood at 36%. Now at 46%. The nature of the staff-related elements sometimes betrays a highly operational reflex on the part of the participants concerned. But it also reflects a shift towards looking at the human component, in the workplace in general and the contact center in particular. The raging war for talent might explain some of it. The rise in the importance of the Net Promoter Score shows that contact center reporting might also be susceptible to trends and hypes.

Service level still rules

It is also possible to look at the level of the individual proposed indicators rather than at the level of the scorecards. In this approach, illustrated in figure 57, 'service level' and 'quality' indicators tie for first place. Over the years, 'service level' has lost its dominance as category. Of the 801 proposed indicators, a quarter is concerned with either workload processing or the quality with which this is done. These two frontrunners come before 'productivity and cost'. This is where variance with the benchmark is most marked, which probably reflects the way participants in the

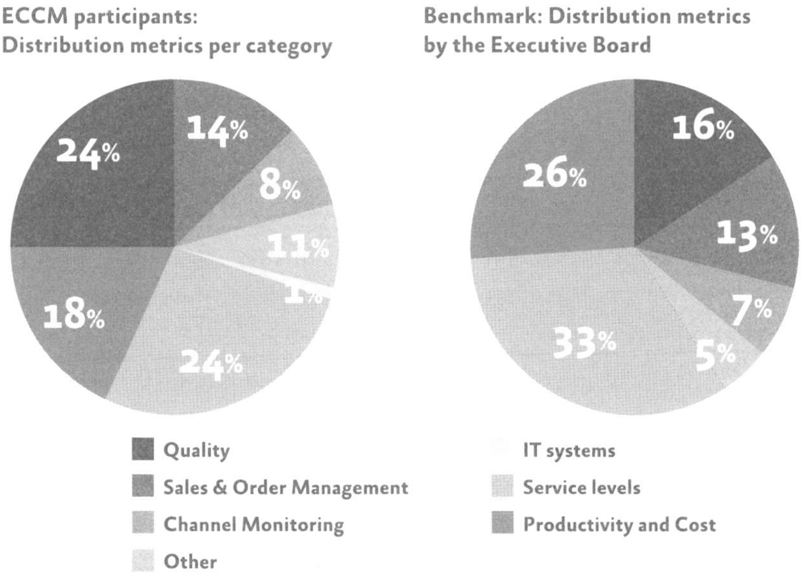

Figure 57: the frequency of metrics

Field research: evolution over time

If we look at this distribution over the years, we get the following picture:

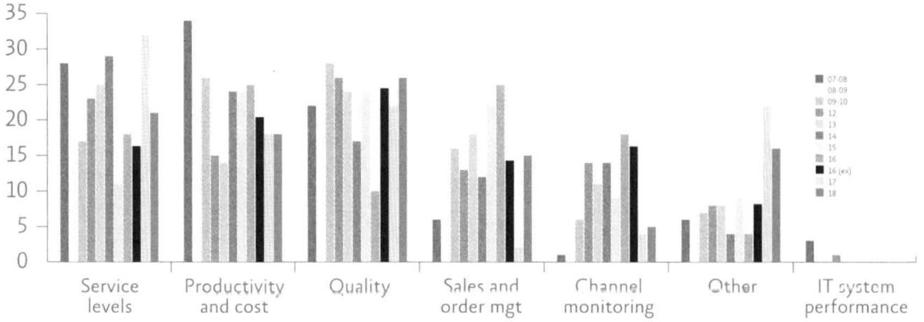

Figure 58: ECCM inputs over time

Just because more scorecards contain a certain category of indicators, does not necessarily mean that the total number of different indicators in that category will also go up. This would be the scenario, if there was more unity of indicators within a category.

Expert Class view their contact centers. It is of course quite possible that other modules earlier in the course program had already inspired them.

With this approach, 'Other' represents a much smaller category. This demonstrates that if this indicator occurs – which has a full effect at the level scorecard in the previous exercise – it is often only with a single isolated indicator. 'Quality' and 'service level' more often occur in combinations of indicators. A scorecard typically contains more than one 'service level' or 'quality' input.

All that now remains is to answer the question of how we can best organize contact center reporting when its purpose is to provide feedback to the organization of which it is a part.

There is nothing wrong with a good model!

To make this clear, it may be useful to first have a look at some of the general – theoretical – models dealing with performance management. These are by no means specific for application in a contact center context, nor do they pretend to be a universal 'passe-partout' solution. Even so, they can still offer us some useful pointers.

More than anything else, over the years they have served as eye-openers for the participants in the Expert Class about the pros and cons of their chosen inputs.

I am certain that they might do the same for you, dear reader.

Model 1: outcome versus output

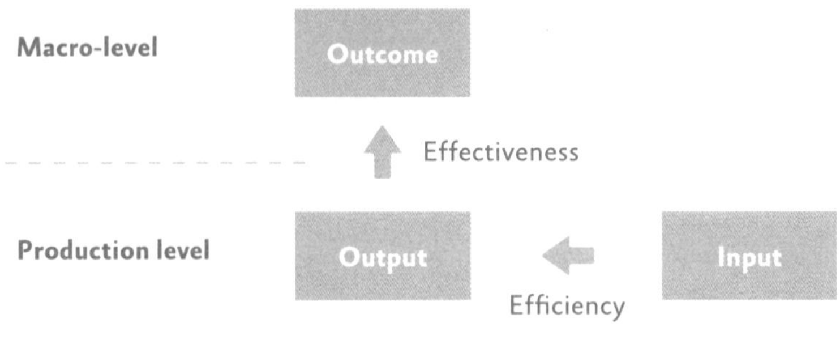

Figure 59: input/output/outcome

A first model of this kind describes the role of an organization in terms of input/output/outcome.

According to this model, the organization strives to achieve a certain outcome, a kind of societal higher purpose or objective at a higher macro-level. To realize this outcome, a concrete output is produced. 'Something' is made or done that will hopefully lead to the successful attainment of the outcome.

To create this output, the organization processes an input. It uses tools and resources in the widest sense of the word to do so.

The manner in which the smallest amount of input is used to create an optimal amount of output is a matter of efficiency.

That the output ultimately generates the desired effect in terms of outcome is a matter of effectiveness.

The police at work...

Let's illustrate the model by applying it to an example not at all related to contact centers. It is a memento of my military service, carried out under the auspices of Andersen Consulting. For this reason, it is perhaps a little dated, but nonetheless still relevant. It describes how the (then) federal police organized speed controls on motorways.

First, they made available a number of resources (inputs), such as manpower and equipment. Using this input, they then 'produced' a number of patrols (outputs), as a result of which some drivers were caught speeding.

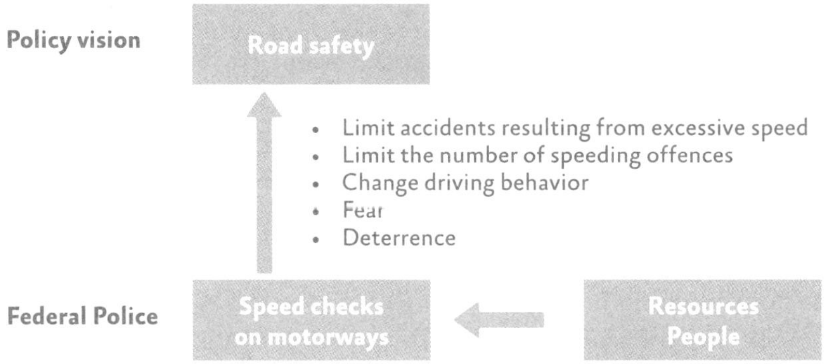

Figure 60: input/output/outcome for speed checks

The offenders are then fined or, in the worst cases, their driving license (and maybe car) is confiscated. This can happen either immediately or at a later stage. However, this output is not the main societal objective. The overall purpose is to increase safety and to reduce the number of accidents and road fatalities.

In other words, there is an implicit belief that increasing the probability that speeding drivers will be caught will act as a deterrent, and thereby lead to more restrained driving behavior. This change in driving behavior will, in turn, reduce the level of irresponsible speeding, so that fewer accidents will happen.

In this way, the final effect is, indeed, an increase in road safety, which can be measured by a drop in the number of traffic fatalities.

The input reporting mentions how many man-hours were made available for the checks, where, at what times, and how much it cost.

The output reporting focuses on the number of vehicles checked, the number of fines issued and offences prosecuted, and the number of convictions in the courts.

But the outcome indicator, which is the one that most interests the political government level and the policy makers, is the ultimate effect of the controls on the behavior of car drivers and its translation into a reduction in the number of fatal accidents.

These same principles also apply in the contact center. Working hours and calls are converted into a number of completed customer contacts, which in turn are translated into customer satisfaction, potential sales, etc. This is all done in the belief that this will eventually contribute to the global results of the organization, both in terms of customer loyalty and profitability.

Of course, up to a certain point it is possible to challenge this argument philosophically. Is customer satisfaction an outcome of the way in which the contact center interactions are dealt with? Or is it more an output of the contact center, which must contribute towards the retention of customers, with the final outcome being repeat sales, average spending, etc.

I will not pretend to have the ultimate answer to this essentially semantic discussion. In the final analysis, it doesn't even matter that much, as long as the relevant reflections are made consciously. In fact, if you ask yourself the question, this is perhaps more important than whatever answer you eventually come up with.

Since this chapter focuses explicitly on reporting to senior management within the organization, the 'outcome' is situated at their level. Viewed from that perspective, 'customer satisfaction with the contact' will be categorized as an output.

Be that as it may, the overall result of the Expert Class most certainly confirms a general strong reflex to focus on outputs. Again, this is hardly surprising. With all we now know about the cost aspect of contact center management, it is only to be expected that there is great pressure on centers to correctly manage the input-output balance.

When contact center managers complain about the unfair picture that is usually painted of their centers, when the contact center claims a role that goes beyond that of a 'cost and call factory', the managers are missing an important

Field research: a natural focus on output

The 'homework' carried out by the participants in the Expert Class in Contact Center Management shows a clear tendency to focus on outputs, as is evident from figure 61. Further details can be found in annex 5.

More than half of the proposed indicators have something to do with output. This again confirms the largely operational approach of the participants to contact center reporting.

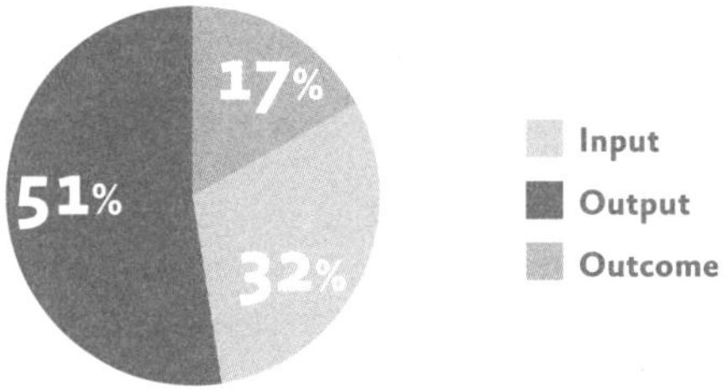

Figure 61: distribution of the indicators of the ECCM participants between an input/output/outcome approach

Only a relatively small minority of indicators (17%) deal with outcomes. In contrast, there are almost twice as many input indicators and three times as many output indicators.

Given these figures, it is possible – no, essential – to question the extent to which reporting correctly reflects the real contribution and performance of the contact center.

opportunity to correct these misconceptions through their own reporting. In fact, it appears they are in danger of doing precisely the opposite. Let's be honest. What is the impression given by the above distribution? Value, profit or cost?

Input and output indicators are unquestionably necessary to run a contact center correctly. You will never hear me say anything different. Ever. But these are probably not the best indicators to use as a feedback instrument to highlight the center's contribution towards the organization as a whole. Certainly not if they require a master's degree in contact center management to be properly understood and interpreted by senior executives and other departments.

The interests and concerns of senior managers are probably not to be found in inputs and outputs, but in outcomes. Unfortunately, these appear much less frequently in contact center scorecards.

This once again creates a field of tension in which both parties risk losing sight of each other.

Of course, it is perfectly possible that in some cases the positioning of the contact center is such that it generates very few (if any) outcome indicators. In all likelihood, this will be the case for most channels and touchpoints, by the way. Similarly, an outcome like 'customer loyalty' is so broad that no single part of the organization can be made responsible for it. In essence, this can do no harm, but the contact center should then at least focus as much as possible on output. Make clear through the 'why' of your output indicators in what way they are genuinely connected to the outcome, the organization's higher purpose.

Model 2: cause and effect

Another way to make clear sense of the input/output/outcome conundrum is to draw up a 'strategic cause and effect' diagram. This shows how different elements influence each other and thereby creates a hierarchy of cause and effect.

This can be very useful in helping you to choose the right performance indicators.

In figure 62[65] customer loyalty is seen as being influenced by customer satisfaction. And one of the driving forces behind that customer satisfaction is product innovation, which in turn is stimulated by investment in research and development.

And at the end of the day, the entire chain must contribute to a better performance of the organization to the benefit of its shareholders.

It is possible to place an indicator for each level of the chain.

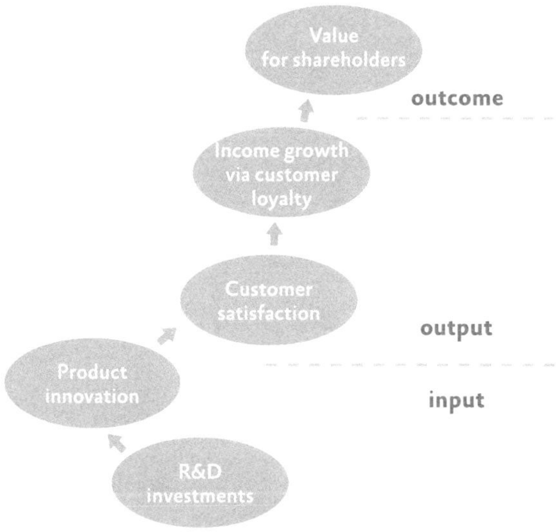

Figure 62: a 'cause and effect' diagram

The 'lower' the position of the indicator in the chain, the more you need to ask whether it really needs to be included in a scorecard intended for senior management. Why would you add a 'cause' to your scorecard, when the 'effect' is available and can also be measured?

In broad terms, it is possible to identify three layers in a 'cause and effect' diagram that correspond to input, output and outcome. The higher up the diagram you go, the more you find the outcomes that have an impact at the organizational level. The lower down you go, the more you will come across inputs.

Figure 63 shows what this kind of strategic map would look like if the indicators chosen by the Expert Class participants were consolidated into a single large diagram.

Once again, a number of observations are worth making:

- The proposed indicators are clearly positioned at different levels. Some of them are positioned right at the very top of the map, at a level that even goes beyond the contact center, and moves into the realms of the performance of the organization as a whole.
- In the most extreme cases, a chain contains a string of more than ten different indicators that are all combined in a cause and effect hierarchy. Even so, all ten were proposed as separate elements in the corporate scorecard exercise.

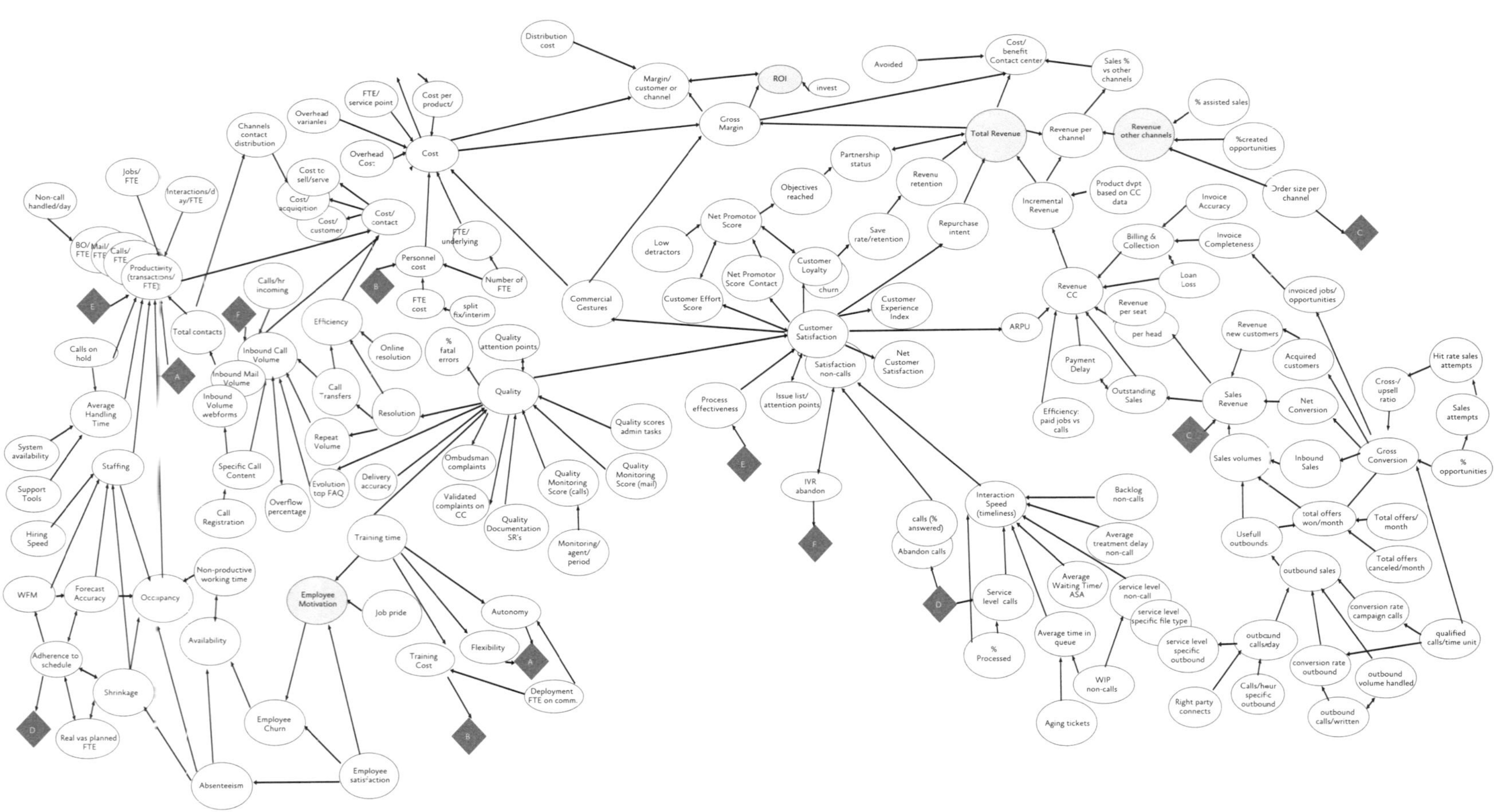

Figure 63: the strategic map of the indicators proposed by the Expert Class participants

Surely in these circumstances the highest positioned indicator would have been sufficient?

- Almost every year it was necessary to create an intermediary link to maintain the logic of the interrelationships. This means that the participants suggested indicators at different points in the chain, but without identifying all the links that lay in between. In figure 63, these are highlighted, showing they are not a participant input, but a necessary logical linking pin. The 'why' of an indicator is not always easy to capture. Some of them are like 'orphans', which cannot be linked to anything and therefore scream long and loud for a 'why' to justify their existence. But not always with success. Okay, we are measuring something but remind me how it is related to an outcome?
- Other connections clearly reflect a belief. Indicators are included because there is a conviction that they measure something that will ultimately have a positive effect on the realities/indicators higher up in the map. But how certain are these connections?
  - A slightly controversial example of this last point is 'employee satisfaction', which is always good for a lively discussion.
  - 'Employee satisfaction' is often included as an indicator, based on the conviction that it will ultimately have a positive influence on customer satisfaction. According to this reasoning, actions relating to employee satisfaction then become… input factors. Leaving aside the fact that there is no scientific evidence to support this claim as it relates to contact centers (see the discussion on the drivers for customer satisfaction in chapter 6), it is nonetheless open to question whether or not this needs to be reported at corporate level.

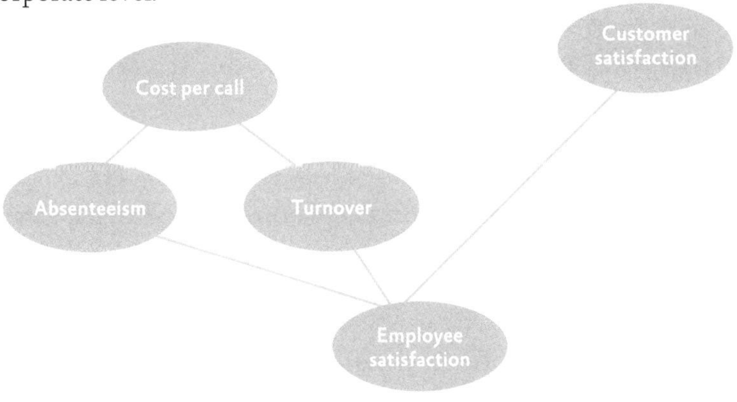

Figure 64: employee satisfaction as a cause for the effect of customer satisfaction

Even when management is convinced by the cause-and-effect cascade of employee satisfaction, as illustrated in figure 64, it is still always legitimate, given the ideally limited number of indicators in a corporate scorecard, to only include 'cost per call' and 'customer satisfaction'.

The other indicators are internal levers, since their nature almost by definition makes them unsuitable as KPIs at the corporate level.

However, a completely different version – and one I have heard passionately defended – is that employee satisfaction is much more than just an input factor. This vision argues that it is the duty of the organization to keep its employees satisfied, almost to the point of this becoming... an outcome. There is a school of thought which believes that employees should be placed explicitly in first position or at least at the same high level as customers and shareholders, so that employee satisfaction merits corporate KPI status. Far be it from me to challenge that school. However I would then expect consistency in the reporting set-up. Intensity of KPI-production and follow-up should then follow, or not? Perhaps it is possible to do an acid test by seeing how frequently the different indicators are measured in practice, because this will say something about the way they are ultimately viewed. Is employee satisfaction really as important as customer satisfaction when one of them is only monitored annually and the other daily? Again, the discussion as such might be more important than the final choice – as long as it is made consciously.

And, just to be clear once more, you will never hear me say that employee satisfaction is not important. I might just have some reservations as we're talking about reporting contact center performance to senior management.

If we know there is a risk of including too many indicators in our reports, it is always a good idea to see how we can look 'upwards' in our map in the most targeted manner possible.

Drawing a cause-and-effect chart is not easy, but it is well worth the effort. At the minimum, this should be an internal exercise for the contact center management. Further involving other parts of the organization can help to promote mutual understanding.

This kind of internal discussion offers an array of benefits:

- The exercise can take as its starting point the full set of indicators that is no doubt already in circulation and use them to either endorse the present method of reporting or radically amend it.

- It puts a number of things on the discussion table in a way that's transparent. Implicit convictions will become quite visible and, in this way, can either be invalidated or validated as shared beliefs.
- The graphic depiction of different connections in a map can be a powerful communication tool, in which the link to the 'higher purpose' of the organization can be made clear. Laying bricks to build a wall or helping to build a cathedral... you probably know the metaphor. The map makes it possible to answer this question for the contact center and its staff in a highly visual way.

Model 3: with thanks to consultancy: from mission to KPI

Why is a KPI important? What exactly is being measured and what is its relevance?

These questions are answered almost automatically if the method of defining KPIs follows a logical process. This process takes as its starting point the 'higher purpose' (from now on, let's just call it an outcome), which is used as the basis for a vision and a mission, which is then systematically translated into a model to create indicators and targets.

Figure 65, inspired by material from Andersen Consulting, describes this methodology.

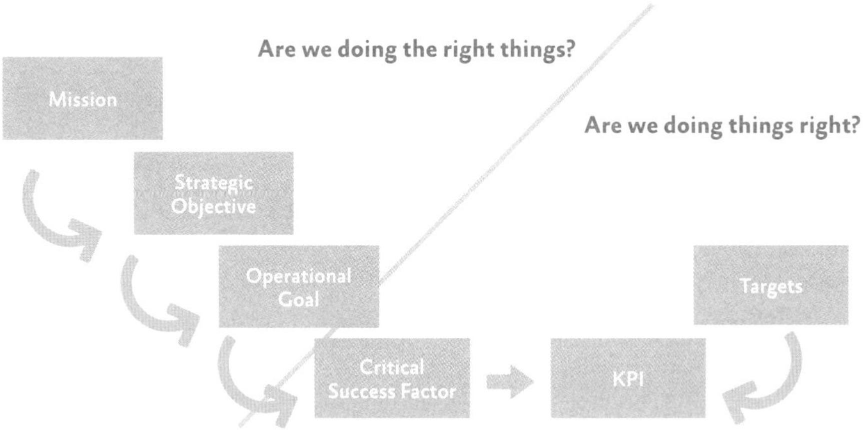

Figure 65: from mission to KPI, consultancy style

An example using a contact center task: dealing with complaints

To illustrate this model, let's have another look at our good-old favorite topic: dealing with complaints.

If the ultimate mission of the contact center is to remove customer uncertainty ('we bring relief', as we saw when discussing the center's value role), then the strategic objective becomes making/keeping customers satisfied.

If the center is convinced that response speed is key in helping to ensure this satisfaction when handling complaints, 'speed' will therefore become a success factor. The number of complaints answered within the agreed time will become the KPI to monitor performance of this factor against a concrete objective.

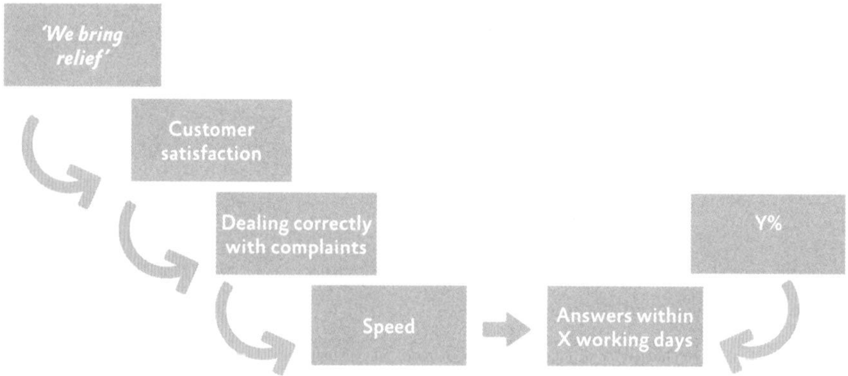

Figure 66: from mission to KPI, contact center style

The overarching mission of the contact center is converted into long-term strategic objectives. What does it need to do to fulfill the mission?

Those strategic objectives are then translated into concrete, tactical-operational, shorter-term goals.

For each goal, a set of critical success factors is determined. What exactly needs to be done, and done well, to ensure the goals are realized? It is at this level of the success factors that Key Performance Indicators are defined and targets formulated. If you apply this thought process consistently and correctly, it will almost 'automatically' result in the necessary follow-up to check that everything is progressing the way you intended.

As figure 65 shows, the focus in the top part of the process is fixed on identifying 'the right things'. The bottom part focuses on how to ensure that those 'right things' are 'done right'. Is the implementation level 'on par' with what is necessary to achieve success at the operational level?

The theoretical approach of this model 'from left to right' guarantees that the center will arrive at the correct KPIs. Applying the same methodology in the opposite direction makes it possible to examine the existing method of reporting critically. Most organizations – and contact centers are no exception – do not start this process with a blank sheet of paper. There is usually already an embedded system of reporting and an existing set of KPIs. This makes it particularly useful to reason backwards, to see if you can distill the objectives and the mission from the things that are reported.

Get ready for a hugely confrontational exercise...

That being said, the exercise as such is once again an ideal platform for group discussion, which will make it possible to:

- clarify and validate the underlying assumptions;
- identify 'orphan' indicators (can every indicator be linked back to a strategically important objective?);

Results from the field research: from KPI to mission

Figure 67 shows an extract from the results of the exercise that was applied to inputs from the participants in the Expert Class in Contact Center Management.

It charts how the different KPIs can be grouped in relation to the strategic objective of customer loyalty,[66] via the operational goal of customer satisfaction.

It should be noted that only one of the KPIs ('customer churn') directly measures the end result, whereas many others focus on the measuring of the success factors, which are assumed to make an indirect contribution to customer loyalty.

In this context, many of the KPIs concentrate on speed, while others relate to the measuring of (primarily internal) quality.

It could be argued that a number of the KPIs dealing with 'customer perception' also immediately measure whether the objective of customer satisfaction has been realized.

Strategic objective	Operational Goal	Critical success factor	Key Performance Indicator
Customer Loyalty*	Customer satisfaction	Quality	% fatal errors
Customer Recommendations			Call transfers
			Delivery accuracy
			Evolution in top FAQ's

Strategic objective	Operational Goal	Critical success factor	Key Performance Indicator
			First Contact Resolution (First time right, measured through customer survey)
			First Contact Resolution (First Time Right, measured through transfer/repeat contacts)
			First contact resolution (not specified)
			Issue list/ Qualitative attention points future
			Log ratio (calls documented/registered)
			Monitoring / agent
			Net promotor score contact
			Objectives achievement rate
			Online resolution
			Respecting commitments
			Quality Documentation SR's
			Quality index
			Quality Monitoring score (calls)
			Quality Monitoring score (mails)
			Quality scores - admin tasks
			Repeat volumes
			Training Time
			Validated complaints on Contact center performance
			Volume ombudsman complaints
		Accessibility	Abandoned calls
			IVR abandon rate
			% calls answered
		Interaction speed	% processed
			Aging tickets
			Average time in queue
			Average treatment delay (non-calls)
			Average Waiting Time calls/Average Speed of Answer
			Backlog non-calls
			Delivery speed
			Processing times
			Same day resolution
			Service level calls
			Service level non - calls
			Service level outbound calls
			Service level specific file types
			Service level specific outbound calls
			WIP non-call transactions

Figure 67: from KPI to mission using ECCM inputs

- identify 'blind corners' (are there objectives that have been insufficiently translated into indicators?);
- eliminate redundancies (do we have too many indicators that are essentially measuring the same thing?);
- visualize perceptions (what are we measuring the most?). The things that organizations measure the most are usually regarded as the most important things, but does this actually tie in with the stated vision and strategy?

Figure 67 illustrates this exercise with part of the input from the Expert Class. You can find the full exercise in annex 6.

These results point to several interesting general lessons. Many of these are in line with our earlier conclusions, be it with a slightly different angle of approach:

- Indicators are positioned at different levels. Measurements are taken at every intermediary stage from left to right.
- There are many different assumptions about causes and effects in terms of success factors and their relationship to certain goals.
- Many of the KPIs actually measure the same success factors. The question then becomes to what extent this involves overlap or redundancy. Is it possible to adopt a more rational approach to the selection of the KPIs? Of course, this phenomenon is to some degree inherent in the way this consolidated summary was developed over a number of years. In a real consolidation discussion, some of the indicators would have been eliminated – and rightly so.
- If these KPIs were being applied in just a single organization, its personnel could be forgiven for thinking that annex 6 is living proof that cost and productivity are measured so heavily that they must form the prime directive. If the center does not want to be seen as a cost center, might it not have been a better idea to balance the emphasis?

Model 4: everything is balance

It is impossible to read any of the recent management literature without coming across the 'balanced scorecard' theory of Kaplan and Norton.[67] The authors concluded that in most organizations the concept of 'performance' is too frequently and too one-sidedly expressed in terms of purely financial indicators.

To be sustainable in the long term, companies not only need to look at what makes shareholders happy, but also at what makes customers happy, at what is important for the optimization of internal processes and at what needs to be done to prepare for the future.

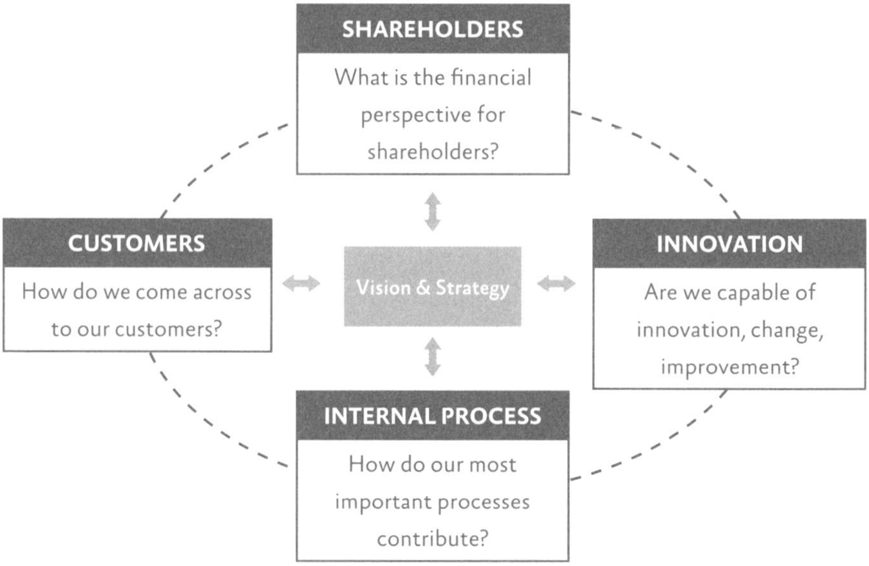

Figure 68: a balanced scorecard

Figure 69: the COPC® vision translated into a balanced scorecard

In this manner, it is possible to create a more balanced picture of the way the company is currently performing.

This methodology has also found its way into contact center reporting.

The COPC®[68] example, which is especially popular in the Netherlands and is specifically geared to the needs of contact centers, takes things a stage further by applying the same reasoning to the way in which KPIs are developed. In this respect, it is worth noting how the methodology depicted in figure 69 closely resembles the methodology we have just described above.

The balanced base of the pyramid implies that the success factors – and therefore, the KPIs derived from them – are spread in a balanced manner across different perspectives.

Note also how 'innovation' in this model is replaced by 'people'. This is not unusual. In fact, I have seen it applied in this way in many balanced scorecards. What's more, it is certainly fitting in contact centers, where the personnel are often the only input factor and, as we saw earlier, an important stakeholder.

Field research: out of balance...

The indicators proposed by the participants in the Expert Class in Contact Center Management completely fail to show this nuanced balance. You can find the full classification of the indicators in annex 7. Figure 70 paints the broad picture.

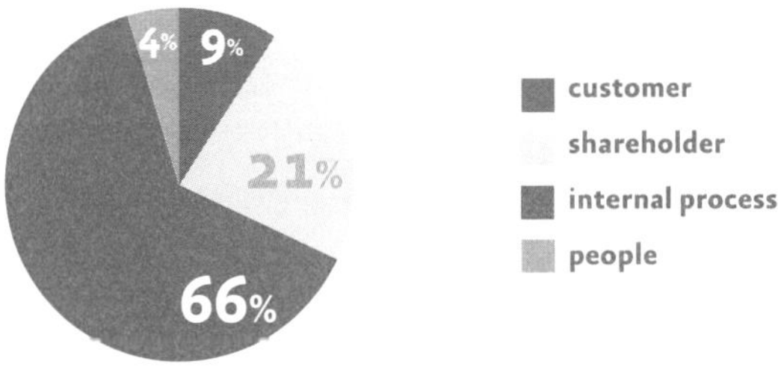

Figure 70: the unbalanced scorecard of the ECCM participants

Indicators with an – internal – process perspective form the large majority. By a landslide. In fact, two-thirds of the proposed indicators relate to internal processes. This once again confirms the highly operational focus adopted by many contact center managers, who even in their reporting to the C-level find it difficult to escape from this narrow vision of things.

In the lessons as part of the 'measurements' module in the Expert Class, the discussion of these results is always lively. Some of the participants cling to their inward-looking approach; others are willing to see an external perspective behind internal processes. This is the case, for example, when the internal processes aim to deliver 'quality', which leads to the tendency to regard this as a customer perspective.

Quality monitoring is a case in point.

There is a conviction that a structural approach to quality, allied to correct monitoring and follow-up, ultimately benefits the customer. But in the final analysis this monitoring, often carried out by using a simple check-list, is no more than an indicator-based method to check the 'correct' implementation of the contact center's own internal rules and regulations for quality. Does the agent follow the prescribed internal processes, yes or no? This then becomes an indicator reflecting compliance, more than customer satisfaction. Hoping you're right about the drivers for satisfaction that it checks up on (and assuming you regularly test this with some regression analysis).

To take the edge of this kind of discussion, I usually make a harsh and a less harsh version of the scorecard – figure 70 reflects the harsh version. Even so, it will come as no surprise that the internal process perspective still takes a good lead in both versions, and that it has consistently done so over the years...

As far as the balanced scorecard is concerned, it can reasonably be asked at which level of reporting this balance needs to be found. Is it at the level of the organization as a whole or is it at the level of the contact center? And in terms of the Expert Class exercise, it can just as reasonably be asked how much balance you can expect if the input is deliberately restricted to five indicators. These are valid subjects for reflection.

Even so, when we are talking about the inclusion of a limited number of contact center KPIs in a corporate scoreboard, you might logically expect a greater focus on customers and stakeholders. Surely that would be more in keeping with the tasks and *raison d'être* of a contact center as we have discussed them so far, wouldn't it?

Yet even in an exercise that artificially attempts to push things in that direction, the results in practice often suggest the contrary.

This is not a value judgment. But I sincerely hope it is food for thought.

Model 5: focus and benefits

In her book *The Real-Time Contact Center* author Donna Fluss introduces an interesting new way to look at contact center performance[69] and therefore at indicators.

She posits, amongst other things, that the value of information from the contact center increases exponentially when it can be shared meaningfully with other departments within the same organization. For her, the contact center is a unique source of insights into customers, market trends, competitors, the possible damage caused by organizational shortcomings, and warning signals in the field of customer loyalty.

She had me hooked straight away...

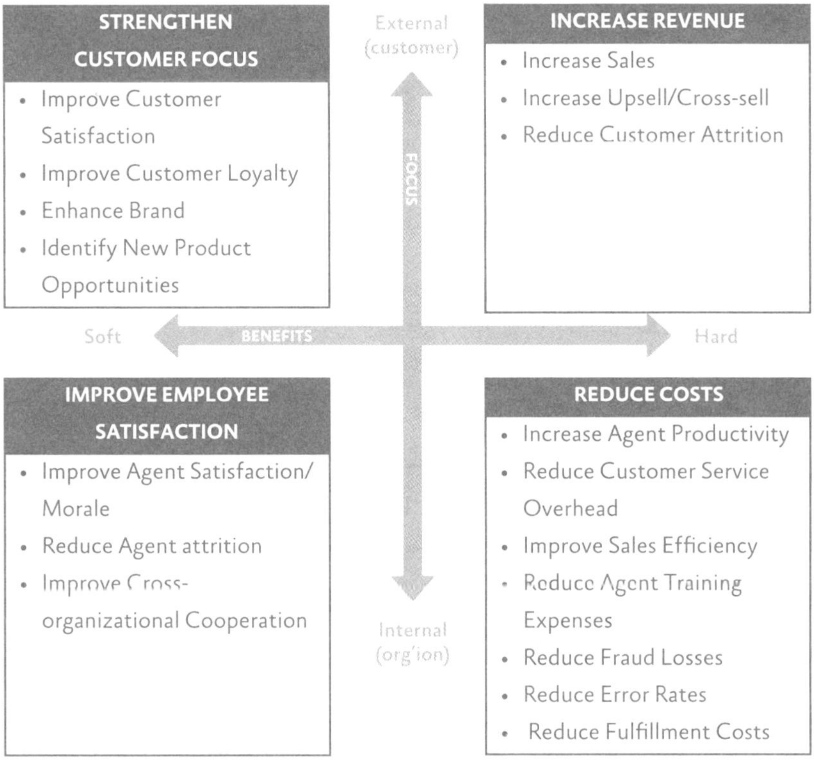

Figure 71: the Donna Fluss model, inspired by *The Real-Time Contact Center*, with DMG Consulting LLC as the source reference

Fluss also introduces the model depicted in figure 71, which outlines the different advantages of performance management.

Field research: the focus on operations reveals itself in the predominance of internally focused KPIs, with a cost impact

When the different input indicators, without taking account of their frequency, are plotted into this model, the results can be seen in figure 72 (see annex 8 for a full summary of the allocation of the indicators).

Figure 72: ECCM KPIs in the Donna Fluss model

The majority of the indicators are concerned with monitoring internally focused, 'hard' benefits. These benefits are often to be found in the fields of productivity and cost.

This is partly explained by the fact that all volume monitoring (referred to in an earlier section as channel monitoring) also falls within these broad fields, but even so...

The resulting image is one of a cost center, focused on cost control. It is only as a kind of second thought that some attention is given to the customer, while the personnel are pushed far into the background.

Painful. Especially so, because on the basis of our discussions during the Expert Center lessons, it is clear that what managers are showing in their reporting is not in line with what they want their centers to be...

In essence, the model recapitulates all the different objectives that organizations can set for their contact centers. It varies little – I am happy to say – from the roles that we defined earlier in this book. But those roles and objectives are then incorporated into a useful model, in which both the focus and the benefits are charted along two axes.

The focus is either external (on the customer) or internal (on the organization). The benefits are either hard (in Euros cash) or soft (non-monetary).

One noticeable aspect of the model is the way it gives the contact center agents a prominent place. The 'people component' is integrated into the greater whole in a logical manner.

As with previous sections, it is interesting to see how the results of our Expert Class exercise fall into this model. It offers an additional insight into the focus, which, as we already know, is largely fixed on operational matters. If there is any truth in the old adage that 'what gets measured, gets done', the insight immediately shows us what we can expect from our contact center managers – and what we need to change.

Do you remember the origin of all these indicators? It was a single question: 'Which five indicators relating to the contact center would you like to propose for inclusion in reporting at the highest level of your organization?'

You can be certain that these indicators tell a story, and will be taken as an indication of how you see – and want to see – the positioning of the contact center.

So if most of your indicators are cost related, how can you complain when people see you as a cost center? High time for contact center managers to take a good and hard look in the mirror...

Don't forget: measuring is not the same a performing!

In the previous section, a strong case was made for contact centers to avoid KPIs at the operational detail level, especially when reporting to the rest of the organization.

Call it a plea for a greater focus on outcome.

At the same time, however, it is important to remember that a KPI must, by definition, also give a clear indication of performance. The contact center will

Net Promoter Score: the one question you have simply got to ask...

Wikipedia describes the Net Promoter Score as follows: 'The Net Promoter Score (NPS) is a management tool that can be used to gauge the loyalty of a firm's customer relationships. It was developed (and registered as trademark) by Fred Reichheld, Bain & Company and Satmetrix. The concept was introduced by Reichheld in his 2003 *Harvard Business Review* article "One Number You Need to Grow". The NPS is based on a single direct question: "How likely is it that you would recommend our company, our product or our service to a friend or colleague?" According to the author, the willingness to put your personal credibility and engagement to the provider in the balance is the best predictor of customer loyalty. A score is usually given on a ten-point scale, following which the NPS is calculated as follows:

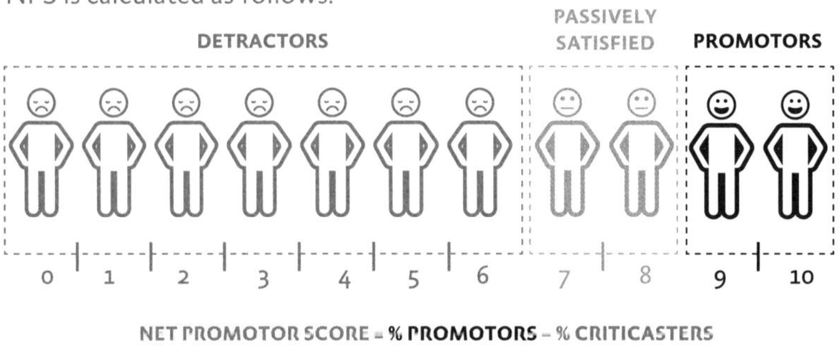

Figure 73: the Net Promoter Score

The final score can vary between -100 (everyone is a detractor) and +100 (everyone is a promoter).

A positive NPS is regarded as "good". An NPS higher than +50 is regarded as "excellent".

While the Net Promotor Score has gained popularity among business executives, it has also attracted controversy from academic and marketing research circles.'

Our field research has certainly confirmed this popularity. This is clear from figure 74, where the first graphic records how many times the participants included this indicator in their scorecard, while the second graphic converts this into a proportion of the total number of participants.

This underlines that the concept has become a major hype in recent years, rising from zero to near dominance in a relatively short space of time. Do you recall how earlier we said that in overall terms the most frequently suggested indicator appeared in the proposals of just more than half the managers questioned? In certain Expert Class editions, the NPS-indicator more than matched this.

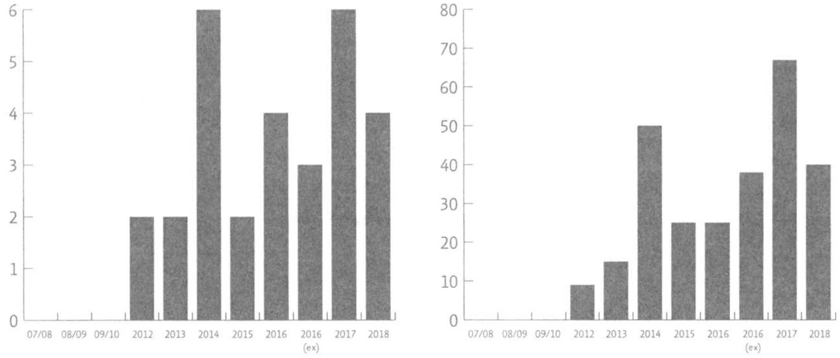

Figure 74: the rise of the Net Promoter Score concept in the Expert Class

either be performing well or not, and this can be measured by monitoring the extent to which it succeeds in reaching its agreed on KPI targets, which in turn reflects the extent to which the critical success factors are being met.

This must not be confused with the role of the contact center as a collector of information, sometimes including data relating to KPIs at the organizational level. Because the contact center is the place within the organization that has the highest concentration of live customer contacts, it is also an extremely useful and efficient survey channel. As a result, frequent use is made of this 'facility' to ask overarching questions relating to various departments.

This places the contact center in the role of the organization's 'measurer', but without actually being 'measured' itself.

We can use an example to clarify this point.

In recent years, the Net Promoter Score (NPS) has become an extremely popular metric. As already mentioned, it now features with increasing prominence among the indicators listed during the Expert Class exercise. NPS has been suggested over the years by 33% of the participating managers, but all these references came from the three editions of the course held since 2012, as shown in figure 74.

The 'single question' about willingness to recommend can easily be included in the industrialized customer surveys that are commonly used for assessing interactions with the contact center. These results can then be extracted and reported.

Even so, it is easy to imagine that this willingness of customers to recommend is dependent on many more factors than the level of service provided by the contact center. This is graphically illustrated in figure 75. And figure 75 is just a quick sketch!

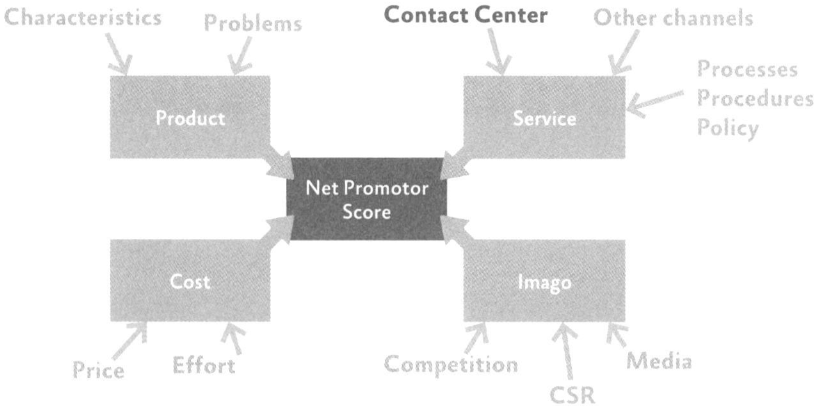

Figure 75: the factors influencing the NPS

Viewed in these terms, the resulting NPS will not be an indicator for the performance of the contact center as such, but is more a reflection of the customer's perception of the organization as a whole.

Changing the question might alter this. For example: 'Based on your interaction with the contact center, has the likelihood increased that you would recommend us to friends and colleagues?' This is what several of the participants in the Expert Center exercise had in mind when they talked about a 'Net Promoter Score for the contact' as an indicator. But I've rarely seen it done this way.

Another alternative is to focus on the 'recommendation worthiness' of the contact center itself. You can do this with a question like: 'Would you recommend the contact center as a channel for this kind of interaction?' Leaving aside the somewhat contrived nature of the question, you might wonder whether you really want to score well. If you are pushing self-service for this particular interaction, a high score will actually be a bad score. In chapter 3, we devoted a whole section to reasons for not encouraging people to approach the contact center. So are we sure that we are now seeking recommendations to do precisely the opposite?

These nuances sometimes come across as bending over backwards to justify including NPS in the KPI-list. I am the last person to try and dissuade contact center managers from this idea, but I would argue that it requires some serious thought in advance about precisely what you want to measure and, more importantly, why. Remember also that in this context the question we asked earlier – 'Do KPIs measure the real performance of the contact center?' – is highly relevant.

It contains several traps we'll have to avoid later in this book. In the same train of thought, the use of input indicators is seldom a good basis for judging performance. The inputs are often something that the contact center more or less 'undergoes' as part of the job. At best, they perhaps have an indirect bearing on the quality of work (for example, the way the avoidance of repeat calls influences total volumes), but no more than that.

Albeit not as a performance measure as such, giving details about input volumes is definitely useful in helping to set the right context, against which actual performance must be judged. A center's reduced accessibility, for example, has a completely different connotation if it coincides with an abnormal and unexpected explosion in incoming volume.

'Divine intervention' is seldom a good explanation for performance

According to the above reasoning, the evolution of a KPI-score indicates whether the performance of the contact center is getting better or worse.

This implies in turn that the contact center management must understand the reasons for the evolution. 'Unexplained' variations suggest that either the managers are not aware of all the levers of performance or else that they do not have all these levers under control.

Sometimes changes in input will be able to clarify variations in contextual terms – hence their importance. An incident that leads to an unexpected increase in calls may, for example, explain a reduced level of accessibility.

A more likely explanation, however, is that the KPI has been formulated at the level of the objective, for which the performance of the contact center is only one factor in the outcome. The more you are inclined to measure aspects of overall customer perception, the greater the risk of assessing things that are not fully under the contact center's control.

Be that as it may, the different theoretical models outlined above can help you from now on to make things more comprehensible and insightful.

You're welcome.

Mythbusting

Contact center indicators are not free from trends and hypes. This was already clear when looking at the evolution of the results of the Expert Class 'homework' over the years.

Some concepts are – temporarily? – hot. Others are regarded *bon ton*, driven by some organizational desire for political correctness. On the other hand, certain KPIs persistently hold on to their aura of truth and appear repeatedly year after year, even though they might not always deserve it.

This is an ideal moment to critically examine some of these myths, in no particular order, and, where possible, bust them. Adam and Jamie in contact center land...[70]

Service level: known and loved, but misunderstood and over-hyped

'Service level' is possibly the mother of all contact center indicators. Traditionally, it gives an indication of the waiting time for calls by quantifying what percentage of calls was answered within a previously set threshold. Twenty and thirty seconds are frequently used as threshold, but there is no universal benchmark.[71]

The term is also used to describe the response speed for cases that do not originate from a telephone call, cases which are usually dealt with in the back office. This KPI-type appears regularly in our Expert Center field research, where the threshold is more likely to be expressed in hours (social media, e-mail) or days (complaints).

Experience suggests that the sensitivity of discussions about service level relates primarily to telephone calls. The focus on service level in this domain is based on the stubborn belief that:

- many contact centers leave customers waiting for far too long before picking up the phone;

The Charter for Customer-friendliness confirms the pressure on waiting times

In 2011, the Belgian contact center world was rudely shaken up by a highly mediatized campaign focused on the perceived customer-unfriendliness of the sector.

In particular, long waiting times were criticized under the slogan 'Pick up!' Bowing to media and government pressure, in June of that year twenty-one companies eventually signed a Charter of Customer-friendliness. Among the pledges made in the charter, the most discussed and the most contentious was the promise to keep customers waiting no longer than two minutes and thirty seconds or to offer them a pro-active call back if this looked likely to happen. No nuance, no flexibility.

In other words, the Charter - which curiously enough made little further explicit reference to call quality - made a clear connection between speed and customer satisfaction.

The signatory companies not only had to comply with this time threshold, but also to report on it accurately and openly.

In the first wave of excitement surrounding the charter, the press - radio, TV, newspapers - gave it considerable attention. The waiting times in the contact centers of the participating companies were rigorously tested, sometimes live on air.

It was clearly a theme that touched a sensitive chord among the general public, especially in Flanders. As far as the companies themselves were concerned, it was more a sensitive nerve – and a painful one at that...

With the disappearance of the Peeters & Pichal program on Flemish radio, who had been very public advocates, the public follow-up of the charter slowly faded away. Some time later, a further eleven companies signed the document, but to much less media interest. The sector made a largely unsuccessful attempt to rehabilitate the concept by suggesting it be used like a kind of quality label, but this idea soon died a quiet death and today the level of follow-up is almost non-existent.

- customer satisfaction is to a large extent dependent on response speed and can therefore be negatively influenced by a poor service level.

As we have already seen, this is a popular indicator, also among the participants in the Expert Class. In fact, it is the second most frequently occurring of all the indicators.

Almost one manager in two (44%) wants to include it in his scorecard for the CEO. Perhaps understandably, as it might be one of the few contact center indicators the CEO has actually heard of.

Leaving aside the question of whether response times really do have an impact on customer satisfaction – I will keep you in suspense on this for now, but you can probably guess where I'm heading – the correct approach to the service level concept first needs a little further clarification.

Service level is expressed as a mathematically calculated number. It is an average of the entire group of calling customers, but only relates to waiting times. It says nothing about individual customer experience.

Figure 76 shows the waiting times for a number of calls.

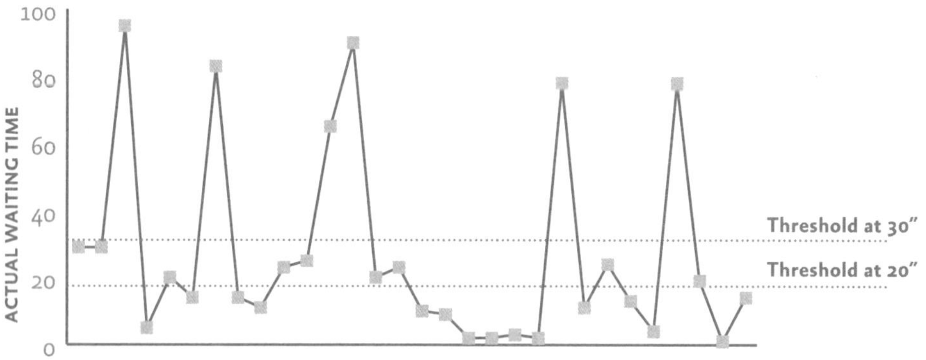

Figure 76: service level in perspective

When the service level is measured against a threshold of thirty seconds, the average success rate is 73%. When it is measured against a threshold of 20%, the success rate falls to 53%. When, in this second case, the denominator excludes callers who had hung up – let's assume 10% – the service level rises again to 66%.

These are three different figures, based on which different conclusions could be drawn in the reporting. But in terms of customer experience, they are identical.

This should make clear that whenever we are talking about service level it is important for the interpretation of the results to always provide details of the threshold time and the method of calculation. It also explains why earlier, back in figure 52, we hammered on the vital importance of high quality when describing the indicator.

In figure 76, at least six customers would raise their eyebrows if they were told that the service level of the company is 'good'. Their waiting experience was anything but good. 'They kept me hanging on the line for more than a minute!'

Because of the way it is calculated, the service level says nothing about the calls that vary from the norm. Just missing the threshold by seconds or missing it by three or thirty minutes: it is all the same within the globality of the calculation. This is why some contact centers prefer to work with an average answer time, known as 'average speed of answer' or ASA.

Even then, care is needed with the interpretation of the results. Consider, for example, the situations depicted for three different contact centers in figure 77.

Based on current opinion about KPIs, and just looking at the numbers, conventional wisdom would probably say that the first two results are better than the third.

But appearances can be deceptive.

The third contact center has much less variability in its answer speeds and therefore comes closer to providing a more consistent and predictable customer experience.

The first contact center has the widest range of variability, with some fairly high peaks. Customer experience at this center therefore depends on the time when you make the call. Random experience, remember?

Which contact center would you prefer to call? Which contact center would you prefer to manage? And how would your answer change as a function of seeing numbers/charts of figure 77?

These variations in answer speeds (and therefore in customer experience) are always hidden. It is an inevitable result of the way service level is calculated and reported. The number included in the scorecard is usually a monthly number; in other words, a global figure for the entire month. This can conceal quite large variations between the individual days.

In the same way, a cumulative figure calculated on a day-basis can also contain a wide range of different customer experiences, depending on the time of the call.

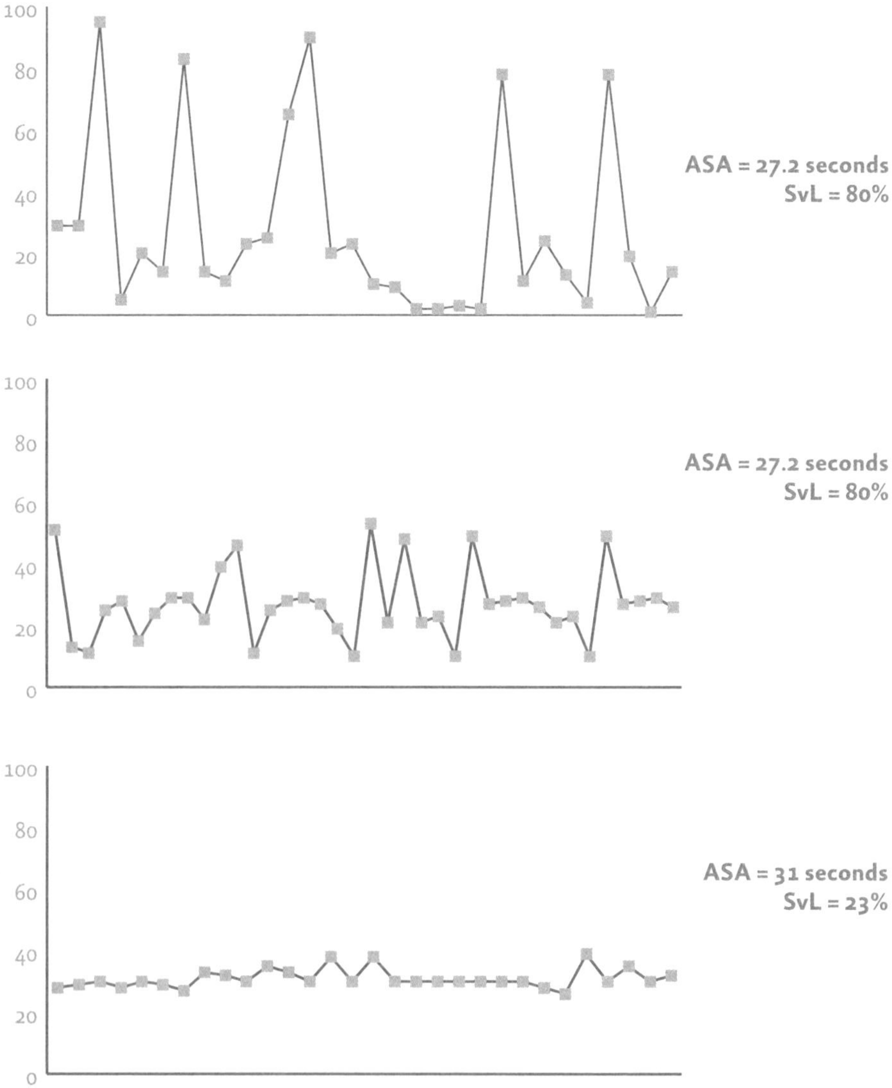

Figure 77: a comparison between contact centers based on service level and average speed of answer

Figure 78 illustrates this phenomenon. It shows how the staffing level in this particular contact center results in a drop of the service level during the – less busy – later hours of the day. However, this only has a marginal impact on the daily average and would probably not be regarded as a problem by the organization. That's if they even notice. However, be sure that the customer calling at 17.15 will know. It's no fun being the statistically irrelevant...

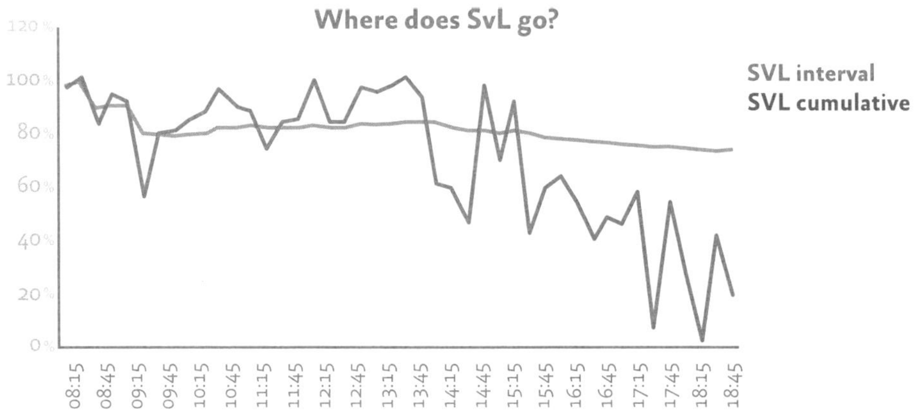

Figure 78: service level over the course of the day

Customer experience in off-peak moments will always remain inadequately highlighted. Even during a globally 'good' day, there will be customers who are (probably) justified in complaining about their individual experience.

For this reason, it is sometimes a good alternative to include a summary of the actual experience of customers in terms of waiting time as part of your contact center report. You can do this by graphically depicting the cumulative distribution of the waiting times, as illustrated in figure 79. This shows that 46% of customers had no waiting time at all, 64% were answered in 30 seconds or less, and so on, with just 0.9% having to wait longer than five minutes.

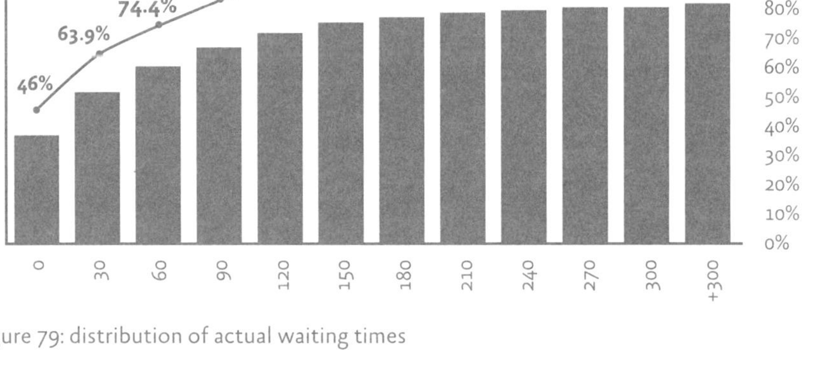

Figure 79: distribution of actual waiting times

Red is green is red

Quite often, the level of achievement for a KPI in relation to its objective is visualized using a relatively simple color code. From nursery school onwards, we are conditioned to associate green with 'good/safe' and red with 'bad/danger'. And it's the same with KPIs: green if you achieve a norm, red if you miss it.

There is nothing wrong with this system; quite the reverse: it is clear and easy to use, and the sight of red figures triggers an emotional response that calls us to action. Because we have also learnt that it is never good to be 'in the red'.

In terms of contact centers, however, there is an important nuance of which you need to be aware: too green can sometimes be the same as red. Service level is a good example. If your score for this aspect is too high, it is probably a sign of over-capacity, which has negative implications for the center's role as a cost center. Perhaps Brad Cleveland was right in figure 46 after all: 'When the service level increases, productivity decreases...'

But the opposite can also be true. Any self-respecting quality auditor will tell you that an indicator that has been in the red for far too long is generally a signal that the management can live with the situation. Otherwise, the necessary remedial actions would already have been taken. When achieving the target is clearly not that important, it may be a good idea to reduce your reported level of ambition. Regarding presentation, it is a better option than having to report a deep red score each month.

Setting over-optimistic targets is seldom good. This is an area where contact centers occasionally shoot themselves in the foot. They formulate a long-term objective or a future ambition, but then measure it in real time. It is smarter to have a series of intermediate objectives, for which your short-term results will obviously appear better, or to link your evaluation color to the speed and direction of the evolution. Measure whether you're heading in the right direction, not whether you're already there...

First time right/first contact resolution: the holy grail

In the trend to replace traditional call platform indicators with metrics more closely related to customer experience, 'first time right/first call resolution' (FTR/FCR) is a clear winner.

That just sounded like real expensive consultancy-speak. Sorry.

Though there is truth in it – as you can derive from FTR's popularity amongst Expert Class participants. It is suggested by about a third of them, which puts it firmly among the top five choices.

Purely as a concept, the 'first time right' principle is the holy grail of contact center management. It combines everything. And I do mean everything. The customer is assisted perfectly at the first time of asking, which boosts his enthusiasm for your organization. At the same time, efficiency levels in the contact center improve through the avoidance of repeat calls or repeat processing.

Couldn't be better, right? An open and shut case.

Unfortunately, in practice it is damned difficult to measure – or at least measure properly. This was again clear in the Expert Class. Selecting the indicator was no problem, but when the participants were asked 'Okay, so how do you measure it?', it was usually red faces all round.

Much depends on how you define the concept. By now you should know that I am not a great fan of semantic discussions, but in this case I will make a brief exception. Clarifying the 'how' will already be so difficult, that we should at least start by clarifying the 'what'.

Thank you, Six Sigma – and others

'First time right' is a concept that originally developed out of Six-Sigma-like quality methodologies, which generally place an emphasis on the correct implementation of processes. In this sense, it is closely related to quality management theory and practice. It is somewhat ironic that the contact center sector, which fights tooth and nail to free itself from its 'call factory' image, should now fall hook, line and sinker for a concept derived from a hard-core production environment.

Traditionally, the scope of the concept covers the full process or the entire organization. From the offset, it is therefore possible to argue that the mere existence of a contact center proves that the organization, as a whole, is not 'first time right' in its functioning. Every question that arrives in the contact center (whether for information or as part of a complaint) proves that something somewhere in the organization has failed. Perhaps the communication was unclear, or the product was defective, or the invoice was wrong. It doesn't really matter. It was not right first time.

Dissection of a concept

'First time right/first contact resolution', as the names imply, assumes that the first time was indeed 'right' in terms of 'resolving' whatever caused the customer to contact you. In other words, a problem was solved or the correct information was given. However, there is a dichotomy here: the 'right' relates to the internal process; the 'resolution' relates to the customer.

Potentially, this can create a field of tension between the two.

Consider, for example, a call from a customer who thinks he has been charged incorrectly. The 'right' explanation may involve referring him to the small print in your conditions of sale. It is unlikely, however, that he will regard this as being 'resolved' to his satisfaction. Or what about the 'right' way to deal with a call about a lost parcel? Anything short of actually finding the parcel while you are talking will not be the 'resolution' the customer was hoping for. So, whose 'resolution' are you actually measuring? United Airlines probably thought that Mrs Irlweg's answer was the 'right' one – or not?

'First contact' rather than 'first call' better reflects the multi-channel experience of today's modern customer. However, honesty compels me to admit that few organizations are able to measure this correctly. There are few CRM systems that can link both shop/office visits and surfing behavior to calls. This means that in practice we are seldom able to move beyond the idea of the 'first call', so that any measuring remains largely focused on the contact center and says nothing about the customer's real overall experience.

Although the two terms are often confused, FTR/FCR is not the same as actually solving the problem by the agent, during the call. FTR/FCR is not just a question of 'online resolution' alone. Perhaps the problem can be solved immediately by the operative on the phone. But perhaps it can't and may first need to pass through several hands before a solution is found. If this does not involve the customer having to call back, from his perspective this is still 'first time right/first contact resolution'. In contrast, measuring 'online resolution' gives insight into the internal efficiency of the organization and the process. How much can and may the front office agent decide and do for himself? This aspect is not necessarily a reflection of the customer's experience. Online, the agent can still get it 'wrong'.

So what do we measure?

Because it is so conceptual, the key question for this indicator is how exactly do you give it concrete shape and form? What exactly do you measure? Various metrics are used in practice, but they each have their advantages and disadvantages.

- As with other customer-related insights, it is always a good idea... to ask the customer himself! 'How many times did you have to contact the center before your problem was solved?' 'Were you given an answer to your question?' These are examples of questions you can easily include in a transactional questionnaire. The main advantage of this is that the information you request certainly reflects the customer's perspective. But there are disadvantages as well. For example, perhaps the customer cannot decide at that moment whether the problem has been solved or not. For a simple information-seeking interaction, it might still be easy for the customer to recognize 'right' (although, if he knows, then why contact in the first place?).

But this becomes more difficult for more complex problems, certainly where follow-up in the back office is required.

As previously mentioned, the customer's perspective on 'resolution' may clash with what the organization considers being 'right'. The customer might be far from satisfied with the solution he has been offered, whereas from the company's point of view the matter has been correctly resolved.

Perhaps the customer is unable to make a distinction between similar but inherently separate facts. What if the invoice next month is wrong 'again', even if the cause was two very different internal factors on each occasion? What if a newspaper is delivered late twice in the same month? How will the customer perceive two consecutive 'first times'?

With this approach, it goes without saying that the company cannot opt to exclude customers who have already taken part in a survey. Worries about possible over-questioning usually lead to the filtering out of customers who are already registered in the database. But in this way, you automatically eliminate repeat calls as well, at least as far as the survey is concerned.

- It is also possible to identify repeat calls on the technical platform itself. Within a period agreed internally, every call received from the same customer – which in practice often means coming from the same telephone number – is taken to be evidence of a non-FCR. Trying to refine this still further to 'calls about the same subject' demands sophisticated (potentially expensive) linkage with the CRM systems, although it is not uncommon to do so. In this case, 'repeat call' then becomes 'call from the same telephone number about the same problem within the same period'. Given this greater complexity, everything depends on documenting the calls in the correct manner.

My experience is that in practice both methods produce broadly comparable results, at least when viewed globally. Detail analyses always reveal inconsistencies, since customer declarations do not always correspond with their actual behavior. Working with repeat calls can (depending on the set-up of the telephone platform and the focus of the reporting) be considerably more complex and require significantly more manual processing than the 'just-ask'-method. It is up to each organization to weigh the pros and cons in its specific context and take its own decision.

- 'Quality monitoring' is a more internally oriented method. The recordings of 'live' conversations are monitored and evaluated in terms of the 'right' procedure. This gives an insight into the extent that agents say and do the right things, viewed from the perspective of the organization and the observer. This is a highly practical method, because the staff can immediately be coached in the best ways to avoid repeat calls. Organizationally, it requires a certain adjustment of the systems set-up, to ensure that enough statistically representative material is collected. Of course, the problem of what is 'right' will remain. Is it what the company observes or what the customer feels?

Customer satisfaction: the alpha and omega

The customer is the start and finish of everything that happens in a contact center. He puts the contact center to work. His satisfaction is the ultimate barometer of how the contact center works and how well it does its job. This is especially true when customer surveys make a distinction between satisfaction with the center and satisfaction with the organization as a whole.

Customer satisfaction was the undisputed number one among the input suggested by participants in the Expert Class in Contact Center Management. It was the only indicator put forward by more than half of the participants. We can therefore reasonably conclude that there is a high degree of consensus about its importance.

As far as the measuring of customer satisfaction is concerned, it is once again true that one size does not fit all. If you only want a kind of global barometer, with a high-level qualitative explanation of the underlying reasons for the scores, the periodic questioning of the customers with whom you have been in contact will probably be adequate, providing you ensure that the selection of the sample population is sufficiently representative. If you prefer, or need perceived objectivity, you can decide to outsource surveying to specialized (independent) firms that will provide you with structured feedback.

However, there are many contact centers who want to use customer satisfaction data as a basis for individualized coaching to their staff. Global averages are no good for this purpose. There needs to be enough individual feedback material for each operative, duly registered, processed and reported. This can be done in a cost-effective way by automatically asking relevant questions by IVR or e-mail after a sufficient number of interactions. Self-evidently, this latter method also offers more scope for customers to make personal comments. It then becomes a matter of not forgetting to read these comments and doing something meaningful with them, particularly if the customer regards the exercise as an additional input channel for follow-up questions.

Here again, there are sufficient options either to do this yourself in-house or to outsource the task to specialized partners, if you so prefer.

The linking of scores to individual operatives makes personalized coaching possible. Linking them to the available background information about the call/case allows a more statistical analysis. For example, it is possible to investigate if certain products and/or processes seem to generate a particular (dis)satisfaction that is not related to the individual operative.

As we will see in more detail later on, the intelligent analysis of this data is a fundamental condition for extracting value from it. It is no longer enough in our modern world to rely on gut feeling to determine possible causes and effects. This is no basis for taking crucial decisions.

The index: the answer to life, the universe and everything

In a relentless attempt to depict the complex world in the simplest possible way, many organizations make regular use of an index, which is a consolidated basket of several underlying indicators.

Mathematically, it is indeed perfectly possible to calculate a weighted average for a number of key elements. The relative weights can reflect priorities, yet still allow performance to be captured in a limited set of indicators.

That being said, the problems with this method are, of course, predictable.

42!

A hilarious illustration of the problem with indices can be found in a scene from the film *The Hitchhiker's Guide to the Galaxy*.[72] I use this frequently during my courses.

A highly intelligent race builds a super-computer called Deep Thought to find the answer to the ultimate question about 'life, the universe and everything'.

And, oh yes, they would like 'something simple'.

In return, the computer asks for the necessary time to make the computation.

After 7.5 million years, Deep Thought returns with the answer... 42!

The consternation among the waiting crowd is huge, but Deep Thought insists the answer is the product of a thorough analysis and is unquestionably correct.

But only if you understand what the right question is, you will properly understand the answer.

According to the super-computer, the key therefore lies in asking the right question.

It still surprises me how this film fragment can cause so many 'aha' moments in a class on contact center management...

Too great a consolidation will result in a meaningless figure. Like 42. To understand evolutions and steer the necessary adjustments, you need to examine the details that you can only find by taking the index apart.

There is a real temptation to use such an index in a contact center environment. The center has masses of numerical data at its disposal and there is often a deep internal conviction that all this data is important, if only a place could be found to store and process it properly. In these circumstances, combining and consolidating looks attractive. Especially when there is room for only a limited number of KPIs. This often happens, for example, around productivity, but it usually generates results that are complex and, ultimately, devoid of any useful conclusions. We are back to 42 again.

Customer effort score: the next best thing

In a notorious *Harvard Business Review* article from 2010,[73] the authors of the Customer Contact Council proposed something they claimed to be an even more powerful KPI than the Net Promoter Score. They argued that it was no longer customer satisfaction or the NPS that were the best predictors of repeat purchases and spending behavior. Both had been toppled from the throne by a new concept: 'customer effort'. This was linked to a new metric: the Customer Effort Score (CES), which was defined as the amount of effort that the customer needed to put in himself, to get his question properly answered.

The authors developed this concept further in their highly recommendable book *The Effortless Experience.*[74] It is a book that will undoubtedly appeal to many a contact center manager, because it is so attuned to operational experience.

Instead of focusing on the impossible-to-copy heroic stories of extreme customer experience, the idea behind customer effort is to keep things manageable by placing the emphasis on the complexity-facing customers. To a degree, this requires you to anticipate the most likely customer follow-up questions and respond to them proactively.

Next issue avoidance: win-win

One of the concrete elements on which it is possible for organizations to work within the context of customer effort is 'next issue avoidance'.

Using statistical insights, it is possible to predict the subject for which any given customer is most likely to next contact you. A customer who first calls for the activation of a service will, for example, in X percent of cases call again within a certain period to ask a 'how to' question. This is predictable – and therefore opens some interesting options. Perhaps you can already capitalize on this knowledge during the original call or maybe you can proactively send an information mail to the customer a short time later.

Providing information offline in this way also helps to keep conversation duration under control.

In fact, with this system we are actually getting closer to the avoidance of calls altogether, as we discussed earlier in the book.

A big future?

A big future is being predicted for the effort score as an indicator for contact center performance.

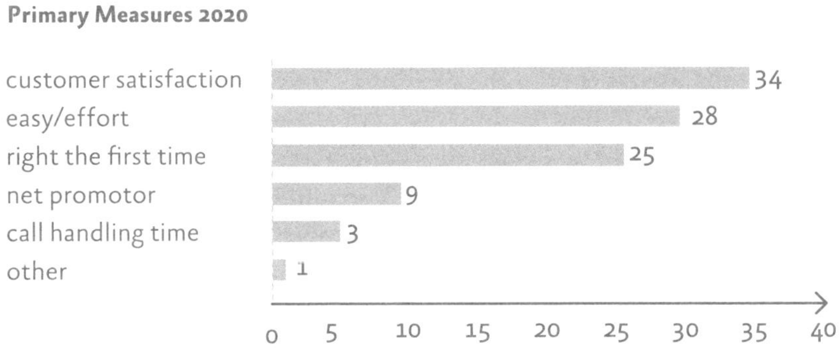

Figure 80: primary contact center measures in the future

In fact, a recent UK study[75] predicts that by 2020 the effort score will have already replaced the Net Promoter as the most important KPI for such performance. Of course, it still has two years to go as we speak... Please notice also how 'customer satisfaction' is expected to remain on top.

It is probably good news for contact centers that Professor Nicola Millard (one of the authors of the study, and someone we have met before, in this book) announced at a recent congress[76] that, according to her calculations, some 67% of the effort score is influenced by just six factors, all of which fall within the operational sphere of influence of the contact center:

- the agent;
- being able to reach the right person;
- customer navigation;
- keeping the customer informed;
- the number of calls needed;
- prompt response and processing.

And the winner is...?

When we are confronted with two hyped indices, the obvious question to ask is which one is better.

The answer, somewhat predictably, depends on the exact question. What do you want to know/measure?

In *Telecommerce 05 2013*[77] a group of researchers detailed the findings of their scientific study on comparing between CES and NPS. Their conclusions were not really surprising. In view of its broader scope (which means that not just the process, but also emotions, brand perception, product and price can also influence the outcome), they argued that the Net Promoter Score is a better indicator for the loyalty of customers, which perhaps immediately confirms that the NPS reflects far more than just the performance of the contact center. The circle – here, at least – is round.

Having said that, the more explicit process orientation of the customer effort score means that it complements the NPS well, certainly for matters relating to customer experience during the actual contact. As such, it deserves its place in the contact center's arsenal of indicators.

And for both indicators, there is – luckily – a growing consensus that the score as such is not the main thing. It should be about being able to close the loop by asking the 'why' follow-up questions. Knowing why a particular score was given reveals the true insights needed to derive improvement actions.

Or will a third dog run away with the bone?

It may seem a bit like the 'washes whiter than white' claim of some washing powders, but during another recent congress[78] yet another 'better' indicator was pushed into the limelight. This is EXQ (customer experience quality), the supposedly new kid on the block when it comes to predicting customer loyalty and word-of-mouth recommendations.

In his book *Measuring Customer Experience*, the author Dr. Phil Claus describes how the quality of the customer experience can be measured and how it is a better predictor than any of the other indicators currently available. In particular, he presents a number of main drivers for this experience, which are listed in figure 81.

Each of the drivers has a set of variables, which can be measured in concrete terms. The number of these variables – to which the respondents gave answers on a seven-point scale – are also shown in figure 81. The questions make use of statements like 'Doing business with XYZ is easy' (variable number 2 in 'service experience'), 'I have confidence in the expertise of XYZ' (variable number 2 in 'brand experience'), or 'XYZ keeps me well informed' (variable number 3 in 'after sales experience').

Will we embrace EXQ in the future as the new messiah amongst the ever-growing field of indicators? I have no idea. Given the way it is presented, it seems very much like a case of the 'strategy map' meets the 'index'. In the 2016 Dutch version of this book, I suggested not to hold your breath just yet. Two years later, I'm glad you didn't. Complex academic research does not always translate into something operationally useful.

Figure 81: Phil Klaus's method for measuring customer experience

At the end of the day, it is down to each individual organization to decide how best to capture feedback from their most important stakeholder: the customer.

Making sure that the reporting is compiled and presented in the best possible manner is at least one thing that the contact center can do to repair its relations with the rest of the organization. The question is: is that enough?

The bpost experience: an indicator for every level

During my time at bpost, different indicators were tested in different ways at different moments during the customer experience.

A general loyalty survey, using also NPS, included at one time a question which asked how easy it was to do business with bpost. Although this resulted in some interesting benchmarks, it was above all noticeable how difficult customers find it to interpret this conceptual idea, both for themselves and for us!

If the 'why' question reveals 'we're used to working this way now', there is very little practical learning to distill.

In this respect, it provided no more additional information than the classical loyalty questions relating to recommendations and repeat purchases – or at least not enough to warrant reconfiguration of the NPS-based loyalty indicator and reporting/communication used throughout the company.

The same question, but now posed in the context of a transactional interaction with the contact center, taught us again that the customer finds it very difficult to distance himself from the concrete issue with which he is confronted. Though this still provided concrete process feedback about the way in which the contact center had dealt with that issue. For this reason, the question was retained, certainly at the contact center level.

As far as the level of the individual agents and their coaching was concerned, we found that the traditional customer satisfaction metrics continued to offer the best results. Subsidiary questions relating to helpfulness and clarity of answers were used as individual performance indicators.

6

'CAN WE FIX IT? YES, WE CAN!'

In the previous chapters we have kind of smashed the contact center dream to pieces. It has become clear that it is not so easy to take on the idyllic role we had in mind, in part because of the silo structure in most organizations, but also in part because the communication of the majority of contact center managers reflects a mindset that is too inward looking.

Even so, the contact center remains a value and profit center. It is just not always recognized as such.

This book does not intend to plunge you into a Valley of Despair, however...

Surely by now we have all had enough of the Calimero-like self-pity and gloom that have dogged contact centers for so long? So, let's use the above conclusions rather as a source of inspiration to actually do something about it.

Calimero? Bob the Builder!

It would be a bit too simple to limit my advice here to: 'Do the opposite of everything you know can go wrong!' It is probably more meaningful, and useful, to set down a number of the possible solutions in a diagrammatic list.

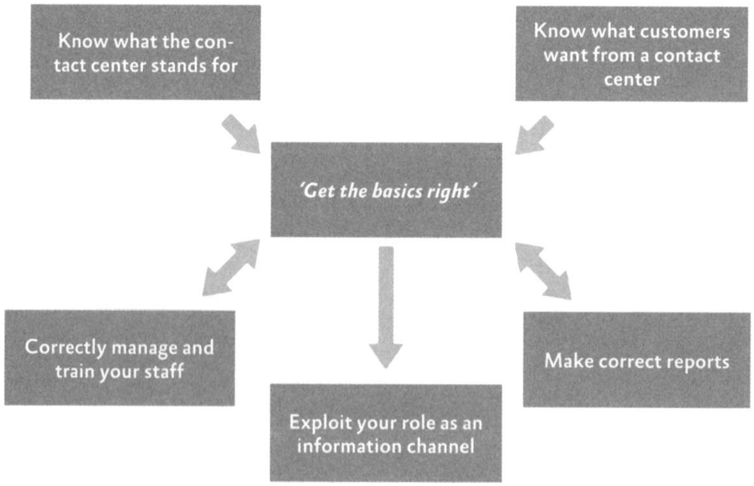

Figure 82: get the basics right

The essence can easily be summarized in a single golden rule:

'Do what you are supposed to do and do it right.'

Take as your starting point the tasks you have been given by the organization and strive to carry them out to a high standard of operational excellence. Create added value, in part by providing new insights. Only then should you think about moving into other less obvious areas of potential interest.

So let's follow the reasoning in figure 82 step by step, to see if we can pave the road toward finding solutions.

Know what the contact center stands for

> 'The performance of a contact center cannot be translated into a number of quantitative details. It is about finding the right balance between the quantitative, qualitative and financial aspects. This balance will be different for each organization. A good contact center is the contact center that best meets the requirements of this previously agreed balance.'[79]

The contact center is not an isolated island. Hopefully, that was the clear message from the previous 200 or so pages!

The contact center always functions within a wider context. Whether internally or externally, it is there to serve the organization. It needs to support the organization's product and service offer for a particular customer segment. It must also meet the expectations of shareholders.

This applies equally to an external contact center. Even though this is a separate company in its own right, it still needs to meet the expectations of the client organization in the support of their activities. In fact, perhaps this is even more necessary for external centers, given the possibility that they can always be replaced by a 'better' competitor.

If there is a main difference between in-house and outsourced contact centers in this area, then – in my experience – it can, paradoxically enough, be found in the fact that those 'expectations' are much more clearly described for the external centers. Service level agreements are defined in very precise terms in formal contracts. Arrangements between internal centers and other departments in the organization are generally much looser.

This general context results in a series of requirements for and expectations of a contact center. This is illustrated in figure 83.[80]

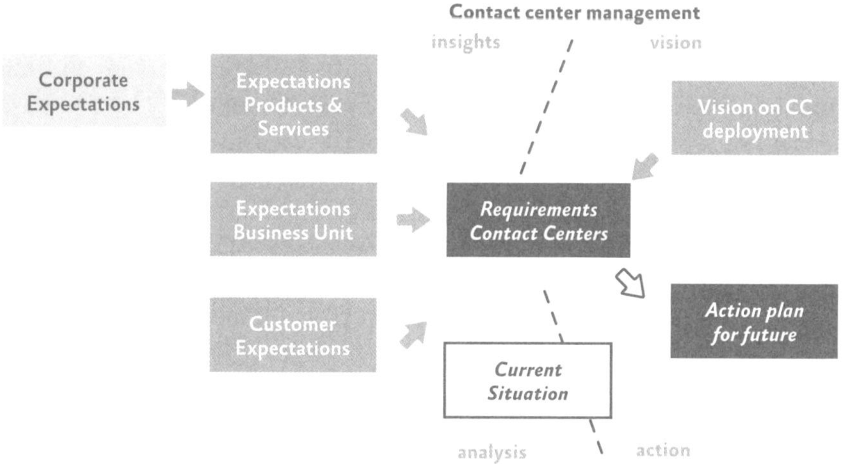

Figure 83: the expectations of the contact center

Of course, the nature of the products and services the contact center is supporting also plays a defining role in setting these tasks and expectations.

For example, it is logical that operating a technical computer helpdesk entails different demands than does providing directory services.

This is also the moment to reflect on whether or not the contact center will take up a sales role.

Note how in figure 83 the 'vision on CC deployment' also plays a part. It should be obvious by now that I didn't expect any self-respecting contact center manager to just sit by idly and play only a passive role in the process. In fact, I expect exactly the opposite.

This is the time for the contract center manager to step up – to be actively involved in helping to crystallize the vision for the center, by making clear to the organization what the center can offer and what levers are needed to make this possible. In doing so, he should not only rely on his own expertise, but also on the lessons he has learnt from customers.

Perhaps all the answers will not be immediately available. But as we saw with '42', the contact center manager must at least be able to ensure that the right questions are asked.

Corporate expectations are very clear for the Carglass contact center
For former contact center manager Stefan Sterk, the expectations his organization had of his contact center were crystal clear:

'Carglass, a contact center with a star
A "star", a chip, a crack... Whoever has a problem with their windscreen immediately thinks of Carglass. The fact that the company has been 'top of mind' for years and looks set to stay that way is due to the three guiding principles by which it swears:

- being easy to reach, always (24/7);
- offering customers appointments at the moments that suit them;
- providing efficient and friendly service, so that the customer will be happy to return to Carglass the next time anything goes wrong.

Step on the gas!
In all three of these main pillars, Carglass's in-house contact center plays a crucial role. It is the beating heart of the organization and heavy investments have been made in the training of its personnel. Staff turnover is remarkably low and efficiency levels are high. Taking action quickly is the most important message drilled into every contact center operative: "The customer has a problem and asks us to solve it as fast as we can. So let's do that!" As soon as you contact Carglass, you are immediately offered an appointment.

Some contact centers can be monotonous places to work. But not at Carglass. There you will find no objectives about "average call times". The core objective is simply to keep the customer happy. Their motto: "Customer satisfaction is our best marketing".

Looking forward
The future of the Carglass contact center is currently focused on the better integration of new channels of contact. Before very long, they hope to respond more intensively to comments on social media, to offer a chat service, and to be reachable via Skype.

More channels mean a greater load of work. The challenge will be to deal with this extra workload without any loss in speed and efficiency, because the customer of tomorrow will be more demanding than ever. But even then, he will still be able to rely on Carglass and its contact center.'

It should be clear that many of the instruments we looked at earlier in the book will come in very handy during this strategic exercise, for example:

- to determine whether the organization's products and processes are suitable for allocating a sales role to the contact center (figure 25);
- to determine the channels of communication that the contact center will use (figure 14);
- to determine the scope of customer questions (figures 33 and 35).

When it really becomes as clear as possible... Corporate expectations for the bpost contact centers on a single slide

Best Quality
Call centers

Corporate expectations for the contact center cogently summarized in terms of:

- customer positioning
- channel support
- primary objectives

An important task:

- dealing with complaints more efficiently
- giving customers a reliable answer quickly
- helping counter clerks in the post office network (redirect calls)

Three core objectives:

- being available
- answering quickly
- assisting with problems immediately

An important contribution: customer satisfaction

Figure 84: bpost expectations for its call center

In 2008, I joined bpost as head of what were then known as 'the residential contact centers'. In that same year, an intensive roadshow was organized with the aim of familiarizing all staff with the company's strategic plan. In particular, the presentation zoomed in on all the departments that would play a role in providing quality service to our customers. With the imminent liberalization of the postal market just months away, this was (and still is) one of bpost's most important priorities. Using the title 'best quality' for the slides on this subject was an immediate yard stick for its level of ambition in this field.

The call center - *a sign of the times: nowadays bpost also refers to them as contact centers* - was one of the departments that merited a slide of its own in this corporate presentation. It contained one of the clearest formulations of executive expectations I have ever seen.

It immediately gave an unambiguous message about the direction in which the contact centers needed to be developed and the way in which their performance needed to be translated into KPI reporting.

Thank you, Johnny Thijs(*)

(*) CEO of De Post at the time

At the end of the day, it is crucial that there should be absolute clarity about the positioning of the contact center and the role it is intended to play. This is not only essential for the center itself, but also for the organization's other departments. This clarity must be the foundation on which all further reasoning is based.

SOUNDBITE

Corporate expectations for the (external) contact center at EDF Luminus are crystal clear.

Then Chief commercial officer Kris Vervaet (now CEO De Persgroep Publishing and Medialaan):

'A contact center must be a department or entity that in addition to achieving its own objectives and KPIs must also support other departments in attaining the company's wider operational results. It is important that it is not only viewed as a cost center (with its often large scale and headcount), but that its ability to make a commercial contribution as a value center is also recognized.

At Luminus, the contact center is a key player, also for purely commercial purposes. In our company, the contact center is not only deployed to provide first line customer service, but also to stimulate cross-selling, upselling and acquisition.

Our internal marketing department ensures that there is a clear vision behind these different tasks, reflecting the creativity and the image the company wants to project. That is what the contact center is expected to put into practice, so that our customer contacts are in line with this vision and our marketing communication. As a result, the customer really feels like he is talking to Luminus.

Why an external contact center?

They offer professionalism and flexibility. In our sector, and especially at EDF Luminus, flexibility is essential, but it is not always easy or even possible to find it in your own organization.

In addition to this professionalism and flexibility, during the selection process we were also looking for a center that was specialized in first line customer contact and offered high-quality technical support to its personnel, so that these operatives could concentrate fully on their conversation with the end customer.

At the same time, we also see the center as being much more than a simple implementer of tasks. We also expect them to contribute to our wider operational thinking. In other words, it is a real partnership.

The success of the contact center is judged in the first instance based on a set of metrics and results. However, this success is underlined by the winning of prestigious sectoral awards, such as the Caviar 'One Call to Move' Awards, the Accessibility Award, etc.

Last but not least, it is vital that the customer experiences that he is being dealt with by a customer-oriented and highly professional organization.'

Know what customers want from a contact center

'Customer satisfaction' is unquestionably one of the primary objectives of any contact center. It is by providing an emotional experience that the center can contribute to the total customer experience. And it is precisely this that creates value.

When setting up a contact center, it is important to have a good understanding of the mechanics of this process. How is customer satisfaction achieved? Leaving aside the specificity and uniqueness of your own organization, do customers have universal expectations which they expect to be met when interacting with a contact center?

The contact center as doctor: *primum non nocere*
Time for a reality check.

When contact centers are contacted by a particularly emotional customer, the first task is to ensure that things don't get any worse.

This observation does nothing to detract from the value story we described in a previous chapter. On the contrary. Even with customers in this mindset, the contact center continues to care for the emotional experience of the organization's most important source of income.

In essence, contact centers need to do what doctors promise to do when they take the Hippocratic oath; namely, never do any harm to anyone.[81] Whatever happens, the contact center agent must never do anything to heighten or – even worse – create negative emotions.

Figure 85: Hippocrates[82]

By blaming the customer for the problem, by using meaningless jargon or by failing to understand what he or she is trying to say, it is possible for the contact center to quite quickly push the customer's temperature up to boiling point and beyond. This is not a good idea.

You can find a similar line of reasoning in the previously mentioned book, *The Effortless Experience*. The authors dismiss the strategy of 'customer delight' as the best approach for dealing with customer contacts. This, they say, is an approach that is difficult to sustain over time. What's more, it doesn't even really work. Research has shown that a bad experience will do more to drive a customer away than a good experience will do to help retain him.

In other words, first make sure that things don't go from bad to worse.

According to Jos Burgers, 'customers love solutions, but they by far prefer to have no problems in the first place'. This demonstrates that those who argue in favor of a rather Machiavellian approach – first create a problem, so that you can solve it with brio – are actually talking nonsense.

The DNA of customer satisfaction revealed

The question about what drives customer satisfaction in a contact center immediately gives rise to all kinds of intuitive theories and gut feelings. People are usually inclined to answer in terms of beliefs and convictions rather than concrete facts, thereby using an unreliable basis to develop biased levers and actions. In this way, all kinds of 'improvement' initiatives are launched, building on what Gerry McGovern in a different context has called 'Senior Management Opinion Syndrome'.[83] That its acronym SMOS translates from Dutch as 'pile of chaos' just about sums it up.

In some ways, this is a strange and unnecessary phenomenon. In Belgium – *and what reason is there to believe this is unique* – the drivers of customer satisfaction in contact centers have been scientifically mapped out for years. In March 2006, Call Metrics (now Möbius), working in collaboration with the University of Ghent, conducted research on this very subject, involving twelve major Belgian companies.[84]

Viewed scientifically and statistically, the results of this research are unambiguous. However, it needs to be noted that the focus of the study was specifically on telephone contacts and made no further comments about the global perception of the company and/or brand.

The one thing that jumps out from the equation is how the perceived helpfulness (CHEFT) of the agent has a huge impact. It is by far the biggest lever leading to customer satisfaction and is responsible for more than half the result. On the reverse side of the coin, this also explains how an agent can do great damage if he fails to pay sufficient attention to this aspect. Fortunately, this is individual behavior that can be coached and trained. And if you get it right, you are already half way down the road that leads to customer satisfaction.

It is also worth noting that the positive effect of 'helpfulness' (+0.7) comprehensively outweighs the negative effect of 'waiting time' (-0.1). The harm to customer satisfaction that is supposedly caused by long waits before calls are answered is one of the most persistent myths in the contact center sector. Hence the reservation demonstrated towards this KPI (and the derived indicator 'service level') in the chapter on reporting. As long as waiting time remains under an agreed upon hygiene level, the impact on customer satisfaction is small.

More surprising, perhaps, is the relatively minor impact of the final outcome of the conversation. It seems that a negative outcome to the conversation for the

Call Metrics (Möbius): the determinants of customer satisfaction

The final results of the study reveal the DNA of customer satisfaction with respect to telephone contact with a contact center in Belgium.

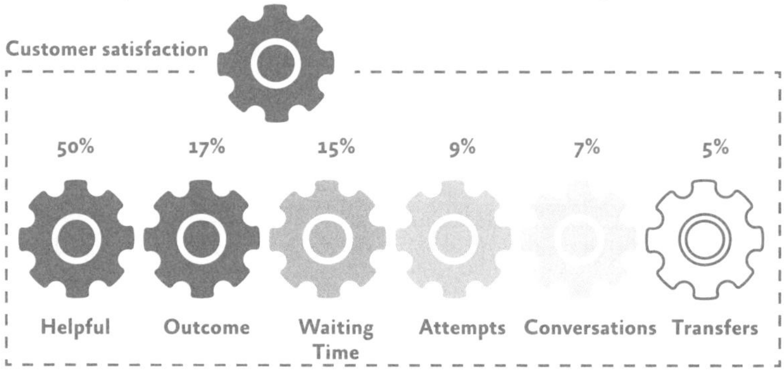

Figure 86: drivers for customer satisfaction

The layout for figure 86 was first devised for a presentation by Horst Remes to the senior management at bpost. It translates the finding of the Call Metric's research into the right levers.

So how does the figure work? If each lever – or perhaps we should call them cogs – makes a full turn, the 'customer satisfaction' cog is turned backwards or forwards by the corresponding amount shown above the relevant individual cog. For example, if the 'helpfulness' cog turns a full circle, equivalent to a gain of one point, the customer satisfaction cog will turn half circle (50%), yielding a gain of half a point.

Purists might prefer to puzzle over the more elaborate calculation that was included in the report of the research findings:

Call satisfaction =

1,5 + 0,7 CHEFT + 0,6 OC - 0,1BWT - 0,3 RCA - 0,2 NRC - 0,3 NT - 0,2 PWT.

Where the abbreviations stand for the following:

- CHEFT: cheft factor,
- OC: outcome conversation,
- BWT: biased waiting time,
- RCA: repeated call attempts,
- NRC: number of repeated calls to solve problem,
- NT: number of transfers,
- PWT: presence of waiting time during conversations.

Good luck with that.

customer – in other words, the problem is not solved – does not necessarily lead to a negative perception of the contact center's performance. *(The noise you can now hear in the background is the explosion of another myth, one that is often used by contact center managers as a defense mechanism.)*

The research suggests that other 'hard' contact center metrics – repeat calls, 'not right first time', transfers – do have an impact, but one which remains marginal in comparison with the positive effect of staff helpfulness.

Are there any other factors? Yes. Are they worth mentioning? No. They don't even make it onto the diagram – although they were thoroughly researched. So CHEFT rules the day, or so it would seem. But what is CHEFT exactly? It is an acronym that stands for:

- Competence,
- Helpfulness,
- Enthusiasm,
- Friendliness,
- Time.

This factor is the biggest lever for customer satisfaction in a contact center. With the competition far behind.

All these crucial drivers are situated at the level of the individual agent's behavior. In other words, they can be influenced by selection, training and coaching. From the point of view of the contact center manager, this is reassuring. It means that to a significant degree transactional satisfaction can be 'manufactured'. Or 'engineering the experience', as the Corporate Executive Board more elegantly refer to it.

Among the study's other more interesting – and perhaps surprising – conclusions is the discovery that there are a number of factors, once thought to be significant, that have no measurable impact on customer satisfaction.

This includes some favorite contact center 'old chestnuts', so traditionalists or those of a sensitive disposition are advised to skip the next paragraph...

- The cost of the call:
  - the argument about whether or not to use a free-phone number for the contact center should be discussed, if at all, from a different perspective than customer satisfaction with the conversation.
- The reason for the call:
  - complaints can just as easily lead to satisfied customers as simple requests for information, provided the agent shows a genuine desire to help the caller.

  - in other words, the way the conversation develops is more important than its cause. This can again help to eliminate an often used (and fundamentally invalid) excuse, popular with both contact center operatives and their managers. If a customer is unsatisfied at the end of a conversation, in the first instance this is not the fault of errors elsewhere in the customer experience chain. The real reason is to be found in the attitude and approach of the contact center and its operatives. And in the process he is allowed to follow, to generate a response that the customer will recognize as 'help'.
- Socio-demographic characteristics of the customer (except for age):
  - clichés about difficult/easy customers no longer hold water, at least as far as ultimate customer satisfaction is concerned.
- Employee satisfaction:
  - the study concludes that in a contact center environment there is no causal relationship between the satisfaction of the center operatives and the ultimate satisfaction of the customer. This has been confirmed by other equally reliable scientific studies.[85]
  - in my experience, trying to argue this point in a contact center environment is like swearing at church. Not only is it 'not done', but it sometimes also provokes a strong negative reaction. It goes directly against a popular belief. There are dozens of arguments you hear to the contrary, including hoary old classics like: 'You can hear a smile through the telephone'. Attempting to show that there is no scientific basis for this kind of comment usually leads to being accused of wanting to create an impersonal, staff-unfriendly working climate.

    It is an emotional subject and it always leads to emotional debate.

    So let me be crystal-clear on this matter. Stimulating employee satisfaction in contact centers is an excellent strategy. It is a really good idea, for many reasons (improved productivity, retention, communication, social dialogues and simply being human). But its value as a main driver for customer satisfaction has never been proven in the contact center. Take good care of your people by all means, because they deserve it. But don't confuse your motives for doing so.

If there was such a thing as a compulsory reading list for contact center managers, in my opinion this Call Metric (Möbius) study should be on it. I am not saying you should follow it blindly and forget everything else. An organization

In the real world, too? bpost confirms the Möbius theory

Inspired in part by the findings of the Möbius study, bpost systematically subjects the results of its customer satisfaction surveys by phone to statistical regression analysis.

After each telephone contact, customers are asked via IVR[86] to express their level of satisfaction about:

- the conversation in general;
- the helpfulness of the agent;
- the clarity of the answer;
- the number of times they needed to contact the center before their question was answered.

I imagine you can see the influence of the CHEFT factor.

The results, together with all other operational data relating to the call, are analyzed using a multi-variable regression model.

The bpost contact center was not one of the twelve centers that took part in the original Möbius study, though the operational results in daily practice continue to confirm that study's findings.

The results for residential postal customers are given in figure 87.[88]

These results show even more clearly than in the original research that satisfaction about the perceived helpfulness of the agent is the decisive factor. Satisfaction about the clarity of the answer comes in second place. The (penalizing) importance of 'not-first-time-right' experiences and the internal transfer of calls was only marginal. No statistically significant differences were found in relation to the nature of the call, the subject and the outcome.

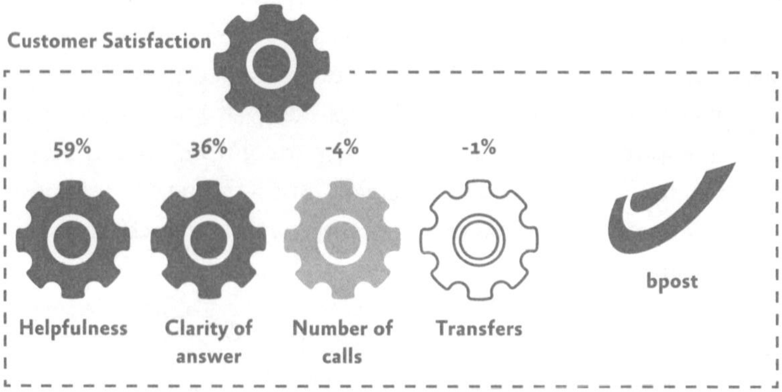

Figure 87: front office customer satisfaction at bpost

These results are practical, because they can be used for the individual coaching of agents. Within bpost a whole program has been set up to translate personalized feedback into individual action plans.

always has the right (and often good reason) to place the emphasis differently. But such a decision must be based on a full knowledge of the situation, its background, the possible alternatives and the possible consequences.

And the same for the back office?

There is much less research material available for customer satisfaction in relation to back office interaction. In part, this is connected with the less measurable nature of back office activities, reflected by the fact that it sometimes still gets called the 'black office'.[88]

Or perhaps the capturing of back office feedback is just more difficult than asking customers to give their impression of a front office conversation by simply pressing the buttons on their telephone?

Or perhaps we all still think too much in terms of a 'call' center, rather than a 'contact' center?

Whatever the reason for this relative lack of information, more insights about the back office's performance in this domain is key. Given the operational context of the contact center, it are traditionally the more complex (and, consequently, the more emotionally charged) cases that find their way to the back office. And as we saw earlier, a number of important communication channels are directly routed there. Customer satisfaction levels in this vital part of the operational set-up are therefore a subject of crucial interest to contact center managers. Unfortunately, the 'blind spots' in research and reporting mean that it is hard to steer towards customer satisfaction, at the moments that might matter most.

For this reason, since the end of 2013 bpost has been investing in the development of satisfaction metrics for its back office. For each closed case, for which the e-mail address of the customer is known an invitation is sent to take part in an online survey to measure levels of satisfaction.[89] The advantage of this system is that it makes it possible to ask open questions about qualitative strengths and points that need improving. Experience so far suggests that a lot of customers are more than happy to take part and willingly submit their comments. The challenge, of course, is then to do something meaningful with this large amount of unstructured feedback. Moreover, the fact that many customers use this feedback as an extra channel to ask follow-up questions means that this channel needs to be monitored and managed.

For lack of any good alternative reference, the questions finally included in the survey were the result of internal brainstorming. As a result, they no doubt reflect – in part, at least – a certain management vision. The aim was to discover levels of customer satisfaction about:

- the general processing of the case;
- the clarity of the answer;
- the proposed solution;
- the speed of response;
- the way in which the customer was kept informed throughout the process.

Two open fields for additional comment were added to the web form to give customers the opportunity to say what they appreciated about the service and what they thought could be improved.

Once again, regression analysis was used to try and identify explanatory reasons for the scores in the operational characteristics of the individual cases. And again, feedback was given to individual members of staff for the purposes of targeted coaching.

Figure 88 depicts the survey results for residential postal customers.[90]

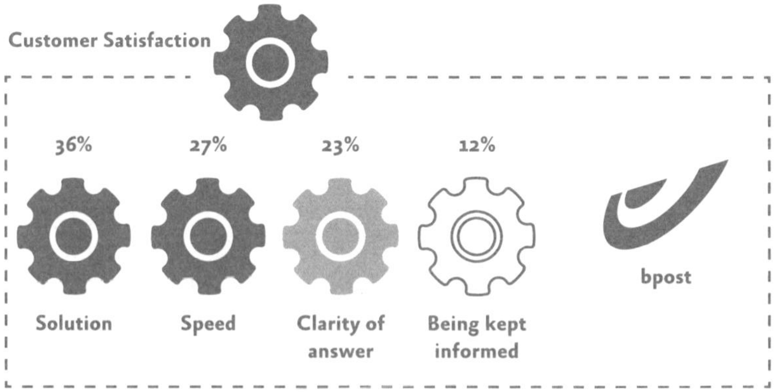

Figure 88: back office customer satisfaction at bpost

Perhaps the most noticeable fact is the way in which the different micro-elements – in contrast to the front office – now have a more evenly spread impact on customer satisfaction. This may suggest that there is a greater mutual correlation between these sub-elements.

Within this more balanced picture, satisfaction with the proposed solution is the most decisive factor, but speed of response, clarity of answer and informative communication also show themselves to be important levers.

As always, however, a degree of caution is necessary when analyzing the results of this kind of action.

The most flagrant example of this is the detail analysis of the 'speed' component. The obvious reflex when seeing the chart is to want to speed up the handling by introducing various process changes. However, deep analysis revealed that this would have no significant effect.

It became clear that there was no correlation between satisfaction about speed and the length of time it actually took to deal with the case from start to finish. A conclusion, as you may recall, that is not so very different from the situation in the front office.

In fact, it transpired that satisfaction about speed was more heavily influenced by the information provided to the customer during the process about its progress.

And so, this becomes the real 'speed' lever and the focus of actions you can put in place to influence satisfaction.

All animals are equal, but...

The basic theory of customer relationship management teaches that there is a need to differentiate when dealing with customer experience.

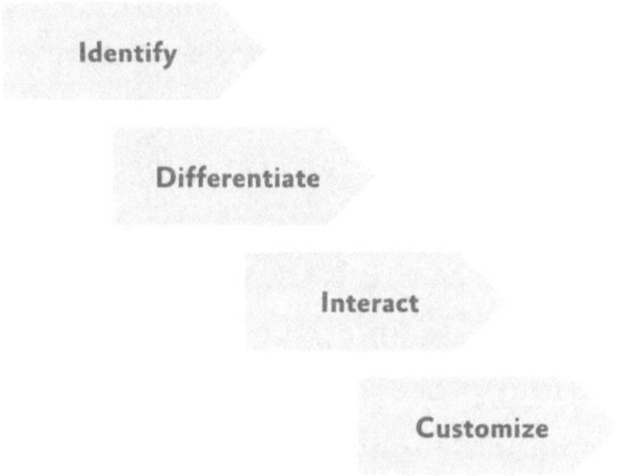

Figure 89: the model for the management of customer relationships, according to Pepper & Rogers

Based on its knowledge of the value of a customer and his specific needs, a company can maximize the personalization of its offers to that customer.

In this way, it is possible to create a unique experience, which the customer will not be able to find elsewhere. This, so the theory goes, makes the customer truly loyal. So, customer insight becomes a competitive advantage.

This kind of differentiation is also possible in the contact center's approach. A customer can be recognized based on a call number, a customer number or some other form of identification, either automatically or as result of questioning by the center's operatives. Whichever method is used, once identification has been made it becomes feasible to build up an approach along the lines of figure 90.

This might include things like:

- the adjustment of the automatic answer menus (IVR), either in function of the needs of the moment or based on the customer's product portfolio;
  - just received an invoice = 'invoice queries' as the first choice in the IVR;
  - doesn't have an internet subscription = option not offered in the menu;
  - current appointments = confirmation of date and time as the first thing the customer will hear in the IVR.
- the routing of the call:

WHO?

- Identity
- Market segment
- Socio/demo
- History
- Portfolio
- Stage in life cycle
- Value
- Potential
- Churn risk
- Influence

WHY?

- Probable reason for call based on history
- Time
- IVR choice
- Called number

WHAT?

- Priority
- Adjusted IVR menu
- Expertise/skills
- Tone of voice
- Flexibility in procedures
- Handling model
- Commercial offers
- Channel choice

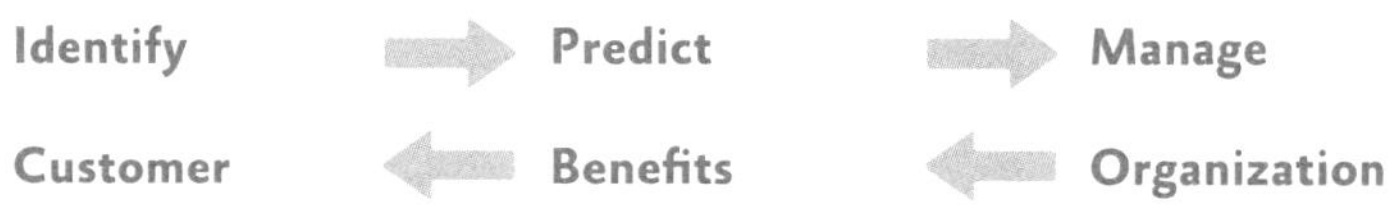

Figure 90: customer differentiation in a contact center approach

- in function of the (probable) reason the customer has given by making a choice in the IVR menu. This then triggers skill-based routing, which is something any half-decent platform should allow without too much difficulty;
- with a certain priority. For example, incoming calls from within your own retail network can be given preference in the queue.
- with sophisticated CRM combinations. For example, Telenet uses the active life cycle of the customer to determine which quality of operative will answer the call ('the best operatives do…'). Belgacom used to route calls from its defaulters automatically to the collections department, irrespective of the choice the caller made in the IVR.

- the degree of freedom the operatives are given to deal with the call as they see fit. How far can they go in the offering of certain solutions and products that deviate from the standard?

These are all questions we saw in a more fragmented form in earlier sections of the book. Of course, the answers will vary from case to case. Each organization will need to work this out for itself and for its contact center.

There are, however, a number of universal truths:

- There are few things so irritating as being asked for details, of which it later becomes clear that they were not used. This is damaging for the perception of 'customer effort'. The identification of the customer must never form an obstacle to the prompt and helpful solution of the initial question.
- The contact center's differentiation must be in line with the general customer strategy of the company. For example, the value assessment of the customer cannot be exclusive to the center.

  The differentiated approach must then be applied consistently in the customer approach at all the other touchpoints. There is no point in giving a malfunction call priority and treating it with greater flexibility, if this is not later confirmed in the technician's visit, either in terms of timing or level of care. The basis for getting these things right is a reliable and good performing CRM system.

  Of course, this argument can just as easily be read in the opposite direction, when it closely approaches our earlier reflection about 'what has the contact center ever done for us?' Why would you consider particular customer groups as a priority in marketing strategies, when in the contact center they are just dumped on the pile with the rest?
- The entire configuration inevitably creates greater complexity for the contact center management.

  However, this complexity can have a return: the final outcome must either be greater internal efficiency and/or increased customer satisfaction.
- Of course, this last point makes it necessary to focus on elements that you know can effectively increase customer satisfaction. This is turn requires measurement and analysis. Customers' hear-say alone is a very flimsy foundation for a re-engineering of processes.
- Different customer segments, almost by definition, do not know or understand each other's different experiences. Do you want to communicate about differentiation to valorize your 'happy customers'? Fine, but remember this means that other customers will almost certainly feel disadvantaged as a result.

  If you communicate that there is a special number for Small and Medium Enterprises (SMEs), manned by product specialists, that is one thing. If you communicate that in the queue for a general number SME-callers will be given priority to the detriment of ordinary members of the public, that is something else.

We saw earlier that in this age of social media the users create their own transparency. As a result, preferential treatments will inevitably be made public, sooner or later. The more flagrant this treatment is, the greater the caution required.

In short, then, these are the most important strategic choices for which the different aspects 'want to', 'must', and 'can' will need to be weighed against each other. During these discussions, the contact center manager can (must?) play an important contributory role, although he should always bow to the logic of the greater organizational whole.

SOUNDBITE

Horst Remes of One Stone on customer expectations

Making choices
Ask your customers exactly what they expect from a contact center and then calculate if you can afford to meet all their wishes. It's a pretty sobering exercise!

The harsh reality is that we need to make choices. And that means we had better choose the things that are really important to our customers. But that's where the problem usually starts.

We make the things we can measure important. In other words, we use ourselves as the yardstick. What we think is important, the customers will also think important – or that's what we believe.

The first error in that reasoning is that we overestimate ourselves as rational beings, so that we forget our own emotional reflex.

What's more, contact center managers know how a contact center works. We can't just turn off that knowledge when it suits us – what is often referred to as "the curse of knowledge". This leads to a second error: we attach exaggerated importance to the things we can measure.

This explains why waiting times can be reduced and "first time right" levels improved, without having any positive effect on customer satisfaction.

Making promises

In reliable scientific research, we see time and again how emotional aspects – like the friendliness and helpfulness of the agent – weigh more heavily than the things that the contact center usually measures.

But in contrast to what you might first think, this emotional aspect is not entirely dependent on the agent. To come across to the customer as being helpful, the agent needs to be able to make promises. A lot of them are afraid to do that, because they can't always trust – often with justification – their colleagues in other departments to make good on those promises.

In fact, experience suggests that it is actually better for customer satisfaction if you occasionally need to go back on your promises – providing you do it proactively and it doesn't happen too often – rather than promising nothing at all.

Strategy

The most successful contact centers form a fundamental part of their organization's business strategy.

The leaders of these organizations regard their telephone operatives as their stormtroopers: they capture territory and bring in vital information about the battlefield.

They provide them with the necessary ammunition; for example, to make promises. They demand absolute loyalty to the objectives and they make those objectives transparent.

And if that strategy is crystal clear, it is much easier to make the right choices.'

Get the basics right

Once it is clear to the contact center what the different stakeholders expect of it, the message becomes a simple one: 'Just do it!'

'Everyone agrees that you can only get added value from customer contact if the foundations are properly laid.'[91]

If, in first place, a contact center manager fails to fulfill his expected role, he loses all right to speak. In comparison with falling short when it comes to the prime role, everything else fades into the background. Philosophical reflections about your contribution to value? You can forget all that, if the organization thinks you have failed to meet the Olympic minimum!

This might sound overly simplistic. But it often boils down to exactly that. Or doesn't it?

Of course, being a contact center manager is a *métier*, a craft – we've just spent a whole book trying to explain this – but sometimes, to repeat the words above, you've just got to do it. No frills, no fancy stuff. Just what is expected of you. Get the basics right.

As far as contact center management is concerned, these basics are:

- making sure that at every moment the most appropriate agent is dealing with the right contact in the correct manner;
- correctly following up the agents in the performance of this task;
- correctly following up the operational results and using them to make necessary adjustments, but without forgetting knowledge management, budget management, applications management, union relations and a thousand and one other things!

But basics are basics.

The first task – correctly determining the need for operatives – is a complex one.

Aspects like call volume and call peaks, which by definition are difficult to predict, need to be worked into some kind of model. Based on a self-imposed ambition in terms of waiting time, you decide the number of operatives you need. Of course, this becomes even more complicated when you start dealing with different languages, different levels of knowledge, different locations, etc.

And once you have got this far, you then need to take account of queuing theory and the possible effects of customers hanging up and calling back later when they can't get through...

Sound complicated? It is. This is why in most contact centers it is done with the help of specialist (work force management) software.

The most recent versions of this software no longer try to calculate theoretical capacity, but are based on staffing simulations for the center, taking account of all possible parameters. The system then churns out the 'right' staff rosters, when new simulations no longer yield a better result.

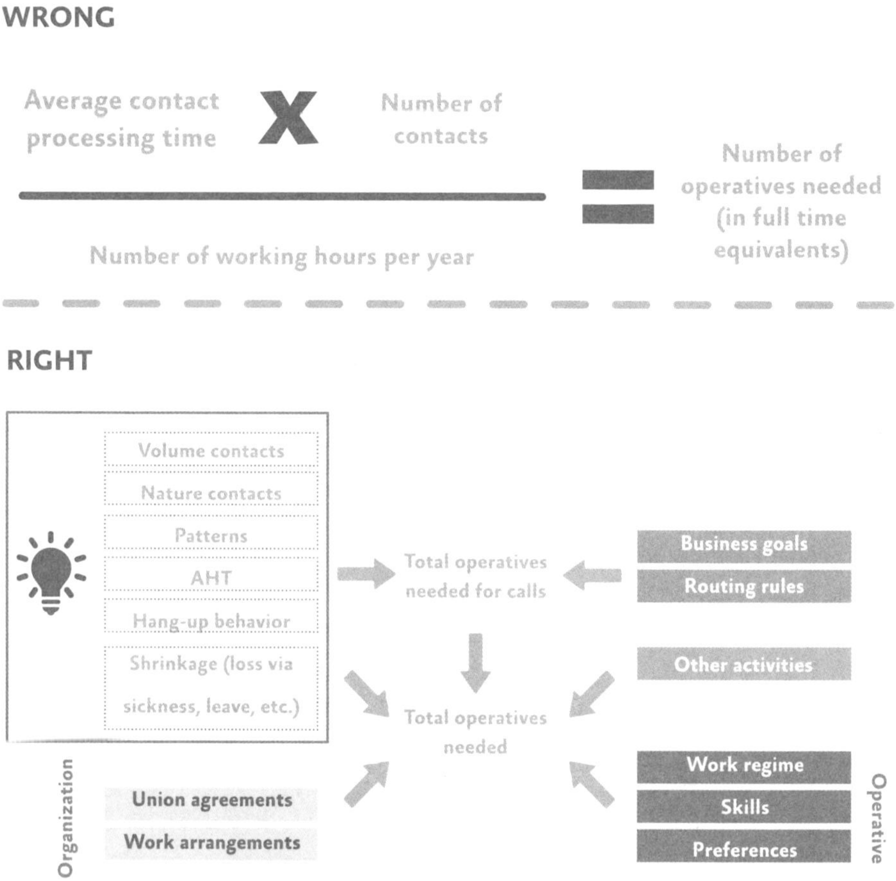

Figure 91: workforce management replaces the rule of three

Benno Schiffer (once of Teletrain, now at Verint):
Work force management (WFM) supports customer care management through the most efficient use of staff and resources

'Today, customer care management needs to constantly balance between the wishes of the customer, the needs of the organization that wants to offer a good level of service, budgetary limitations and staff expectations.

To make all this possible, we use a WFM process based on five key building blocks: forecasting, capacity planning, scheduling, intra-day management, and reporting/analysis.

During the forecasting process, we try to estimate as accurately as possible the likely future amount of work. This means not only looking at the expected work volume per type and contact channel, but also the expected handling time.

An estimate also needs to be made of the occupancy rate and the productivity and utilization ratios of the different groups of staff.

In capacity planning, the predicted work volumes and handling times – which together form the workload – are offset against the number of staff and their above-mentioned ratios. This makes it possible to identify on a day-by-day basis possible moments of over- and understaffing. This in turn allows us to make operational decisions about recruiting, annual leave policy, training, etc.

The third step is the actual allocation of the staff to the different services within the center, taking account of any contractual obligations and any personal or department-specific agreements that have been made. Every effort is made to match the necessary number of operatives as closely as possible to what is needed to achieve the desired level of service on an interval basis.

After that, we turn our attention to intra-day management, which involves following up on the workload (traffic management) and the staff (adherence management), so that we can compare this information with our earlier predictions about the amount of work and the number of hours. If we find any serious deviations, these can immediately be corrected by using one of a number of previously agreed upon scenarios.

The final phase in the process is the reporting of our efficiency metrics and KPIs. This information is then analyzed, so that we can further optimize our operational processes, where necessary.'

This is also the reason why the cost calculation of contact center support cannot be based on a simple rule of three, as demonstrated in figure 91. It is essential that the contact center management is involved in the calculation to provide necessary nuance and clarification. We have already seen (in the chapter on cost centers) the problems it can cause if this is not the case.

Of course, the contact center manager is then faced with the challenge – and the obligation – to explain in a credible manner why his actual requirements are much higher than with the simplistic rule of three approach.

Working with priorities

The priority pyramid

It helps to deal with the basics correctly if you can visualize them as priorities.

Even with a limited number of (corporate level) indicators, there is a kind of hierarchy of importance, on the basis of which the contact center is judged and directed. As a possible source of inspiration, below you can find visualizations of the way I have looked at contact centers during my tour of duty in Belgacom and bpost. These visualizations are loosely based on Maslow's hierarchy of needs pyramid.

This pyramid contains the most important objectives, which are also communicated internally in exactly the same manner. Each element has its own measurable KPI. Depending on the current level of performance in relation to objectives, these can be colored red or green. This makes it possible to see at a glance how the contact center is performing against its basic requirements.

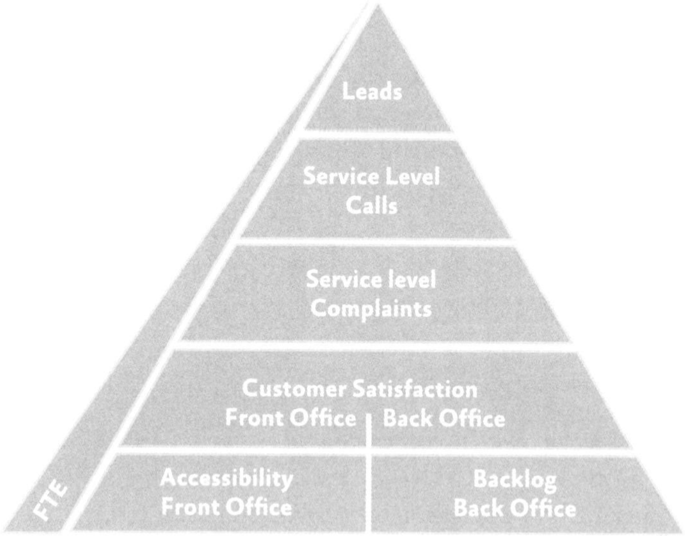

Figure 92: the contact center priority pyramid according to Smets

The first priority of the contact center is to deal with whatever the public throws at it: calls, cases, interactions and all the other functions related to the different channels of communication it supports. Some of these things will be handled by the front office; others by the back office. Both offices stand on an equal footing, in keeping with the yin-yang metaphor we used earlier in the book.

For calls this is typically expressed in terms of accessibility: what percentage of calls were answered? For offline interactions, this is usually translated as the avoidance of backlogs, which could be monitored by the number of days of work in the pipeline at any one time.

In essence, this first step in the pyramid tells us whether the contact center is able to cope with the incoming volumes of work or whether it has hopelessly lost control.

Abandoned calls kill

In June 2016, Flemish newspapers ran a tragic story about 46-year-old Stefan W., who had been found dead in his apartment. His phone logs showed unsuccessful attempts to reach the emergency services. He tried three times but could not get through. It was reported that the emergency helpdesk at that time was swamped (no pun intended) with calls related to damages caused by a heavy thunderstorm. Damages... not life-threatening emergencies. This incident inspired the creation of separate contact numbers in case of weather conditions.

But just imagine being the contact center manager...

Fortunately, for most contact centers the effects of a sub-par accessibility are far less dramatic. But when being confronted with unacceptable abandon rates, contact center managers should feel every bit as sick.

When the incoming volumes are processed, the next (self-evident) priority is to see that they are processed as well as possible. In this respect, the customer is the only relevant barometer of quality. All other operational indicators come very much in second place. For this reason, transactional customer satisfaction enjoys a high priority in its own right. As previously mentioned, this needs to be measured in both the front office and the back office.

The next level in the pyramid looks at the handling of cases – typically complaints, but also 'other communication channels' cases' – in the back office, to see if they are being dealt with within the agreed time (service level). In some ways, it may seem counter-intuitive to come across this element in isolation at this position in the pyramid. When assessing his level of satisfaction, is it not likely that the customer will take all aspects of the service into account, including the time it took? So why show it separately here? And why should it be globally more important for the back office than service level is for the front office? After all, in recent years the question of service level has become increasingly mediatized, so that in certain organizations it now has a near sacred status.

Well, yes, it does. However...

The reference to the back office at this stage of the pyramid is primarily justified by the fact that very often in these cases a specific commitment is given to the customer. General conditions frequently contain explicit time limits, with which the organization is bound to comply on pain of sanction. These limits remain largely unknown, hidden in the small print. But when a case is passed on to the back office, the customer will be informed of these time limits in person. This explicitly created expectation must then be met. And this means that it must be separately monitored and followed up.

One cautionary note of advice though. If the back office measures service level only on closed cases, then it might paint a picture way too green. In a 'Last In First Out' approach, your service level remains great, but in the meantime others are aging badly. Service level as an indicator needs to be coupled with an overview of the pending cases and their evolution – hence the reason for putting the backlog at the bottom row of the pyramid.

This time commitment is less explicit for the front office. True, in Belgium the Charter for Customer-friendliness contains a maximum answer time of 150 seconds, but this is one of those things that is best covered with the cloak of charity – or forgetfulness.

The net result of all this is that the front office service level only appears at the next step of the pyramid. Its promises are much less clear-cut. Even so, its appearance at all is again something of a surprise. Didn't we just see in a previous section that its influence only had a marginal effect on customer satisfaction?

Yes, we did. But...

Not talking at all about response speeds in a priority pyramid for contact centers would just be too big a culture shock for everyone else in the organization. It is one of the most well-known of all KPIs (even at executive level), so that not to mention it would seem suspicious at best and smack of a cover-up at worst.

Besides, the operational management of a contact center demands that the notion of service level is followed up, even if only to serve as a necessary parameter in your work force management engine. And yes, I'll admit, I am just rationalizing the sad fact that I have never managed to get rid of it as a senior management reporting element.

As far as I am concerned, you can drop this KPI, if you can get away with it. If you can't – and you probably won't be able to – make sure that it is not allocated an unhealthily disproportionate place of importance in your list of priorities.

In purely service-oriented contact centers, the concrete commercial support of sales tends to be something of an add-on. This explains why 'leads' comes at the top of the pyramid and in this sense is subordinated to all your other more important priorities. This is perfectly in line with corporate expectations.

The entirety of your operations, embracing all your priorities, then needs to be weighed against the available budget. In the pyramid, this is translated into a number of FTEs, which is always the biggest driver of costs and the element that is most subject to influencing. Including the budget reality in your priorities sends out a powerful and unambiguous signal that cost management is an important part of your 'basics'. Putting it as a transversal layer avoids artificial priority discussions. You're supposed to do all of it, at the lowest possible cost. Your DNA, remember...?

In view of what we already know, it is also possible to break a lance for the inclusion of another transversal layer. For example, 'employee satisfaction' could (must?) be one such possibility, allowing you to ensure that the achievement of the other, more externally focused indicators will not happen at the expense of your own staff. Again, it would certainly send a powerful visual signal to your organizational colleagues.

However, its inclusion in the pyramid would require this satisfaction to be measured and reported on a regular basis. If it is only done sporadically – and in some companies that means just once a year – the results are so statically ill-defined against the other parameters that the exercise becomes meaningless. That is the only reason for the non-inclusion of this element in figure 92.

A sales role can influence the order of the pyramid

In a contact center that explicitly profiles itself as a sales channel, the order – and therefore the importance of the different needs – can change.

This is illustrated in figure 93.

'Sales' still comes behind 'customer satisfaction' in the pecking order. This makes it very clear that the 'sales is service' – ambition takes on a high priority, but not at the expense of annoying the customer with an avalanche of inappropriate commercial talk.

However, it is equally clear that 'sales' has certainly pushed service level farther down (or in the pyramid higher up) the order.

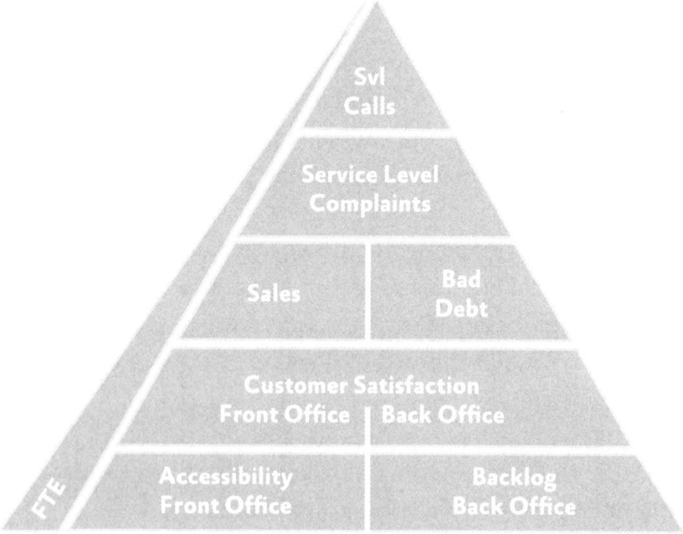

Figure 93: a sales role changes the priorities

To ensure that the enthusiasm for sales success does not lead to too much creativity, which may result in orders that are never completed, the notion of collectability has also been introduced via the 'bad debts' KPI.

Correct guidance of agents

The entire pyramid is built upon the performance of the contact center staff, who, each in their own function, need to carry out their task correctly day after day.

You can regard this as the operational counterpart of the fact that FTEs are by far and away the largest cost element.

In other words, 'doing the job' is the cornerstone on which the entire contact center edifice is built.

The base of the basics, as it were...

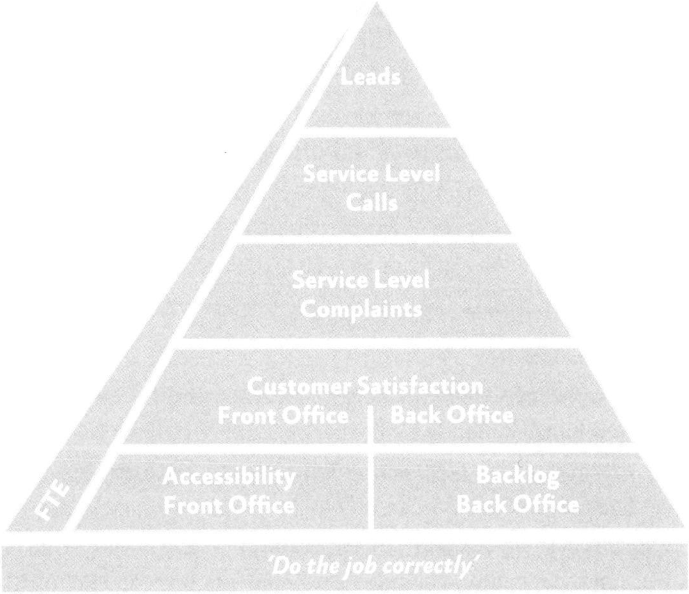

Figure 94: 'do the job correctly' is the basis for everything

The emphasis on employees and their individual behavior is consistent with our earlier observations about the drivers of customer satisfaction.

Making sure that your people (can) do their job correctly is therefore at the very core of contact center management. It is the key to getting the basics right.

Can creative and empowered agents really make the difference?

The importance of the behavior of employees often leads to bold and forthright claims. Some argue that the human factor is the biggest differentiator of all in service provision. In an era in which companies resemble each other more and more in every other aspect, their people are often the only thing that can make a difference. Products can be copied, technology is increasingly standardized, processes are converging toward a series of universal best practices, and prices are generally fixed by mutual consent. Nowadays – for the time being at least – your employees are the only element in your value chain that can't be cloned.

Be honest: it sounds better and is a bit more politically correct than 'seeking to create mindless telephone slaves, who are chained to the platform and only allowed to read off a number of brain-numbing, soul-destroying standard scripts...'

As I said: bold and forthright claims...

The 'people make the difference' argument is certainly valid. It also coincides with what we see in practice, especially given the modern-day evolution towards more complex calls. By definition, these are less capable of being dealt with by standard and self-service answers. As a result, they can only be handled by a human employee who must have the skill and ability to search for an often far from obvious and creative solution. To make this possible, he must be given the freedom by his managers to 'color outside the lines' or, if he is sufficiently empowered, to even move those lines to a different position.

Just another contact center

During a 2015 Contact Center Congress, a clear majority (90%) of contact center representatives labeled their center as a differentiator for their organization. They associated this position however mainly with strategy and value, organization and culture, and processes. Nothing really contact center-specific.

68% considered their contact center to be different from others. Again, however, the same explaining variables prevailed, putting 'people' only fourth in a list of five.

There seems to be a gap between the dream and reality...

(Contact Center Professional 3.0 – workshop Organization and Leadership – Jan Smets – CCLA Contact Center Congress 17/11/2015

Harry Potter in contact center management?

Sadly, it is not possible to just wave a magic wand and turn all your agents into creative and empowered geniuses. Until further notice, the contact center is not run by Harry Potter...

And still, this is what some organizations seem to hope will happen. They decree top-down that from now on their employees will be given all the freedom they need to better serve the customer. In other words, they push the responsibility for sustainable success firmly onto the shoulders of their personnel. And then they wonder why things don't turn out the way they had planned...

Unfortunately, this top-down imposition of empowerment ignores decades of contact center management that went in the opposite direction! It takes no account of a past when strict adherence to procedures and rules was the order of the day, when it was thought that the best way to achieve 'quality' was by

Change to strange?

The model depicted in figure 95 is an interesting way for us to consider if and how a contact center or its operatives can be a competitive differentiator. It is based on the description I once heard Dan Cable give about his 'change to strange' theory.[92]

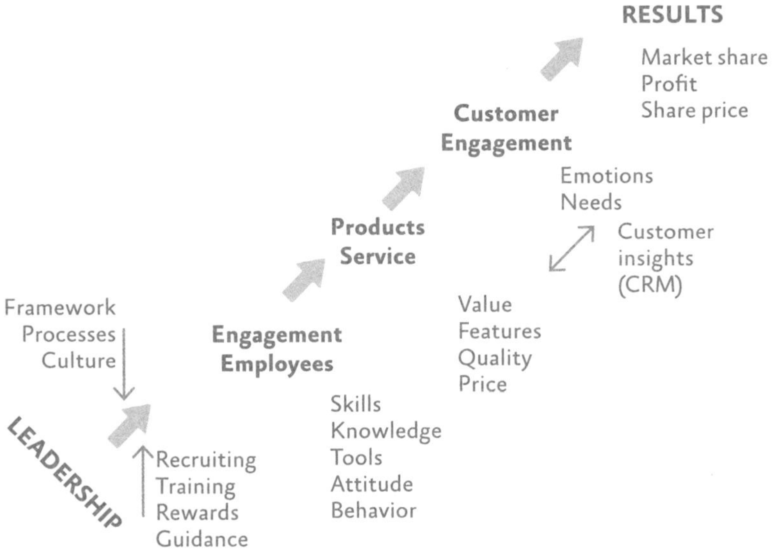

Figure 95: change to strange

According to Cable, every company is searching for 'extraordinary' results, irrespective of the manner in which they are expressed. In this sense, 'strange' therefore means 'exceptional', rather than 'odd' or 'crazy'.

Of course, this is true. No mission statement in the world has the ambition to make its company 'average'.

They always want to be the best, strongest or most successful at what they do.

These extraordinary results can only be achieved if customers are exceptionally loyal or are prepared to pay extra to buy your products or services. This is only likely to happen when they regard those products and services as being equally extraordinary, as something that they are unable to find in the same form anywhere else. Perhaps these products and services have become so personalized (customer relationship management) that it is difficult for someone else to provide them.

These products and services are created by employees, who – to carry logic through – must also be extraordinary. Extraordinarily committed, skilled or (let's be cynical for a moment) cheap.

The role of the managers in this organization is to create a framework in which the employees are able and allowed to do this. This is the basis of leadership.

So much for the theory. Time to take a look in the mirror of practice. Is your contact center an 'extraordinary' factor for your organization? A factor that sets you apart from the competition? If so, how? What are you doing that is so different from everybody else? What have you got that they haven't?

Or you can apply the same reasoning specifically to the contact center. What extraordinary results are you chasing? What do you need in the chain to effectively achieve those results in a sustainable manner? What are your operatives extraordinarily good at?

CallExcell, a Belgian external contact center, is proud to boast that it is 'not just another contact center', a claim it seeks to make good by the 'extraordinary' way it deals with its customers and its personnel and the 'extraordinary' manner in which it profiles itself so explicitly in the market. This is the banner, as it were, behind which their employees march to success.

So what are things like where you work?

slavish obedience to the 'right' internal guidelines. These were the days when quality monitoring was intended first and foremost to check not quality, but compliance, to see how far everyone had followed their instructions. If this was supposed to be empowerment, it was no more than empowerment to obey.

In many contact centers, creativity – another key element of the new creed – is almost as much of an unwelcome guest as empowerment. In bank contact centers, for example, and certainly since the banking crisis of 2008, managers keep a tight control over what customers are told. Too much creativity in this direction would almost certainly not be greeted with applause.

Okay, perhaps to some extent this is understandable. Unbridled ingenuity in every conversation would hardly be in keeping with the aim of providing a 'consistent and intentional' approach that is necessary for the creation of a brand experience, as shown in figure 43. This is something that the contact center already finds difficult enough as it is.

Employees will inevitably find that being empowered has its limits, although this was almost certainly not made clear at the start. In these circumstances 'confusion' is the best of a series of bad outcomes that one can hope for.

Exploring the playing field: the bigger box

There needs to be crystal clear communication with employees about what 'doing the job well' really means. All too often they are addressed in vague, general terms that leave them none the wiser: 'Just do what you think is right and use your common sense'. They are left to fill in the details for themselves. Is it any wonder that things sometimes go wrong?

How do you draw an owl?[94]

So what are the agents supposed to do with these vague basic instructions (if you can call them that)? How are they expected to give concrete practical expression to something so nebulous?

'Use your common sense' is often more a cover for a lack of preparation than a genuine evolution towards greater staff empowerment.

This is something that managers need to be honest about. When they tell their operatives to use their common sense, what they really mean is that they need to guess what the manager would do in the same circumstances and then do just that.

This is the kind of 'guidance' you find being given to operatives all the time. For a contact center, this is the equivalent of the 'how to draw an owl' illustration you can find on the internet.[93] Drawing 1 is the advice the managers give. Drawing 2 is what the operatives are expected to provide.

How to draw an owl:

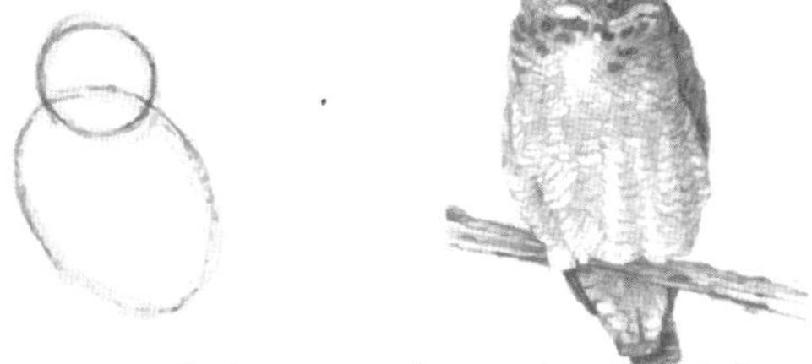

1. Draw some circles 2. Draw the rest of the owl

The task of making things clear is the heavy responsibility of... those responsible!

Giving correct guidance to contact center operatives implies the customers' needs as a starting point, and a precise translation of what this means in terms of 'doing the job correctly' from figure 94. Being able to make this crystal clear to the operatives in precise and concrete terms is crucial. For this reason, it was a key element in a multi-year change program that bpost initiated in its contact center, in collaboration with the Cohen Brown management and advice group. This basic philosophy is not exclusive to contact centers – the post offices have also been using it for years with success – but it works just as well. It is summarized in what is known as the 'success triangle'.

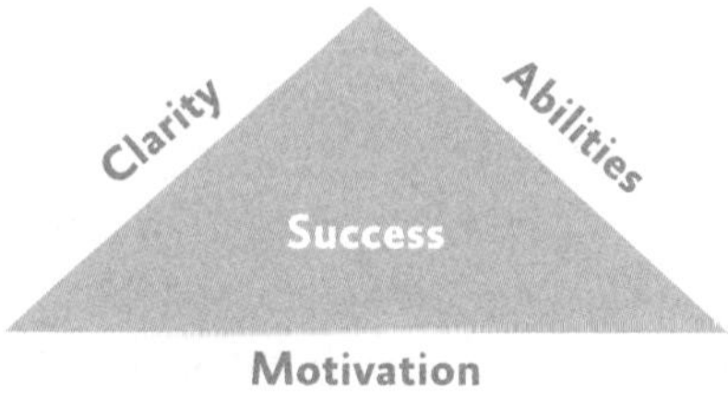

Figure 97: the success triangle© Cohen Brown

In this approach, 'success' comes as a result of being very disciplined in answering three questions:

- Is it clear? Are the objectives transparent and do the operatives fully understand what is expected of them in terms of the tasks they perform?
- Do the operatives have the necessary knowledge and resources to carry out those tasks correctly?
- What does the organization do to guarantee success and to encourage operatives to perform their duties to an ever higher standard, day after day? How is motivation kept at a high level?

Applying this model consistently creates a common language, makes performance discussable and allows you to pinpoint causes of non-performance. Is it a question of not 'knowing how to', 'not being able to' or 'not wanting to'?

A balance needs to be found between a clear definition of the basic rules of the game and the room for maneuver that the operatives are allowed within those limits. In short, were not talking about 'out-of-the-box' thinking; we are talking about creating a new and bigger box.

The guidelines for what is allowed and what isn't need to be defined with precision. On the one hand, this gives the personnel something concrete to hold on to, while on the other hand it gives the organization a certain reassurance that nothing too radical will happen.

Once that room for maneuver has been clearly established, the operatives must be free to move within it autonomously.

But this does not mean that they should simply be left to their own devices. They need to be coached in how to use this freedom properly. You can compare it with a football match. During the game itself, the circumstances are fairly unpredictable and the players need to be able to deal with the unexpected. But if they are coached well enough and train hard enough in advance, they can be ready to cope with most of the things they will face on the pitch. Almost every game situation can be simulated and analyzed. Patterns of play can be learnt until the right reaction almost becomes a reflex. This is also how combat units train in the army.

Something similar can be applied in contact centers. Role playing and situation scenarios can help to prepare operatives for 'what if' situations. In this way, they can develop the right habits in a 'safe' environment, with clear feedback and answers to questions about whether those habits constitute what the managers regard as 'good'.

Having said that – and if my personal experience has any value as a reference – many operatives don't really enjoy classic role-playing exercises. But listening together to actual recorded conversations, discussing them and commenting on them, and exchanging practical tips and techniques is an equally good alternative. As long as it allows to make the limits of the new big box visible and shows them how to deal with all that extra space.

Consequently, in this field the management of the contact center and of the organization in general plays a more important role than the operatives themselves. The managers not only create the framework within which the operatives

'Few people are capable of doing great things. Many people are capable of doing small things with great love.'

Mother Theresa

will work and the processes they will use, but must also secure initial acceptance and then further perpetuate this 'new' way of working.

What kind of behavior is rewarded within the organization? What are the new hero stories?

An internal hero story in which an operative is praised because he was involved in the longest call ever but in the end still managed to help the customer brilliantly,[95] will have a better effect on staff morale than the ticking-off of an operative because he did not follow the right procedure.

The first unfortunate comment made by a team leader to an operative can cause irreparable damage.

Primum non nocere (part deux)

We already encountered Hippocrates' principle earlier, in relation to customers. The same applies for contact center management when it comes to their agents.

In September 2018, a leading Flemish magazine ran a series of articles on 'shitty jobs'[96]. First of the lot: contact center agent. Based on first-hand experience from an outsourcer, an interview with an insider depicted a hellish working environment, in which agents were forced to mimic scripts, recorded only for Big Brother control purposes, were underpaid and over-pushed, had to work with sub-optimal tools and were followed to the bathroom to make them respect their scheduled breaks. All this resulted in quite literally burning up agents, typically within an 18 month time frame.

Talk about painting a negative picture. The blame is put on (most often telco) clients, squeezing the contact center for costs.

The interviewee... someone from the HR-department.

Well then... shame on you!

Not for being a whistle-blower. But for being in a position to actually do something about it, and failing. Management has a crushing responsibility in this. Period.

*'Contact centers do not operate.
Contact center agents do.'*

Bart Dietz

Never under-estimate the role of first-line leadership

Hopefully, we are now all in agreement that the behavior of the agents is the decisive factor in the successful performance of the contact center.

The very foundation. Right?

But the manner in which they are guided is also a huge 'basic to get right'.

According to Bart Dietz,[97] five years of scientific research at the Erasmus University of Rotterdam has consistently led to the same conclusion: what leaders do with their agents is more important than who the agents are. Roughly 70% of the variation in performance at agent level is explained by who the leaders are and how they act, rather than by differences between the agents themselves. In short, how well the contact center functions is primarily ensured by the first-line management.

In other words, success is created by a group of people... about whom the contact center leader traditionally does not have a great deal of insight. It is a typical characteristic that almost every moment of an agent's time at work can be monitored and controlled. In fact, there is a kind of 'Big Brother' syndrome, which actually makes some operatives feel uncomfortable. There is no comparable supervision of the team leaders, notwithstanding their huge influence.

It is hardly surprising, then, that Dietz's lecture on 'leadership' is embedded as a fixed (and highly praised) element of the Expert Class in Contact Center Management.

Its scope is too broad to be summarized easily. And quite frankly, it is a subject that is worthy of a full book in its own right. It deserves better than to be shamelessly summarized here. But that being said...

A selection from his '10 lessons for contact center managers'[99] so explicitly supports the storyline we have been telling that it would be a pity not to use it (briefly):

1. In terms of performance, 'removing agent stress' works better than 'improving motivation'. Stress can be removed by creating sufficient clarity, avoiding work overload and avoiding ambiguous messages. This is clearly related

to the success triangle and the precise delineation of the playing field – our bigger box.

2. Pro-social motivation works. In a contact center, it is certainly possible to motivate operatives by making clear to them what they do and what effect and impact this has on others.[99] Please connect the dots for yourself between this part and the emotional charge of the contact and the whole 'value' story.
3. Communication improves motivation.
   It is impossible not to make the link between the need to make expectations explicit and the need for individual feedback that we have mentioned repeatedly throughout the book.

But I am relieved that you have now heard it all from someone else as well...

Translating correctly into KPIs and reporting

The potential pitfalls involved in setting up a good reporting system have already been discussed at length.

The full implementation of the techniques for setting up a balanced scorecard, based on the vision and mission of the contact center, should really help you in this respect. What's more, these techniques are no more than a chapter old... so everything should still be fresh in your memory! So why not get started?

The previously mentioned Corporate Executive Board has also given us a good summary of the most important lessons. When you need to report contact center performance 'upstairs', it is always a good idea to follow the handy rules set down in figure 98.

Upward Management Rules

- Limit to one page
- Align with corporate goals
- Give key points for area above/below target
- Provide metric interpretation summary

Figure 98: golden advice from the Corporate Executive Board's 2007 Customer Contact Council Research

The advice to limit the number of indicators and to align them with the general objectives of the organization has since become standard. It is also self-evident that the reader of the dashboard (in other words, 'the boss') should be helped to correctly understand and interpret the results.

Play your role as an information channel

Another thing we looked at earlier – again in some depth – was that one of the most important ways for the contact center to create added value is to distill information from the market place. This information can relate to a wide variety of subjects: your own products and services, your customers, your competitors, the market itself. Much, if not most, of the underlying data is already present in the center as a result of the role it plays in centralizing customer feedback. However, to turn that data into useful information requires an effort that is atypical for most contact centers.

It is atypical because most of the multiple operations in a contact center are done in real time. Within that short window of time there is not much room for a detailed analysis. In fact, it is unreasonable even to expect it. As result, this analysis is one of the few things not done in real time.

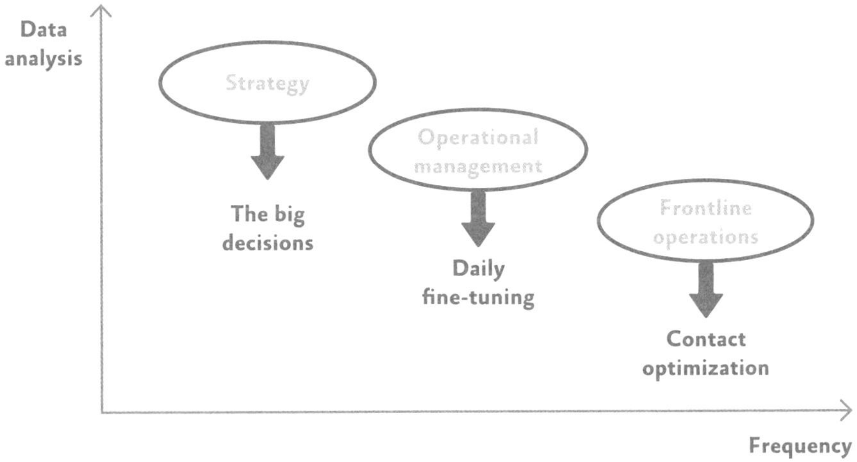

Figure 99: data analysis in the contact center

(inspired by Christophe De Clercq, Executive Class in Contact Center Deployment, THOCC, June 2013)

Even so, agents must still be able to find the right response/action within the duration of the contact. This means that the results of the previously processed and analyzed data must be made available to them in real time by the platform system they are using.

Operational management takes place at a higher level than contact-per-contact thinking.

The available KPIs must allow management to make the right decisions in terms of resource deployment. Intelligent analysis of what is happening and insights into the different mechanisms and levers must make it possible for the contact center management to make – the right – operational decisions

The 'big' strategic decisions, which are more usually taken at the organizational level rather than within the contact center, are few and far between. When they do need to be made, this requires a much more thorough analysis and distillation of relevant insights. This is the point where 'data' really does need to become 'information'. To support these big decisions effectively, the contact center must be prepared to switch its focus away from combating systems and concentrate instead on the identification of patterns.

Without wishing to use the fashionable new buzz phrase 'big data', it should nonetheless be obvious that in-depth analytical skill and a certain affinity with data must feature among the list of competencies for the contact center managers of the future.

'Data is the new oil', according to Christophe De Clercq (Eneco)

'Nowadays, you often hear it said that "data is the new oil". It is a good analogy. It took mankind tens of thousands of years to discover that oil existed, but at a certain point we realized that it was sitting in the ground under our feet and that its possibilities were limitless – if only we could get at it in the right way.

You can say the same about data. Every company has got it but we are now only just realizing what we can do with it. The result is a new industrial revolution. The frontrunners in Silicon Valley already know what this means: "Big data is not a trend, it's reality... If you're not involved with data, you're history!" I heard this as long ago as the summer of 2014 in an inspirational presentation at the Institute for the Future.

But what are these possibilities, exactly? And are they as limitless as everyone is saying? In essence, it is possible to distinguish three levels of value creation:

1. Strategic intelligence: the analysis of huge mountains of data to make important strategic decisions;
2. day-to-day intelligence: the classic A/B test, where the results of a particular action are tested against a control group, is a perfect example;
3. real-time use: without a doubt the most interesting but also the most under-exploited form of value creation!

Every contact center is bursting at the seams with so-called "business rules". These rules are designed in such a way that their correct application should lead on average to the best possible result. I sometimes like to compare these rules with a "one-size-fits-all" t-shirt. These always look ridiculous, because they very clearly don't "fit all". They are either much too big or much too small!

Even worse than these business rules are the essentially random decisions supposedly taken on the basis of "gut feeling".

The great value of data for contact centers is the way that it can make each customer contact more relevant. Customers do not have average or random expectations and the same is true for the agent in the contact center. I advise you to search in your own contact center for business rules or gut decisions of the kind I have mentioned above, both of which are applied hundreds of times each day. I guarantee you will be amazed at what you find!'

7

CONCLUSION

'There is a difference between knowing the path, and walking the path.'
The Matrix

Every wise lesson has a conclusion. But how do you conclude a story without end? There is still no such thing as a 'definitive truth' about contact center management. And it was never my intention to write one.

Perhaps the absence of a neatly rounded finish is a conclusion in itself.

Nowadays, many people predict a perfect storm[100] when it comes to future dealings with customers. Thanks to the proliferation of social media and the ease of access to telecommunications and the internet, consumers are now in a position like never before to really seize power. Their expectations are evolving, not only in terms of quality but also in terms of the greater personalization of service. Tolerance thresholds are getting lower and it was never so easy to turn a complaint into an irresistible online and offline movement.

'Je suis client.'[101]

The contact center will need to get used to this new situation. It has no choice.

There is no conclusion, only next steps

Trying to predict the future and to leave tangible traces of those predictions is always tricky. On the one hand, it inevitably dates your work. On the other hand, it also makes it very easy to later look back and see how outdated content has become and how childishly naive the 'prophet' now seems. You have probably been at presentations where the speaker refers to the film *Back to the Future 2*, which at the time (1989) painted a highly futuristic vision of what things would be like... on the 21st of October 2015. Let's just say that reality had not yet overtaken Zemeckis' fantasy by the time I was applying the finishing touches to the Dutch version of this manuscript. And it still has yet to, three years later.

Of course, if your predictions hit the nail well and truly on the head, then you are praised as a 'visionary', if not the 'messiah'.

At a New Year's reception of the Contact Center Leaders Association,[102] I once risked making some predictions about the immediate future of the contact center.

In the Dutch version, finalised by end 2015, I took the bold step in committing those predictions irrevocably to paper. Fate would decide just how embarrassed I would likely feel in a few years' time. But now, three years later, I still feel comfortable enough to repeat them in the English version, without any 'cheating-in-retrospect'. I did not add that much. Maybe, I might have been on to something then?

1. Customer-oriented thinking 2.0 has arrived, but does not always work to the advantage of the contact center.

   It is almost as if everyone has 'rediscovered' the customer. 'Customer-orientation' is hailed as the creed that will lead us all to commercial salvation. Some of the sentiments associated with this trend tend to turn the clock back to the bad old days – at least as far as contact centers are concerned. Pleas for greater attention to 'the personal touch' and 'proximity', especially when preached by marketing departments, seem to assume that contact centers have regressed into the old-style impersonal 'call factories'. Perceptions and gut feeling are back in fashion and are the bases on which (often strange) channel decisions are taken. It has once again become *bon ton* to depict the contact center as something distant, dispassionate and, ultimately, unfriendly.

   It is going to take an awful lot of sustained evangelism from the contact centers to turn this picture around.

2. The economic crisis will continue to be an ally for the contact center.

   Even in these harsh times, it remains an indisputable economic reality that a contact center is a very efficient – probably the most efficient – way to deal with large volumes of customer interactions. If or when more expensive channels seek to attract more contacts, to justify (in part, at least) their cost, this will be very difficult for them to objectify financially. Since the crisis is predicted to last for several more years, this is a fact that will continue to play in the contact center's favor.

3. On the other side of the coin, this same harsh economic reality will ensure that there is permanent pressure on the cost component of the contact

center. The possibilities for outsourcing and off-shoring as viable alternative options will remain, certainly in a globalized and highly connected context. The quest for self-service will start from – projected – customer experience arguments, but will inevitably get translated into significant cost-saving mantras. As we saw, avoiding the need for a contact is the most customer-centric level of service. But the fact that it allows you to de-staff, and cut costs, will generate even more fervent advocates, especially in Finance and C-suites. The contact center manager will struggle to separate goal from consequence.

4. The demise of the telephone will be predicted time and time again... but it will survive anyway.

   Chat will probably be positioned as the first of the phone's successors for 'modern' customer contact. Funnily enough, this claim is often argued from an economic standpoint.

   Its advocates point to the fact that an average agent can deal efficiently with on average 2 or 3 chats at the same time[103] or else highlight the possibility of automating chat sessions with the help of so-called avatars. The benefit for the organization is cost reduction. The benefit for the customer is put forward as a kind of multi-tasking: he can ask his question while simultaneously carrying on with other more relevant things.

   For a number of companies chat is indeed the next logical step in their development of new communication channels. If, for example, you sell internet applications, it would look pretty odd if you didn't offer this channel. Chat is a more natural lever to push digital self-service. An agent pushing the right web-page during a chat, is a more natural flow than a verbal (human or IVR) reference. This makes it an appealing complement to digital alternatives. And chat is a natural step towards automated chatbots.

   Even so, I predict that the telephone will live to fight another day.

   Leaving aside the value of its low-threshold access, the telephone is still the shortest and quickest way to get in touch with another human being of flesh and blood, with whom you can conduct a real conversation. As long as customers continue to experience emotions and have personal stories they wish to share in a direct process of dialogue, the contact center will remain an important element in the total customer 'package'. Given the emotional link, this human contact could even become a powerful differentiator. 2018 radio ads for a Belgian insurance company describe failed attempts at self-service, and end with an 'aah, a human being' moment of relief from the customer when calling the contact center. Or as a consultant once put it, as human contacts become scarcer, they will receive more value. Quod erat demonstrandum.

Smaller relative share of the telephone might not mean less absolute volumes of calls. Chat and maybe other communication means will probably get added as a channel – primarily because the companies themselves in many cases seem keen to stimulate it – but it will be a story of 'as well as' and not 'instead of' the telephone. Of course, this means more new channels for the contact center to support, with the inevitable consequences this will have for organizational complexity and individual skill sets.

5. In the battle to prove its ability to create added value, the analysis of the data possessed by the contact center will be crucial.

We have lived through the era in which the primary role within the contact center was that of the workforce manager. For many years, the essence of contact center management was the ability to efficiently and effectively make use of the available resources – mainly personnel – to achieve the best possible results. Today, the balance is shifting towards roles and functions that exploit the mass of information held in the center. This involves not only the structuring of insights, but also the statistical and analytical identification of real operational levers.

In a lecture, I once referred to this as the Doctor Who syndrome. This TV hero has... two hearts. The contact center of tomorrow will have this as well. In addition to its traditional WFM heart, it will develop a new – and more strongly beating – analytical heart.

In this field, science will replace craftmanship and the data analysts will be the valves that keep the center's analytical heart pumping. This is a competence that is typically scarce, and not only in contact centers. Bridging this knowledge gap will be a major challenge for the future and will undoubtedly be a domain where vendors will profile themselves.

6. Customer effort will increase in importance as a concept, particularly in a contact center environment.

This prediction does not exactly constitute a huge leap in the dark. Many others have also predicted much the same thing, including Nicola Millard (see chapter 5). The concept is based on a perfect win-win reasoning: win for the customer, whose life is made easier, and win for the organization, which is able to avoid unnecessary work, with all the economic benefits this implies. The contact center will increasingly become the place where opportunities for all kinds of improvements are discovered and reported. In this way, it will contribute towards the reduction of its own volumes.

7. Homeworking will fundamentally change the operational organization of contact centers in the future.

   With the further congestion of our roads, the all-too-common failure of public transport to meet public needs and the growing importance of the work-life balance, homeworking is a social trend that is destined to increase dramatically. In many companies it is already being applied extensively for white collar employees. However, the companies who also allow this for their contact center employees are much thinner on the ground. In the worst cases, some companies allow homeworking for every echelon except for the contact center! In one sense this is paradoxical, since the very basis of the function involves 'working at distance'. What's more, the wide range of monitoring possibilities makes managing contact center activity easy to follow almost irrespective of where it is carried out.

   Certainly, where there is currently a need to work large but tight shift regimes, the possible reduction of pressure on the personal work/life organization of staff is an argument in favor of homeworking. This internal pressure is set to become unsustainably heavy in the future.

   The main challenge to homeworking in this context is not technical, but relates to the historical manner of leading, supporting and coaching contact center agents. Still today, this is heavily based on a 'command and control' approach, rooted in the manager's physical presence. This would necessarily need to be replaced by a model based more on trust.

   Perhaps we need to wait for a ground-breaking trendsetter, a successful example that can convince the rest of the sector to follow. In 2015, the Dutch VANAD was able to create this kind of momentum in the Netherlands. The Belgian external contact center IPG has also been copied to a certain degree by others in the same field. And I lack the necessary modesty to not mention bpost here, which in part of its contact center environment allows up to three days a week of homeworking, in a very, very conservative environment. Or to paraphrase YouTube: 'It will be the first followers that transforms the lone nut into a movement'.[104]

The further expansion of homeworking will also make it possible for contact centers to attract new kinds of employees. The collective sectoral search for ambitious school-leavers may soon become a thing of the past. It may well be replaced by the recruitment of slightly older, slightly more empathic operatives, who are only prepared to step (back) into the labor market on certain conditions.

Graeme Codrington has already predicted it: if you look at the activities of a contact center at the meta-level, the idea of 'spending the whole day on the telephone talking to strangers about this, that and the other' seems more like something we can imagine our mother doing than our daughters.

Sorry, mum...

Moreover, homeworking also offers the possibility to deal more efficiently with certain shifts. This makes it something worth considering in objective cost reduction terms. This applies equally to premises and other related building costs.

In any case, homeworking might fundamentally alter the relationship between the contact center management and its employees.

8. In the future, the battle for the contact center will be fought increasingly in the back office.

Most contact centers have a front office that is more or less optimally organized. Of course, there is always room for improvement but investments in recent decades in call platforms, desktop software, workforce management and other such innovations have leveled the front office playing field. The battle there has already been fought and the victorious vendors have divided the market cake between themselves. Nowadays, there are very few companies who will think lightly about switching their technology.

In comparison, the back office is much less developed, which opens the prospect of being able to make further efficiency gains. According to a study by Genesys, 28% of back office time can be classified as 'unproductive'.[105] Pressure on costs will ensure that efforts are made to capitalize on this potential. Reducing the distance between front and back at the organizational level, something I already admitted being in favor of, will further accelerate this tendency.

The killer gain will be made by the contact center that can succeed in correctly translating the specificities of its back office into systems solutions. This requires much more than simply copying the mechanics of the front office. The work of the back office is fundamentally different in terms of flow: cases are given to an operative who in many instances hangs on to it for quite some time, gradually and sequentially dealing with it in fits and starts, as the information he needs to solve it is received from in and outside the organization. The actual working time is therefore not the same as the total turnaround time. The first determines the workload planning, but the two together determine the customer's perspective. And that's different from a call. Very different.

9. Different technical solutions will converge. Distribution platforms will be able to complement their integrated case dispatching with their own planning tools. Planning platforms that already use your volume and reflect your working processes could use that easily to do dispatching. This is just one example, but I predict that in the years ahead we will see a titanic battle between the major suppliers, who will each come from their historical angle of approach to try and conquer the entire contact center from front to back. Only the strong will survive, or the very specialized, providing they can integrate with the giants. The contact center will be increasingly seen as one channel in a whole suit of an omnichannel with a need for overarching system infrastructures. There will be interesting price tags to all of this...

10. In a world in which the universal truth about contact centers has not yet been discovered, the main source of information and inspiration is... the contact center professional himself.

    Contact centers can learn a lot from each other by sharing best practices and exchanging relevant stories, not only about the things that work but also about the things that go wrong. It will not happen very often that these operational tips and tricks contain anything of strategic or competitive value, so there is no need for secrecy. In Belgium, there is certainly still room for improvement in this respect, although organizations like the Contact Center Leaders Association and ContactCenters.be are attempting to make progress in this direction. However, it are the contact center managers themselves who need to display more willingness to look over the wall and talk to their neighbors.

Be the change you seek in the world

All these things imply that it is essential for the contact center manager to leave his current state of near perfect isolation.

It is his duty to understand what his center can mean for the rest of the organization and he must then translate that meaning into concrete action. In this way, he can become an effective bridge builder between the operational reality of customer experience and the design of products, services and processes.

Leaving the discussions about the cost and value center to one side, perhaps the most important thing is how the contact center – and its management – sees itself.

Nobody is ever going to get the role they really want handed to them on a plate. You've got to be prepared to fight for it.

'The future,' an Orange commercial once declared, 'is bright'. It is up to contact center professionals to grab that future by the scruff of the neck and make it their own.

The balancing act

In the introduction, we already made the comparison between a contact center manager and a plate juggler in a Chinese circus. To come full circle, we can do no better than to show another balancing trick that the contact center manager needs to repeat day after day.

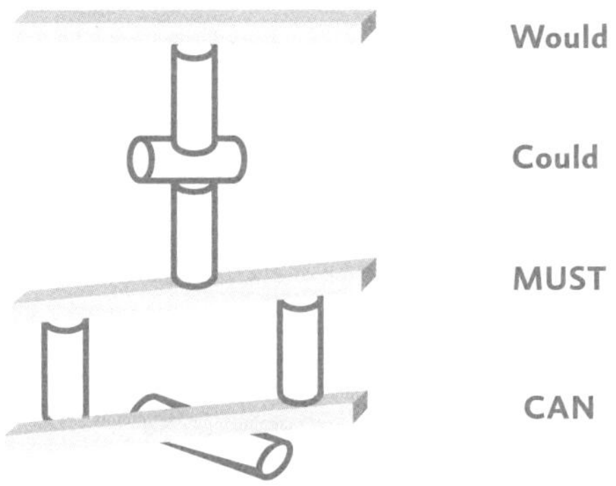

Figure 100: the contact center balancing act

As a contact center manager, there are no doubt lots of things that you would like to do.

There are no doubt lots of things you could do, based on the huge volume of customer contacts you process each day.

Never forget, however, all the things that you must do, the things that the organization as a whole expects you to do. Do them well. An audience that is left frustrated and disappointed rarely applauds.

And the foundation on which all your work depends and which you need to keep in mind is what you can do, given the resources at your disposal. Never stop pushing your boundaries, but realize full well where they are.

Forget this and you will hit the ground with a bump. For real.

Do it right and you are certain to make a difference.

As Seth Godin has said: *'Now has always been a good time to start'*.

I sincerely wish you all the best of luck.

Jan Smets

"For too long the contact center has been seen as a cost to serve; a necessary but unsexy part of the business. No longer. As organizations become increasingly omni-channel, the contact center is becoming an experience centrer – the hub for engaging with customers across all the channels. For some brands, the contact center is an important experience and touchpoint in its own right. One person who understands this and has transformed contact centers, is Jan Smets. In his terrific book he shares with us the tools for doing so."

Shaun Smith, bestselling author of *On Purpose. Delivering a Branded Customer Experience People Love*

"Staying ahead of customer expectations for service has never been more complex than it is today. The relationship between businesses and consumers is being revolutionized by technology advancements. Industry professionals, now more than ever, need a practical guide to understand the opportunity – and *Contact Center Management* rises to the occasion."

Merijn te Booij, Chief Marketing Officer Genesys

"Jan is a real practical man. Down to earth with a huge experience running one of the largest Contact Centers in Belgium. Jan also has a clear vision about the future and that makes this book very interesting. When day-to-day practice and vision come together, it makes a book readable. Last but not least, Jan also has an enormous sense of humor. It is always fun to hear him speak. For me Jan is a living legend in the Belgium Contact Center world and I really admire him."

Ad Nederlof , Executive Chairman Vanad Group

"Contact centers are a crucial part of most organizations' customer engagement strategy. Jan Smets' vision and experiences described in this book provide valuable insights to anyone trying to evolve their contact center from a cost center to a vital part of the organization that improves both the customer experience and the bottom line."

Marije Gould, Vice President of Marketing, EMEA at Verint

"A must-read for anyone who wants in on discussions regarding the management of contact centers."

Marc Buelens, author of *Bye Bye Management*

"Contact centers play a key role in improving customer relationships. The world of contact centers is currently undergoing tremendous changes. This book provides excellent insights, and helps you embark on a journey towards the contact center of tomorrow."

Steven Van Belleghem, author of *Customers the Day after Tomorrow*

ANNEXES

ANNEXES

1. 'Yes, but': countering the objections to the introduction of a sales role in the contact center.
2. 'Measurement' homework in the Expert Class in Contact Center Management.
3. List of indicators as given by the participants in the various editions of the Expert Class in Contact Center Management.
4. Typology of the indicators from the Expert Class in Contact Center Management.
5. Indicators from the Expert Class in Contact Center Management, plotted in categories based on input/output/outcome.
6. The indicators from the Expert Class in Contact Center Management, included in a 'mission to KPI model'.
7. The indicators from the Expert Class in Contact Center Management, distributed over an (un)balanced scorecard.
8. The indicators from the Expert Class in Contact Center Management, in the model introduced by Donna Fluss/DMG Consulting.

Annex 1:

'Yes, but': countering the objections to the introduction of a sales role in the contact center

(amended from an internal Belgacom/Proximus document)

'Killer phrase'	Possible answer strategy
Customers don't/ won't want this/ customers will never accept this.	Says who? What is the factual basis for that statement? Refer to other companies in the sector who have done this successfully. Point to figures relating to customer satisfaction, if you have them. Show that 'sales' has no negative impact. If you don't have figures, start measuring. Emphasize that the process must ensure correctness and that the customer will have the final say at all times.
Sales are not a service. The two things are contradictory.	What is so wrong with our offer that we genuinely believe we are doing our customers a favor by not offering it? Is satisfying a (perhaps unspoken) need of the customer not a service? Sales will not replace service. The initial question of the customer will always be answered first.
The... won't like it (fill in the possible objector in your specific case, but 'unions' are the most likely suspect).	Probably not. So make sure you have smoothed the path as transparently as possible. If you really can't counter this 'killer phrase', then you probably need to revise your approach.
The staff won't want this/won't be able to do it.	Why should we underestimate our own staff? Are they so inferior to staff in other contact centers where sales already works well? 'Want to' is relative. It is a non-negotiable part of the job, as formally described 'Won't be able' is a matter of technique. Foresee a trajectory of supporting this change, in which training and coaching are the central elements. Refer to this regularly in discussions.

'Killer phrase'	Possible answer strategy
It will never work.	It is certainly a good idea to run a trial project, for which you need to select a group of well-motivated operatives. Use their results as evidence and their experience in your communication. If even the best and most motivated agents fail to achieve convincing results during the trial, you have a problem.
Sales targets clash with other objectives.	With an approach in which the initial question of the customer is always correctly dealt with first, conflicts with other customer-related KPIs are not very likely. Even so, check your process KPIs to make sure there are no ambiguities. If (God help you) you have 'conversation length' as a KPI, then it may indeed be difficult to avoid a conflict of interest. In such cases, adjust your coaching indicators.
This is (yet another) extra burden for contact center staff.	How exactly does this increase the workload? We are not asking people to take more calls or work more hours. We are simply extending the length of the individual conversations. In essence, this adds no more work than when, say, a new product is introduced and the contact center operatives need to learn new answers about it.
What's in it for me?	Here you can naturally refer to the incentives and variable rewards that you are probably planning to support the project. But it is risky to talk exclusively in these terms. It is better to talk about the extra service we will be providing for customers; about the pride people will feel about being able to make an additional contribution to the success of the organization; about the fact that the employees will learn additional skills that will add value to their personal professional baggage.

Annex 2:

'Measurement' homework in the Expert Class in Contact Center Management

In preparation for the module 'Measurement' in the Expert Class in Contact Center Management, the participants were given the following task as 'homework':

> 'Imagine that I am someone important in your organization, someone whose name is only mentioned in whisper. The CEO, the general manager, whatever you like... Now imagine that you are the leader of the contact center – front and back office – in that organization.
>
> You bump into me in the lift and I ask, 'How are things?' Slightly flattered by the fact that I actually know who you are, you naturally answer: 'Good'.
>
> I ask another question: 'How are things in the contact center?' Even happier that I also know where you work, you of course answer 'Great!' again.
>
> Just as I am getting out of the lift, I turn around, hold the door open and say: 'I think that we need to pay more attention to the contact center at the executive level. In any case, I want our corporate dashboard to say something about it. Send me five indicators that you think we should use to monitor the center's performance. Could you do it straight away, perhaps? Thanks!'
>
> You take a deep breath, rush to your office and start preparing your answer to my question...'

The participants are given the task:

- to provide an answer relatively quickly: you don't keep the CEO waiting and you can reasonably assume that contact center managers already know (or should know) what their most important indicators are;
- to answer as if they were really communicating directly with the CEO;
- to only suggest indicators for which they can report real actuals; in other words, no politically correct 'We don't have this/can't do this, but think that we should have it, because it sounds good';
- to do this individually and not collude with other participants, not even when they work for the same organization.

This homework is given early enough in the course that it cannot be influenced by changing insights from what the participants have already learnt.

Annex 3:

List of indicators as given by the participants in the various editions of the Expert Class in Contact Center Management

Guidelines: how should you read this list?

The basis for this list is the answers of 138 participants in the Expert Class in Contact Center Management during the period 2007 to 2018. KPIs were grouped when the available information made it absolutely clear that the participants meant exactly the same thing. Even if there was only a marginal difference in interpretation, similar KPIs were nonetheless treated as being separate. This was also the case when the method of measurement was fundamentally different.

The KPIs are listed alphabetically and in function of their frequency.

The relative frequency percentage (as a proportion of the 138 participants) has been rounded off to the nearest whole number.

Indicator	Frequency	Relative frequency
Customer Satisfaction (via survey)	70	50,7%
Service level calls (% calls answered within x seconds)	61	44,2%
Accessibility/abandon rate (% calls answered/not answered)	58	42,0%
First Call Resolution (First Time Right, measured through transfer/repeat contacts)	43	31,2%
Quality Monitoring Score (calls)	42	30,4%
Gross conversion (sales on calls)	34	24,6%
Net Promotor Score	29	21,0%
Service level non-call transactions (% non-call contacts answered within given delay)	24	17,4%
Inbound call volume	21	15,2%
Average Waiting Time calls/Average Speed of Answer	20	14,5%
Employee Satisfaction	20	14,5%
Revenue	19	13,8%
Occupancy/agent utilization	18	13,0%

Indicator	Frequency	Relative frequency
Illness/absenteeism	16	11,6%
Gross Margin	15	10,9%
Handling time/average handling time calls	13	9,4%
Cost/ contact	9	6,5%
First Call Resolution (First time right, measured through customer survey)	9	6,5%
Handling time non-call transactions	9	6,5%
Productivity	9	6,5%
Employee Churn	8	5,8%
Calls/FTE	7	5,1%
Cost	7	5,1%
FTE cost	7	5,1%
Incoming Complaints/incidents volume	6	4,3%
Service level mails (% mails answered within given delay)	6	4,3%
Contacts per customer	5	3,6%
Cross-sell ratio/revenue	5	3,6%
Customer churn	5	3,6%
Sales volumes	5	3,6%
Adherence/real activity vs. planned	4	2,9%
Backlog non-calls	4	2,9%
Customer Effort Score (survey)	4	2,9%
Customer Satisfaction (client company)	4	2,9%
Log ratio (calls documented/registered)	4	2,9%
Net Promotor Score for contact (type)	4	2,9%
Quality Monitoring Score (mails)	4	2,9%
Service level outbound calls (% calls done by certain deadline)	4	2,9%
% fatal errors	3	2,2%
Costs vs. budget	3	2,2%
Forecast accuracy (correctness of volume forecasts)	3	2,2%
Inbound mail volume	3	2,2%
Issue list/attention points	3	2,2%
IT System availability	3	2,2%
Number of FTE	3	2,2%
Repeat volume	3	2,2%

Indicator	Frequency	Relative frequency
Service level specific file type	3	2,2%
Specific call/Service Request content	3	2,2%
Total contacts	3	2,2%
Total transactions/FTE	3	2,2%
% opportunities/calls (calls resulting in identified sales opportunity)	2	1,4%
Average outbound calls/day	2	1,4%
Avoided cost/contact	2	1,4%
Conversion rate outbound calls	2	1,4%
Cost per customer	2	1,4%
Margin/channel	2	1,4%
Non-call contact volumes	2	1,4%
Outbound sales	2	1,4%
Qualified calls/time unit (hr, day)	2	1,4%
Revenue per seat/FTE	2	1,4%
Revenue/contact	2	1,4%
Save-rate competition/retention rate	2	1,4%
Service level Back Office complaints	2	1,4%
Service level social media (% social feeds handled within certain deadline)	2	1,4%
Staffing	2	1,4%
Total offers/sales canceled/month	2	1,4%
Validated complaints on Contact center performance	2	1,4%
# outbound calls/written order	1	0,7%
% assisted sales (sales in agencies supported by contact center)	1	0,7%
% created opportunities agencies (lead generation towards physical channel)	1	0,7%
% processed sales	1	0,7%
Aging tickets	1	0,7%
ARPU (post-call revenue increase in Average Revenue per User)	1	0,7%
Autonomy increase	1	0,7%
Availability (login time)	1	0,7%
Average payment delay	1	0,7%
Average time in queue	1	0,7%
Calls on hold	1	0,7%

Indicator	Frequency	Relative frequency
Calls/hour incoming	1	0,7%
Channels Contact distribution	1	0,7%
Commercial gestures	1	0,7%
Complaint handling	1	0,7%
Conversion rate campaign calls	1	0,7%
Cost of acquisition	1	0,7%
Cost to sell/serve	1	0,7%
Cost variables	1	0,7%
Cost/FTE	1	0,7%
Cost/product/client	1	0,7%
Cross selling	1	0,7%
Customer churn intention	1	0,7%
Customer loyalty	1	0,7%
Customer Satisfaction non-calls (survey)	1	0,7%
Customers acquired	1	0,7%
Delivery accuracy	1	0,7%
Delivery speed	1	0,7%
Deployment FTE on communication	1	0,7%
Distribution cost	1	0,7%
Efficiency: paid jobs vs. calls	1	0,7%
Evolution in top FAQs	1	0,7%
First contact resolution (not specified)	1	0,7%
Forecasted revenue	1	0,7%
FTE/underlying business volumes	1	0,7%
Hiring speed	1	0,7%
Hitrate (sales/sales attempts)	1	0,7%
Immediate resolution rate	1	0,7%
Inbound sales	1	0,7%
Inbound volume webforms	1	0,7%
Incremental revenue/marketing experience	1	0,7%
Interaction quality	1	0,7%
Interactions/FTE/day	1	0,7%
Investments	1	0,7%
Invoice accuracy	1	0,7%

Indicator	Frequency	Relative frequency
Invoice completeness	1	0,7%
IVR abandon rate	1	0,7%
Job pride employees	1	0,7%
Loan loss	1	0,7%
Low detractors	1	0,7%
Monitorings/agent/period	1	0,7%
Net conversion	1	0,7%
Net margin / hour	1	0,7%
Non-call contacts handled/day	1	0,7%
Non-call transactions / FTE	1	0,7%
Objectives achievement rate	1	0,7%
Ombudsman complaints	1	0,7%
Online resolution	1	0,7%
Order size /channel	1	0,7%
Outbound volume handled	1	0,7%
Outstanding sales	1	0,7%
Overflow percentage calls	1	0,7%
Overhead cost	1	0,7%
Partnership status	1	0,7%
Process Effectiveness	1	0,7%
Processing time	1	0,7%
Product (new) development based on contact center data	1	0,7%
Productivity: Back office files / FTE	1	0,7%
Productivity: mails / FTE	1	0,7%
Profitability action	1	0,7%
Quality index	1	0,7%
Quality of documentation Service requests	1	0,7%
Quality scores - admin tasks	1	0,7%
Real vs. planned FTE	1	0,7%
Reduction of recurrent calls	1	0,7%
Repurchase intent (survey)	1	0,7%
Resolution	1	0,7%
Respecting commitments	1	0,7%
Revenue new customers	1	0,7%
Revenue retention	1	0,7%
Revenue vs. budget	1	0,7%
Revenue/channel	1	0,7%
Right Party Connects	1	0,7%

Indicator	Frequency	Relative frequency
Sales % contact center versus total Sales	1	0,7%
Sales attempts/calls	1	0,7%
Sales vs target	1	0,7%
Sales/head	1	0,7%
Same day resolution	1	0,7%
Shrinkage (work force management terminology, % FTE that cannot be deployed)	1	0,7%
Split interim - fix FTE	1	0,7%
Total offers/month	1	0,7%
Training cost	1	0,7%
Training time	1	0,7%
Transaction quality	1	0,7%
Unproductive working time	1	0,7%
Upsell ratio	1	0,7%
Volume per contact category	1	0,7%
Work force management	1	0,7%
Work-in-process volume of non-call transactions	1	0,7%

Annex 4:

Typology of the indicators from the Expert Class in Contact Center Management

Inputs as taken into account

Channel Monitoring	
Inbound call volume	21
Incoming Complaints/incidents volume	6
Contacts per customer	5
Log ratio (calls documented/registered)	4
Forecast accuracy	3
Inbound mail volume	3
Repeat volume	3
Specific call/Service Request content	3
Total contacts	3
% opportunities/calls (calls resulting in identified sales opportunity)	2
Non-call contact volumes	2
# outbound calls/written order	1
Calls/hour incoming	1
Channels Contact distribution	1
Evolution in top FAQs	1
Inbound volume webforms	1
Non-call contacts handled/day	1
Outbound volume handled	1
Reduction of recurrent calls	1
Volume per contact category	1

IT Systems	
IT System availability	3

Productivity and Cost	
Occupancy/agent utilization	18
Illness/absenteeism	16
Handling time/average handling time calls	13
Cost/ contact	9
Handling time non-call transactions	9
Productivity	9
Calls/FTE	7
Cost	7
FTE cost	7
Adherence/real activity vs planned	4

Productivity and Cost (continued)	
Costs vs budget	3
Number of FTE	3
Total transactions/FTE	3
Average outbound calls/day	2
Avoided cost/contact	2
Cost per customer	2
Margin/channel	2
Qualified calls/time unit (hr, day)	2
Staffing	2
Availability (login time)	1
Commercial gestures	1
Cost of acquisition	1
Cost to sell/serve	1
Cost variables	1
Cost/FTE	1
Cost/product/client	1
Distribution cost	1
Efficiency: paid jobs vs. calls	1
FTE/underlying business volumes	1
Interactions/FTE/day	1
investments	1
Loan loss	1
Net margin / hour	1
Non-call transactions / FTE	1
Online resolution	1
Overflow percentage calls	1
Overhead cost	1
Process Effectiveness	1
Processing time	1
Productivity: Back office files / FTE	1
Productivity: mails / FTE	1
Profitability action	1
Real vs planned FTE	1
Shrinkage (work force management terminology, % FTE that can not be deployed)	1
Training cost	1
Unproductive working time	1

Service Level	
Service level calls (% calls answered within x seconds)	61
Accessibility/abandon rate (% calls answered/ not answered)	58
Service level non-call transactions (% non-call contacts answered within given delay)	24
Average Waiting Time calls/Average Speed of Answer	20
Service level mails (% mails answered within given delay)	6
Backlog non-calls	4
Service level outbound calls (% calls done by certain deadline)	4
Service level specific file type	3
Service level Back Office complaints	2
Service level social media (% social feeds handled within certain deadline)	2
Aging tickets	1
Average payment delay	1
Average time in queue	1
Delivery speed	1
IVR abandon rate	1
Outstanding sales	1
Same-day resolution	1
Work-in-process volume of non-call transactions	1
Same-day resolution	1
Service level BO complaints	1
Service level escan documents	1
Service level letter/fax	1
Service level mail	1
Service level outbound campaign	1
Service level outbound contacts	1
Service level outbound prospects	1
Service level social media	1
WIP non call transactions	1

Quality	
Customer Satisfaction (via survey)	70
First Contact Resolution (First Time Right, measured through transfer/repeat contacts)	43
Quality Monitoring Score (calls)	42
First Contact Resolution (First time right, measured through customer survey)	9
Customer Satisfaction (client company)	4
Quality Monitoring Score (mails)	4
% fatal errors	3
Validated complaints on Contact center performance	2
Calls on hold	1
Complaint handling	1
Customer Satisfaction non-calls (survey)	1
Delivery accuracy	1
First contact resolution (not specified)	1
Immediate resolution rate	1
Interaction quality	1
Invoice accuracy	1
Monitorings/agent/period	1
Objectives achievement rate	1
Ombudsman complaints	1
Quality index	1
Quality of documentation Service requests	1
Quality scores - admin tasks	1
Respecting commitments	1
Transaction quality	1
Transaction quality	1
Quality of documentation SRs	1
Recommendation rate	1
Respecting commitments	1
Transaction quality	1

Sales Order Management	
Gross conversion (sales on calls)	34
Revenue	19
Gross Margin	15
Cross sell ratio/Revenue	5
Sales volumes	5
Conversion rate outbound calls	2
Outbound sales	2
Revenue per seat/FTE	2
Revenue/contact	2
Save-rate competition/retention rate	2
Total offers/sales canceled/month	2
% assisted sales (sales in agencies supported by contact center)	1
% created opportunities agencies (lead generation towards physical channel)	1
% processed sales	1
ARPU (post-call revenue increase in Average Revenue per User)	1
Conversion rate campaign calls	1
Cross-selling	1
Customers acquired	1
Forecasted Revenue	1
Hitrate (sales/sales attempts)	1
Inbound sales	1
Incremental Revenue/marketing experience	1
Invoice completeness	1
Net conversion	1
Order size /channel	1
Repurchase intent (survey)	1
Revenue new customers	1
Revenue retention	1
Revenue vs budget	1
Revenue/channel	1
Sales % contact center versus total Sales	1
Sales attempts/calls	1
Sales vs target	1
Sales/head	1
Total offers/month	1
Upsell ratio	1

Other	
Net Promotor Score	29
Employee Satisfaction	20
Employee Churn	8
Customer churn	5
Customer Effort Score (survey)	4
Net Promotor Score for contact (type)	4
Issue list/attention points	3
Autonomy increase	1
Customer churn intention	1
Customer loyalty	1
Deployment FTE on communication	1
Hiring speed	1
Job pride employees	1
Low detractors	1
Partnership status	1
Product (new) development based on contact center data	1
Resolution	1
Right Party Connects	1
Split interim - fix FTE	1
Training time	1
Work force management	1

Annex 5:

Indicators from the Expert Class in Contact Center Management, plotted in categories based on input/output/outcome (in alphabetical order)

Indicator	Outcome	Output	Input
# outbound calls/written order			X
% assisted sales (sales in agencies supported by contact center)		X	
% created opportunities agencies (lead generation towards physical channel)		X	
% fatal errors		X	
% opportunities/calls (calls resulting in identified sales opportunity)			X
% processed sales		X	
Accessibility/abandon rate (% calls answered/not answered)		X	
Adherence/real activity vs planned			X
Aging tickets		X	
ARPU (post-call revenue increase in Average Revenue per User)	X		
Autonomy increase	X		
Availability (login time)			X
Average outbound calls/day		X	
Average payment delay		X	
Average time in queue		X	
Average Waiting Time calls/Average Speed of Answer		X	
Avoided cost/contact		X	
Backlog non-calls		X	
Calls on hold			X
Calls/FTE		X	
Calls/hour incoming			X
Channels Contact distribution			X
Commercial gestures		X	

Indicator	Outcome	Output	Input
Complaint handling		X	
Contacts per customer			X
Conversion rate campaign calls		X	
Conversion rate outbound calls		X	
Cost	X		
Cost of acquisition	X		
Cost per customer	X		
Cost to sell/serve	X		
Cost variables		X	
Cost/ contact		X	
Cost/FTE			X
Cost/product/client	X		
Costs vs budget		X	
Cross-sell ration/revenue		X	
Cross-selling		X	
Customer churn	X		
Customer churn intention	X		
Customer Effort Score (survey)	X		
Customer loyalty	X		
Customer Satisfaction (client company)		X	
Customer Satisfaction (via survey)		X	
Customer Satisfaction non-calls (survey)		X	
Customers acquired		X	
Delivery accuracy		X	
Delivery speed		X	
Deployment FTE on communication			X
Distribution cost		X	
Efficiency: paid jobs vs calls		X	
Employee Churn			X
Employee Satisfaction			X
Evolution in top FAQs		X	
First Contact Resolution (First time right, through customer survey)		X	
First Contact Resolution (First Time Right, through transfer/repeat contacts)		X	

Indicator	Outcome	Output	Input
First contact resolution (not specified)		X	
Forecast accuracy			X
Forecasted Revenue			X
FTE cost			X
FTE/underlying business volumes			X
Gross conversion		X	
Gross Margin	X		
Handling time non-call transactions			X
Handling time/average handling time calls			X
Hiring speed			X
Hitrate (sales/sales attempts)		X	
Illness/absenteeism			X
Immediate resolution rate		X	
Inbound call volume			X
Inbound mail volume			X
inbound sales		X	
Inbound volume webforms			X
Incoming Complaints/incidents volume			X
Incremental Revenue/marketing experience	X		
Interaction quality		X	
Interactions/FTE/day		X	
Investments			X
Invoice accuracy		X	
Invoice completeness		X	
Issue list/attention points		X	
IT System availability			X
IVR abandon rate		X	
Job pride employees			X
Loan loss		X	
Log ratio (calls documented/registered)		X	
Low detractors	X		
Margin/channel	X		
Monitorings/agent/period			X
Net conversion		X	
Net margin / hour	X		

Indicator	Outcome	Output	Input
Net promotor score	X		
Net promotor score for contact type	X		
Non-call contacts handled/day		X	
Non-call contact volumes			X
Non-call transactions / FTE			X
Number of FTE			X
Objectives achievement rate		X	
Occupancy/agent utilization			X
Ombudsman complaints			X
Online resolution		X	
Order size /channel		X	
Outbound sales		X	
Outbound volume handled		X	
Outstanding sales		X	
Overflow percentage calls			X
Overhead cost		X	
Partnership status	X		
Process Effectiveness		X	
Processing time			X
Product (new) development based on contact center data			X
Productivity		X	
Productivity: Back office files / FTE		X	
Productivity: mails / FTE		X	
Profitability action	X		
Qualified calls/time unit (hr, day)		X	
Quality index		X	
Quality Monitoring Score (calls)			X
Quality Monitoring Score (mails)			X
Quality of documentation Service requests		X	
Quality scores - admin tasks			X
Real vs planned FTE			X
Reduction of recurrent calls		X	
Repeat volume		X	X
Repurchase intent (survey)	X		

Indicator	Outcome	Output	Input
Resolution		X	
Respecting commitments			X
Revenue	X		
Revenue new customers	X		
Revenue per seat		X	
Revenue retention	X		
Revenue vs budget	X		
Revenue/channel	X		
Revenue/contact		X	
Right Party Connects		X	
Sales % contact center versus total Sales	X		
Sales attempts/calls			X
Sales volumes		X	
Sales vs target	X		
Sales/head		X	
Same day resolution		X	
Save-rate competition/retention rate		X	
Service level Back Office complaints		X	
Service level calls (% calls answered within x seconds)		X	
Service level mails (% mails answered within given delay)		X	
Service level non-call transactions (% non-call contacts answered within given delay)		X	
Service level outbound calls (% calls done by certain deadline)		X	
Service level social media (% social feeds handled within certain deadline)		X	
Service level specific file type		X	
Shrinkage (work force management terminology, % FTE that cannot be deployed)			X
Specific call/Service Request content			X
Split interim - fix FTE			X
Staffing			X
Total contacts			X

Indicator	Outcome	Output	Input
Total offers/month		X	
Total offers/sales canceled/month		X	
Total transactions/FTE		X	
Training cost			X
Training time			X
Transaction quality		X	
Unproductive working time			X
Upsell ratio		X	
Validated complaints on Contact center performance		X	
Volume per contact category			X
WIP non-call transactions		X	
Work force management			X

Annex 6:

The indicators from the Expert Class in Contact Center Management, included in a 'mission to KPI'

Strategic objective	Operational Goal	Critical success factor	Key Performance Indicator
Customer Loyalty	Customer satisfaction	Quality	% fatal errors
Customer Recom-mendations			Call transfers
			Delivery accuracy
			Evolution in top FAQs
			First Contact Resolution (First time right, measured through customer survey)
			First Contact Resolution (First Time Right, measured through transfer/repeat contacts)
			First contact resolution (not specified)
			Issue list/ Qualitative attention points future
			Log ratio (calls documented/registered)
			Monitoring / agent
			Net promotor score contact
			Objectives achievement rate
			Online resolution
			Respecting commitments
			Quality Documentation SRs
			Quality index
			Quality Monitoring score (calls)
			Quality Monitoring score (mails)
			Quality scores - admin tasks
			Repeat volumes
			Training Time
			Validated complaints on Contact center performance
			Volume ombudsman complaints
		Accessibility	Abandoned calls
			IVR abandon rate
			% calls answered
		Interaction speed	% processed
			Aging tickets
			Average time in queue
			Average treatment delay (non-calls)
			Average Waiting Time calls/Average Speed of Answer
			Backlog non-calls
			Delivery speed

Strategic objective	Operational Goal	Critical success factor	Key Performance Indicator
			Processing times
			Same day resolution
			Service level calls
			Service level non-calls
			Service level outbound calls
			Service level specific file types
			Service level specific outbound calls
			WIP non-call transactions
	Revenue retention	Customer churn	Repurchase intent (survey)
			Save-rate competition/retention rate
		Customer Perception*	Contract extension/project continuation
			Customer Effort Score (survey)
			Customer experience index
			Customer Satisfaction (client company)
			Customer satisfaction (via survey)
			Customer Satisfaction non-calls (survey)
			Low detractors
			Net customer satisfaction
			Net Promotor score
			Net Promotor Score for contact (type)
			Partnership status
Gross Margin	Incremental Revenue	Revenue per seat	# outbound calls/written order
Margin/channel			Cross-selling
Revenue/channel			Efficiency: paid jobs vs calls
			Inbound sales
			Order size /channel
			Outbound sales
			Product (new) development based on contact center data
			Revenue new customers
			Sales Revenue
			Sales volume
			Sales/head
			Total offers canceled/month
			Total offers won/month
			Total offers/month
		ARPU	ARPU (post-call revenue increase in Average Revenue per User)

Strategic objective	Operational Goal	Critical success factor	Key Performance Indicator
		Net conversion	% opportunities Average outbound calls/day Conversion rate campaign calls Conversion rate outbound calls Cross/upsell ratio's Customers acquired Gross conversion (sales on calls) Hitrate (sales/sales attempts) Outbound volume handled
		Collect Revenue	Average payment delay Invoice accuracy Invoice completeness invoiced jobs/opportunities Open invoice amount vs sales
	Revenue support other channels*	Lead generation	% assisted sales (sales in agencies supported by contact center) % created opportunities agencies (lead generation towards physical channel)
	Distribution cost Cost/channel	Cost/contact	Calls/hour incoming Channels Contact distribution Commercial gestures Cost of acquisition Cost/customer Cost/product/client FTE cost FTE/underlying business volumes Inbound call volume Inbound mail volume Inbound volume web forms Number of FTE Overhead cost Specific call content Split interim - fix FTE Staffing Training cost Yearly contacts / customer
		Employee churn	Employee Satisfaction Employee Turnover Job pride employees

Strategic objective	Operational Goal	Critical success factor	Key Performance Indicator
		Productivity/efficiency	Absenteeism/illness
			Adherence/real activity vs planned
			Autonomy increase
			Availability
			Calls / hour specific outbound types
			Calls on hold
			Deployment FTE on communication
			Flexibility
			Forecast accuracy
			FTE/service point
			Handling time transactions
			Hiring speed
			ICT system availability
			Immediate resolution rate
			Interactions/FTE/day
			Jobs/FTE
			Non-call contacts handled/day
			Occupancy/agent utilization
			Online resolution
			Process Effectiveness
			Productivity: Back office files / FTE
			Productivity: mails / FTE
			Qualified calls/time unit (hr, day)
			Real vs planned FTE
			Right Party Connects
			Sales attempts/calls
			Shrinkage
			Support tools
			Total contacts
			Transactions/FTE
			Unproductive working time
			WFM
	Cost/benefit contact center	(Relative) Cost drivers*	% sales vs. other channels
			Avoided cost / contact
			Cost variables
			Loan loss
			Overflow percentage calls
			Reduction incoming calls

Annex 7:

The indicators from the Expert Class in Contact Center Management, distributed over an (un)balanced scorecard (in alphabetical order)

Indicator	Customer	Shareholder	Internal process	Innovation (people)
# outbound calls/written order			X	
% assisted sales (sales in agencies supported by contact center)			X	
% created opportunities agencies (lead generation towards physical channel)			X	
% fatal errors			X	
% opportunities/calls (calls resulting in identified sales opportunity)			X	
% processed sales			X	
Accessibility/abandon rate (% calls answered/not answered)			X	
Adherence/real activity vs planned			X	
Aging tickets			X	
ARPU (post-call revenue increase)		X		
Autonomy increase			X	
Availability (login time)			X	
Average outbound calls/day			X	
Average payment delay			X	
Average time in queue			X	
Average Waiting Time calls/Average Speed of Answer			X	
Avoided cost/contact		X		
Backlog non-calls			X	
Calls on hold			X	
Calls/FTE			X	
Calls/hour incoming			X	
Channels Contact distribution			X	
Commercial gestures		X		
Complaint handling			X	
Contacts per customer			X	
Conversion rate campaign calls			X	
Conversion rate outbound calls			X	
Cost		X		
Cost of acquisition		X		
Cost per customer		X		
Cost to sell/serve		X		

Indicator	Customer	Shareholder	Internal process	Innovation (people)
Cost variables		X		
Cost/ contact			X	
Cost/FTE			X	
Cost/product/client		X		
Costs vs budget		X		
Cross-sell ratio/revenue			X	
Cross-selling			X	
Customer churn	X			
Customer churn intention	X			
Customer Effort Score (survey)	X			
Customer loyalty	X			
Customer Satisfaction (client company)	X			
Customer Satisfaction (via survey)	X			
Customer Satisfaction non-calls (survey)	X			
Customers acquired			X	
Delivery accuracy			X	
Delivery speed			X	
Deployment FTE on communication			X	
Distribution cost		X		
Efficiency: paid jobs vs calls			X	
Employee Churn				X
Employee Satisfaction				X
Evolution in top FAQs			X	
First Contact Resolution (First Time Right, measured through transfer/repeat contacts)			X	
First Contact Resolution (First time right, measured through customer survey)	X			
First contact resolution (not specified)			X	
Forecast accuracy			X	
Forecasted revenue			X	
FTE cost			X	
FTE/underlying business volumes			X	
Gross conversion			X	
Gross Margin		X		
Handling time/average handling time calls			X	
Handling time non-call transactions			X	
Hiring speed			X	
Hitrate (sales/sales attempts)			X	

Indicator	Customer	Shareholder	Internal process	Innovation (people)
Illness/absenteeism				X
Immediate resolution rate			X	
Inbound call volume			X	
Inbound mail volume			X	
inbound sales		X		
Inbound volume webforms			X	
Incoming Complaints/incidents volume			X	
Incremental revenue/marketing experience		X		
Interaction quality	X			
Interactions/FTE/day			X	
Investments		X		
Invoice accuracy			X	
Invoice completeness			X	
Issue list/attention points	X	X	X	X
IT System availability			X	
IVR abandon rate			X	
Job pride employees				X
Loan loss		X		
Log ratio (calls documented/registered)			X	
Low detractors	X			
Margin/channel		X		
Monitorings/agent/period			X	
Net conversion		X		
Net margin / hour		X		
Net promotor score	X			
Net promotor score for contact type	X			
Non-call contacts handled/day			X	
Non-call contact volumes			X	
Non-call transactions / FTE			X	
Number of FTE		X		
Objectives achievement rate			X	
Occupancy/agent utilization			X	
Ombudsman complaints			X	
Online resolution			X	
Order size /channel		X		
Outbound sales		X		
Outbound volume handled			X	
Outstanding sales			X	
Overflow percentage calls			X	

Indicator	Customer	Shareholder	Internal process	Innovation (people)
Overhead cost		X		
Partnership status	X			
Process Effectiveness			X	
Processing time			X	
Product (new) development based on contact center data				X
Productivity			X	
Productivity: Back office files / FTE			X	
Productivity: mails / FTE			X	
Profitability action		X		
Qualified calls/time unit (hr, day)			X	
Quality index			X	
Quality Monitoring Score (calls)			X	
Quality Monitoring Score (mails)			X	
Quality of documentation Service requests			X	
Quality scores - admin tasks			X	
Real vs planned FTE			X	
Reduction of recurrent calls			X	
Repeat volume			X	
Repurchase intent (survey)	X			
Resolution			X	
Respecting commitments			X	
Revenue		X		
Revenue new customers		X		
Revenue per seat		X		
Revenue retention		X		
Revenue vs budget		X		
Revenue/channel		X		
Revenue/contact		X		
Right Party Connects			X	
Sales % contact center versus total Sales		X		
Sales attempts/calls			X	
Sales volumes			X	
Sales vs target		X		
Sales/head			X	
Same day resolution			X	
Save-rate competition/retention rate			X	
Service level Back Office complaints			X	

Indicator	Customer	Shareholder	Internal process	Innovation (people)
Service level calls (% calls answered within x seconds)			X	
Service level mails (% mails answered within given delay)			X	
Service level non-call transactions (% non-call contacts answered within given delay)			X	
Service level outbound calls (% calls done by certain deadline)			X	
Service level social media (% social feeds handled within certain deadline)			X	
Service level specific file type			X	
Shrinkage (work force management terminology, % FTE that cannot be deployed)			X	
Specific call/Service Request content			X	
Split interim - fix FTE			X	
Staffing			X	
Total contacts			X	
Total offers/sales canceled/month		X		
Total offers/month		X		
Total transactions/FTE			X	
Training cost			X	
Training time				X
Transaction quality			X	
Unproductive working time			X	
Upsell ratio			X	
Validated complaints on Contact center performance			X	
Volume per contact category			X	
WIP non call transactions			X	
Work force management			X	

Annex 8:

The indicators from the Expert Class in Contact Center Management, in the model introduced by Donna Fluss/DMG Consulting

External
(customer)

FOCUS

Strengthen Customer Focus

% fatal errors
Accessibility/abandon rate (% calls answered/ not answered)
Aging tickets
Average time in queue
Average Waiting Time calls/Average Speed of Answer
Backlog non-calls
Calls on hold
Complaint handling
Customer churn
Customer churn intention
Customer Effort Score (survey)
Customer loyalty
Customer Satisfaction (client company)
Customer Satisfaction (via survey)
Customer Satisfaction non- calls (survey)
Evolution in top FAQs
Interaction quality
Issue list/attention points
IVR abandon rate
Log ratio (calls documented/registered)
Low detractors
Net promotor score
Net Promotor Score for contact (type)
Objectives achievement rate
Ombudsman complaints
Partnership status
Quality index
Resolution
Respecting commitments
Service level Back Office complaints
Service level calls (% calls answered within x seconds)
Service level mails (% mails answered within given delay)
Service level non-call transactions (% non-call contacts answered within given delay)
Service level social media (% social feeds handled within certain deadline)
Service level specific file type
Transaction quality
Validated complaints on Contact center performance

Increase Revenue

% assisted sales (sales in agencies supported by contact center)
% created opportunities agencies (lead generation towards physical channel)
% opportunities/calls (calls resulting in identified sales opportunity)
% processed sales
ARPU (post-call revenue increase in Average Revenue per User)
Average payment delay
Conversion rate campaign calls
Conversion rate outbound calls
Cross-sell ratio/revenue
Cross-selling
Customers acquired
Forecasted revenue
Gross conversion (sales on calls)
Gross Margin
Hitrate (sales/sales attempts)
inbound sales
Incremental revenue/ marketing experience
Invoice completeness
Margin/channel
Net conversion
Net margin / hour
Order size /channel
Outbound sales
Outstanding sales
Product (new) development based on contact center data
Repurchase intent (survey)
Revenue
Revenue new customers
Revenue per seat/FTE
Revenue retention
Revenue vs budget
Revenue/channel
Revenue/contact
Sales % cc vs total
Sales attempts/calls
Sales volumes
Sales vs target
Sales/head
Save-rate competition/ retention rate
Service level outbound calls (% calls done by certain deadline)
Total offers canceled/ month
Total offers/month
Upsell ratio

Soft **BENEFITS** **Hard**

Soft BENEFITS Hard

FOCUS

Improve employee satisfaction

Autonomy increase
Deployment FTE on communication
Employee Churn
Employee Satisfaction
Hiring speed
Job pride employees

Reduce Costs

outbound calls/written order
Adherence/real activity vs planned
Availability (login time)
Average outbound calls/day
Avoided cost/contact
Calls/FTE
Calls/hour incoming
Channels Contact distribution
Commercial gestures
Contacts per customer
Cost
Cost of acquisition
Cost per customer
Cost to sell/serve
Cost variables
Cost/ contact
Cost/FTE
Cost/product/client
Costs vs budget
Delivery accuracy
Delivery speed
Distribution cost
Efficiency: paid jobs vs calls
First Contact Resolution (First time right, measured through customer survey)
First Contact Resolution (First Time Right, measured through transfer/ repeat contacts)
First contact resolution (not specified)
Forecast accuracy (correctness of volume forecasts)
FTE cost
FTE/underlying business volumes
Handling time non-call transactions
Handling time/average handling time calls
Illness/absenteeism
Immediate resolution rate
Inbound call volume
Inbound mail volume
Inbound volume webforms
Incoming Complaints/incidents volume
Interactions/FTE/day
Investments
Invoice accuracy
IT System availability
Loan loss
Monitorings/agent/period
Non-call contacts handled/day
Non-call contact volumes
Non-call transactions / FTE
Number of FTE
Occupancy/agent utilization
Online resolution
Outbound volume handled
Overflow percentage calls
Overhead cost
Process Effectiveness
Processing time
Productivity
Productivity: Back office files / FTE
Productivity: mails / FTE
Profitability action
Qualified calls/time unit (hr, day)
Quality Monitoring Score (calls)
Quality Monitoring Score (mails)
Quality of documentation Service requests
Quality scores - admin tasks
Real vs planned FTE
Reduction of recurrent calls
Repeat volume
Right Party Connects
Same day resolution
Shrinkage (work force management terminology, % FTE that cannot be deployed)
Specific call/Service Request content
Split interim - fix FTE
Staffing
Total contacts
Total transactions/FTE
Training cost
Training time
Unproductive working time
Volume per contact category
Work force management
Work-in-process volume of non-call transactions

Internal (org'ion)

Bibliography and sources of inspiration

The library:

- Accenture & Montgomery Research (2006). *Defying the Limits volume 6: Delivering the Branded Customer Experience.* San Francisco: Montgomery Research.
- Adams, S. (1996). *The Dilbert Principle.* New York: HarperCollins Publishers.
- Altitude Software (2013). *European Contact Center Benchmark Platform – Whitebook 2013.* www.altitude.com.
- Anderson, C. (2006). *The Long Tail.* New York: Hyperion.
- Anderson, K. & Zemke, R. (1991). *Delivering Knock Your Socks Off Service.* New York: AMACOM.
- Anton, J. & Webb, K. (2005). *Contact Center Management 'By the Numbers'.* Santa Maria: The Anton Press.
- Belgacom (2007). *House of Development.* Belgacom/Vlerick Leuven Ghent Management School.
- Bianchi, R. & Janauskas, M. (2010). *Are you listening to your call center?.* McKinsey & Company.
- BRW Group (2009). *Imago onderzoek Nederlandse contact centers.* www.Brw.nl.
- BT/Avaya (2012). *The Autonomous Customer Report.*
- Burgers, J. (2006). *Klanten zijn eigenlijk nét mensen.* The Hague: Sdu Uitgevers.
- Cable, D. (2007). *Change to Strange.* New Jersey: Pearson, Education.
- Call Center IQ (2014). *Call Center Executives Priorities Report.* Aspect Solutions.
- Call Metrics (2006). *TelephoneX-Ray: Determinants of call satisfaction. Research report.* Call Metrics/Möbius & University of Ghent.
- Cantor, B. (2015). *The Evolution of Contact Center Performance.* Call Center IQ.
- Carlzon, J. (1987). *Moments of Truth.* New York: HarperCollins Publishers.
- Caroll, D. (2012). *United Breaks Guitars.* New York: Hay House, Inc.
- Clapperton, G. & Vanhoutte, P. (2014). *The Smarter Working Manifesto.* Oxford: Sunmakers.
- Cleveland, B. & Mayben, J. (1999). C*ontact enter management. In volle vaart vooruit.* Heerhugowaard: F & G Publishing.
- Cleveland, B. (2004). *Woordenboek contact center management.* Heerhugowaard: F & G Publishing.
- Cockerell, L. (2013). *The Customer Rules.* London: Profile Books Ltd.

- Compare Business Products (2013). *The Effect of Poor Customer Service and What To Do About It.*
- COPC (2007). *COPC® Performance Management System COPC - 2000® CSP Standard.*
- Covey, S. (1992). *The Seven Habits of Highly Effective People.* London: Simon & Schuster Ltd.
- Davey, N. (2014). 'Emotional vs transactional loyalty: is it more important to win hearts or minds'. www.mycustomer.com.
- Dietz, B. (2009). *Managing (Sales)people Towards Performance. HR Strategy, Leadership and Teamwork.* Rotterdam: Erasmus Research Institute of Management.
- Dixon, M., Freeman, K. & Toman, N. (2010). 'Stop trying to delight your customer'. *Harvard Business Review.* July-August 2010. 116-122.
- Dixon, M., Toman, N. & Delisi, R. (2013). *The Effortless Experience.* London: Penguin Portfolio.
- Dumortier, J., Lanciers, E., Verkinderen, F. & Walrave, M. (2002). *Customer Contact Centers.* Mechelen: Kluweruitgevers.
- Eichfeld, A., Morse, T. D. & Scott, K. W. (2006). 'Using call centers to boost revenue. McKinsey on banking.' *The McKinsey Quarterly.* May 2006.
- Executive Board – Customer Contact Council (2007). *Effectively Monitoring and Communicating the Health of the Contact Center Function.*
- Ferment, M. (2010). *Customer Service 7.0.* Ferment Management BV.
- Fluss, D. (2005). *The Real-Time Contact Center.* New York: AMACOM.
- FOD Economie (2012). *Charter voor Klantvriendelijkheid.*
- Friedman, L. G. & Furey, T. R. (1999). *The Channel Advantage.* Oxford: Butterworth-Heinemann.
- Gallagher, R. (2013). *The Customer Service Survival Kit.* New York: AMACOM.
- Genesys (2007). *Whitepaper 'How Contact Centers Can Drive A Higher Net Promoter Score'.*
- Genesys (2007). *Whitepaper 'The Dynamic Contact Center'.*
- Genesys Global Survey (2008). *The Executive Disconnect.* Genesys. (Also published in *Customer Contact Magazine 3*, 2008.)
- Godin, S. (2007). *Permission Marketing.* London: Pocket Books.
- Greenberg, P. (2010). C*RM at the Speed of Light.* New York: McGraw Hill.
- Güngör, H. (2007). *Emotional Satisfaction of Customer Contacts.* Vossiuspers-University of Amsterdam.
- Heller, J. (1961). C*atch22.* New York: Simon & Schuster.

- Hinssen, P. (2010). *The New Normal*. Ghent: Mach Media.
- Hinssen, P. (2017). *The Day After Tomorrow*. Ghent: Nexxworks.
- Hsieh, T. (2010). *Delivering Happiness*. New York: Business Plus.
- Intelli Response (2013). *Death of the Contact center*. www.intelliresponse.com.
- Intelli Response (2015). *Customer Effort Score. Stop making it hard to be your customer*. www.intelliresponse.com.
- James, E. L. (2011). *50 Shades of Grey*. London: Vintage Books.
- Kaplan & Norton (1996). *The Balanced Scorecard*. Boston: Harvard Business School Press.
- Klaus, P. (2015). *Measuring Customer Experience*. Houndmills: Palgrave Macmillan.
- Koole, G. (2013). *Call Center Optimization*. Amsterdam: MG Books.
- Linthout, G. & Fijnvandraat, W. J. (2009). 'De voelsprieten van een wendbare organisatie'. *Customer Contact Magazine, 6*. 8-14.
- McGovern, G. (2010). *The Stranger's Long Neck*. London: A & C Black Publishers Ltd.
- Millard, N. (2014). *Leading with the Customer Experience*. Frost & Sullivan Webinar.
- Millard, N. & Alcock, T. (2014). *Superagent 2020: The evolution of the contact center*. British Telecom.
- Orwell, G. (1945). *Animal Farm*. London: Secker and Warburg.
- Peppers, D. & Rogers, M. (2011). *Managing Customer Relationships*. Hoboken New Jersey: John Wiley & Sons, Inc.
- Peppers, D. & Rogers, M. (2005). *Return on Customer*. New York: Currency Doubleday.
- Philipse, H. J. H. L. (1997). *Succesvol Team- en Projectmanagement in Dynamische Callcenters*. Woerden: Beerens Business Press BV.
- Porter, M. (1985). *Competitive Advantage*. New York: Free Press.
- Price, B. & Jaffe, D. (2008). *The Best Service is No Service*. San Francisco: Jossey-Bass.
- Reichheld, F. (1996). *The Loyalty Effect*. Boston: Harvard Business Review Press.
- Reichheld, F. (2006). *The Ultimate Question*. Boston: Harvard Business Review Press.
- Reichheld, F. & Markey, B. (2011). *The Ultimate Question 2.0*. Boston: Harvard Business Review Press.

- Remes, H. (2012). *Wachten.* Möbius Business Redesign NV.
- Rowling, J. K. (1997). *Harry Potter and the Philosopher's Stone.* London: Bloomsbury Publishing Plc.
- Sinek, S. (2011). *Start with Why.* London: Portfolio Penguin.
- Smets, J. (2016). *Contact Center Management.* Leuven: LannooCampus
- Smith, S. & Milligan, A. (2015). *On Purpose.* London: Kogan Page Ltd.
- Smith, S. (2006). *White paper 'Customer experience happens in the contact center'.* Cincom.
- Streukens, S. (2004). *Return on Services.* Maastricht: Sandra Streukens.
- Syngro (2013). *Briefing paper 'How to compete on customer experience'.* www.syngro.com.
- Syngro (2013). *Briefing paper 'Measure to Manage: three customer experience metrics'.* www.syngro.com.
- Syngro (2014). *Briefing paper 'Customer Effort Score: making life easy for customers.* www.syngro.com.
- Syngro (2014). *Briefing paper 'Why Do Customers Tolerate Bad Service?'.* www.syngro.com.
- Teunter, L. & Maijers, A. (2013). 'Wat is de beste metric?' *Telecommerce, 05.* 38-39.
- The Ascent Group (2009). *First Call Resolution.* www.ascentgroup.com.
- The House of Contact Centers (2013). *Onderzoek kanaalpreferentie.* Contact Centers Leaders Association.
- The House of Contact Centers (2018). *Kanalen & Customer Journey – tussen droom en daad.* Thocc – Data Stories.
- Thompson, C. (1993). *'Yes, but...' The Top 40 Killer Phrases and How You Can Fight Them.* New York: HarperCollins Publishers.
- Tops, H. & Massant, A. (2014). 'The personal touch'. *Efma Journal 241.*
- Van Belleghem, S. (2010). *De Conversation Manager.* Leuven: LannooCampus; Culemborg: Van Duuren Management.
- Van Belleghem, S. (2012). *De Conversation Company.* Leuven: LannooCampus; Culemborg: Van Duuren Management.
- Van Belleghem, S. (2014). *When Digital Becomes Human.* Leuven: LannooCampus; Culemborg: Van Duuren Management.
- Van Belleghem, S. (2017). *Customers the Day After Tomorrow.* Leuven: LannooCampus; Culemborg: Van Duuren Management.
- Van den Brink, M. (herziene druk 2003). *Implementatie en optimalisatie van het contact center.* Heerhugowaard: F & G Publishing.

- Vander Pouw Kraan, D. (2011). *Managing your workforce as a competitive advantage.* Plan Men International.
- Van Gurchom, M. (2014). *Customer Experience in de praktijk.* Amsterdam/Antwerp: Business Contact.
- Van Bel, J. (2007). *Kloteklanten.* Amsterdam: Kluwer.
- Van Moorst, A. (2004). *Strategische sourcing van customer care.* BBPbv.
- Van Moorst, A. & Kjellerup, N. (2008). *Key Performance Indicators in Customer Service.* TOTEM Seminar.
- Van Rhee, J. R. (2015). *Sales isn't service isn't sales isn't...* Expert Class Contact in Center Management.
- Van Vliet, V. & Rozendaal, J. (2009). 'Empathie is het toverwoord'. *Customer Contact Magazine, 7/8.* 32-36.
- Verint (2018). *Defining the Human Age.*
- Vianen, M. & Van Vliet, G. (2004). *Contact centers, een open boek.* Coniche International.
- Welch, J. (2005). *Winning.* New York: HarperCollins Publishers.

The media library:

- Caroll, D. (2009). *United Breaks Guitars.* Dave Caroll Music; http://www.youtube.com/watch?v=5YGc4zOqozo
- De Strangers (1979). *Bade Rijkswacht.* Decca.
- EA Sports. (2015). *Fifa 16.* Sony Playstation4.
- MC Fioti (2017). *Bum Bum Tan Tan.* Island. Universal.
- Prince (1987). *Sign of the Times.* Paisley Park Records/Warner Bros.
- Psy (2012). *Gangnam Style.* YG. Universal Republic. School Boy; http://www.youtube.com/watch?v=9bZkp7q19f0
- REM (1987). *It's the end of the world as we know it.* I. R. S.
- Sunrise Avenue (2006). *Fairytale gone bad.* Capitol Music.
- Walk The Moon (2014). *Shutup and Dance.* RCA.
- *Doctor Who (1963-...).* BBC.
- *House MD* (2004-2012). Heel & Toe Films, Shore Z Productions, Bad Hat Harry Productions.
- *The Call Center* (2013-2014). BBC.
- Brooker, C. (2011-....). *Black Mirror.* Channel 4 – Netflix.

- Chapman, K. (1998-2012). *Bob the Builder*. Hot Animation. Chapman Entertainment. HIT Entertainment.
- Chazelle, D. (2016). *La La Land*. Summit Entertainment.
- Fleisher, R. (1967). *Doctor Dolittle*. APJAC Production. 20th Century Fox.
- Jennings, G. (2005). *The Hitchhiker's Guide to the Galaxy*. Touchstone Pictures.
- Monty Python (1979). *The Life of Brian*. Hand Made Films.
- *Mythbusters (2002-...)*. Discovery Channel.
- Pagot, T. (1963). C*alimero*.
- Raimi, S. (2002). *Spiderman*. Columbia Pictures.
- Robinson, P. A. (1989). *Field of Dreams*. Gordon Company.
- Sartre, J. P. (1943). *Huisclos*.
- Spielberg, S. (1993). *Jurassic Park*. UniversalPictures.
- Wachowski Brothers (1999). *The Matrix*. Warner Bros.
- Wise, R. (1965). *The Sound of Music*. 20th Century Fox.
- Zemeckis, R. (1989). *Back to the Future II*. Universal Pictures.

When Jan speaks...

2007-2018. *Expert Class Contact Center Management.* University of Antwerp Management School/The House of Contact Centers.
- Vision, mission, strategy
- Synergy and integration
- Measurements

2007. *From lip service to real service.* Mechelen. Contact Center Café.

2008. *Musings on contact center management.* Utrecht. CCMA tenth anniversary.

2008. *Wie anders? From Postoffice to Contact Center.* Contact Center Congress ToteM.

2009. *The House of Dolittle.* Möbius lunchtime lectures.

2011. *Contact Center Management Strategie en Werkprocessen.* Kluwer.

2012. *Care is Core, so what is the Cure?* Mechelen. Contact center Congress CCLA.

2013. *Integrating Social Policy/Processes into the Contact Center.* Nice. Frost & Sullivan Exchange.

2013-2015. *CRM – The concept.* Master Customer Management. School for Customer Management.

2014. *Gaining insight from your contact center to drive value back into the business and increase performance.* Londen. IQPC Contact Center Exchange.

2014. *Leading with the Customer Experience: 10 Strategies in 20 Minutes.*

Frost & Sullivan Webinar.

2014. *Your agents are your competitive differentiator: embedding a culture of*

empowerment and creativity. Lissabon. Frost&Sullivan Exchange.

2015. *Contact Center Professional 3.0.* Mechelen. Contact Center Congress CCLA.

2015. *Het Janusperpectief.* Melsbroek. CCLA New Year's reception.

2015. *Smashing Silo's.* Copenhagen. Frost & Sullivan Exchange.

2015. *WFM in Back Office: what's in it for me?* Noordwijk-aan-Zee. Verint

Exchange.

2016. *Seeing with New Eyes.* Eindhoven. Verint Exchange.

2016. *Seizing the Moment.* Utrecht. GSummit Genesys.

2017. *Driving Front Line Behavior Towards Customer Oriented Change.* Brussels. Shingo Institute Conference.

2017. *Driving Front Line Behavior Towards Customer Oriented Change. B*udapest. Frost & Sullivan Exchange.

2018. *Van klachtendienst tot hart van de dialoog.* Gent. Vlaamse Vereniging van Steden en Gemeenten.

End notes

1. Cantor, B. (2015). *The Evolution of Contact Center Performance.* Call Center IQ.
2. Research reported in the digital THOCC newsletter no.0, December 2014.
3. In an international research study, published in Call Center IQ (Brian Cantor, 2015), the respondents gave themselves a score of 3.37/5 for the extent to which they were able to reach contact center objectives. Without additional insights into the sample and the methodology, it is impossible to further compare the two results. But the realization that things can always be improved seems to be a universal given for self-critical contact center leaders.
4. Altitude Software (2013). *European Contact Center Benchmark Platform – Whitebook 2013.* www.altitude.com.
5. The House of Contact Centers (2013). *Onderzoek kanaalpreferentie.* Contact Centers Leaders Association.
6. Cleveland, B. (2004). *Woordenboek contact center management.* Heerhugowaard: F & G Publishing.
7. Dumortier, J. & Lanciers, E. & Verkinderen, F. & Walrave, M. (2002). *Customer Contact Centers.* Mechelen: Kluwer uitgevers.
8. Cleveland, B. (2004). *Woordenboek contact center management.* Heerhugowaard: F & G Publishing.
9. DMG Consulting, as reported by Stefan Kauck, Senior Business Consultant at Genesys, in 'Beyond the contact center: back office integration', during the Genesys User Day (24/9/2015).
10. Altitude Software (2013). *European Contact Center Benchmark Platform – Whitebook 2013.* www.altitude.com.
11. Reference to Sinek, S. (2011). *Start with Why.* London: Portfolio Penguin.
12. Graphic loosely based on a presentation by Totem® Businessarchitects, but shamelessly taken out of context to illustrate a point. Sorry gents!
13. 'From Plain Old Telephony System to Pretty Amazing New Stuff', an expression that has stayed with me from an Andersen Consulting lecture, somewhere.
14. For the marketing novices amongst you, 'Keeping up with the Joneses' is an English expression referring to the typical consumer tendency to watch what the neighbors are buying, as a benchmark of social class. Failing to 'keep up with the Joneses' is regarded as a sign of socio-economic or cultural inferiority. (Wikipedia). You can also see this copy-cat behavior in companies...
15. *Webster's Dictionary* online.
16. 80% of Belgians know what Twitter is, but only 7% use it (study Insites Consulting - www.peoplesphere.be).
17. http://www.youtube.com/watch?v=9bZkp7q19f0
18. Anecdote noted during Genesys G-force, Barcelona 2012.
19. 'United breaks guitars'. http://www.youtube.com/watch?v=5YGc4zOqozo
20. Caroll, D. (2012). *United Breaks Guitars.* New York: Hay House Inc.
21. Greenberg, P. (2010). *CRM at the Speed of Light.* New York: McGraw Hill.
22. In 2011, this story was front page news in the Netherlands, when cabaretier Van 't Hek took the contact centers to task for the unfriendly way they dealt with customers. The direct reason was that a telecom provider had given his son the brush-off when he made a complaint and persisted in refusing to help him until his more famous father intervened. But their sudden change of heart failed to have the desired effect with the wider public when it became known.
    In Flanders, the incident was the inspiration for the Radio1 program *Peeters and Pichal* and their campaign 'Pick up!', which turned the glare of media publicity primarily on contact center waiting times. This initiative was one of the reasons that later led to the famous (or notorious) Charter of Customer-friendliness, in which companies formally committed themselves to make greater efforts on behalf of their customers, with an emphasis on respecting certain speed of response criteria.
23. The House of Contact Centers (2018). *Kanalen & Customer Journey - tussen droom en daad.* THOCC - Data Stories.
24. The Autonomous Customer Report, BT/Avaya. 2012.
25. *Leading with the Customer Experience: 10 Strategies in 20 Minutes.* Frost & Sullivan, 2014.
26. Van Belleghem, S. (2010). *De Conversation Manager.* Leuven: LannooCampus; Culem- borg: Van Duuren Management.
27. Peppers, D. & Rogers, M. (2005). *Return on Customer.* New York: Currency Doubleday.
28. Porter, M. (1985). *Competitive Advantage.* New York: Free Press.

29. Cockerell, L. (2013). *The Customer Rules*. London: Profile Books Ltd.
30. Definition taken from the presentation '4C Consulting'.
31. Carlzon, J. (1987). *Moments of Truth*. New York: HarperCollins Publishers.
32. Belgacom House of Development, Belgacom and Vlerick Leuven Ghent Management School, 2007.
33. Hsieh, T. (2010). *Delivering Happiness*. New York: Business Plus.
34. Inspired by the whitepaper *'Customer experience happens in the contact center'*, ascribed to Forum Corporation, 2002.
35. Davey, N. (2014). *Emotional vs transactional loyalty*. www.mycustomer.com
36. NPS: Net Promoter Score – see the discussion of this concept in the chapter on contact center reporting.
37. Call Center IQ. *Contact Center Excellence*. London UK, 01-02 June 2014.
38. Anderson, K. & Zemke, R. (1991). *Delivering Knock Your Socks Off Service*. New York: AMACOM.
39. Van Rhee, J. R. *Sales isn't service isn't sales isn't...* Expert Class Contact Center Management 20/2/2015.
40. Figure inspired by Friedman, L. G. & Furey, T. R. (1999). *The Channel Advantage*. Oxford: Butterworth-Heinemann.
41. From the film *Field of Dreams*, 1989.
42. BRW Image research contact centers 2009, performed by RMI Market Research, as mentioned in Vliet, V. & Rozendaal, J. (2009). 'Empathy is the magic word'. *Customer Contact Magazine*, no. 7/82009.
43. Inspired by the theory of *Killer Phrases*, from: Thompson, C. (1993). *"Yes, but..." The Top 40 Killer Phrases and How You Can Fight Them*. New York: HarperCollins Publishers.
44. Van den Brink, M. (revised edition 2003). *Implementatie en optimalisatie van het contact center*. Heerhugowaard: F & G Publishing.
45. FOD Economy (10-22-2012). Charter for Customer-friendliness.
46. Call Metrics (2006). *Telephone X-ray: Determinants of call satisfaction. Research report*. Call Metrics/Möbius & University of Ghent.
47. Price, B. & Jaffe, D. (2008). *The Best Service is No Service*. San Francisco: Jossey-Bass.
48. Inspired by Linthout, G. & Fijnvandraat, W. J. (2009). 'The feelers of a flexible organization'. *Customer Contact Magazine no.6*. 2009. 8-14.
49. Call Metrics. (2006). *Telephone X-ray: Determinants of call satisfaction. Research report*. Call Metrics/Möbius & University of Ghent.
50. Accenture research in UK & US. (2006). Cited in: *Delivering Branded Customer Experience:* having to repeat information to different agents is the number two frustration of customers.
51. McGovern, G. (2010). *The Stranger's Long Neck*. London: A & C Black Publishers Ltd.
52. Covey, S. (1992). *The Seven Habits of Highly Effective People*. London: Simon & Schuster Ltd.
53. Contact Center Café on the Charter of Customer-friendliness THOCC/CCLA, 7/3/2013.
54. Figure loosely inspired by the whitepaper 'Customer experience happens in the contact center'. Source: Smith, S. & Wheeler, J. (2002). *Managing the Customer Experience: Turning customers into advocates*. New Jersey: Pearson Education.
55. Genesys research 'The Executive Disconnect', as published in *CCMA* no.3, 2008.
56. Cleveland, B. & Mayben, J. (1999). *Contact center management. In volle vaart vooruit*. Heerhugowaard: F & G Publishing.
57. Executive Board - Customer Contact Council (2007). *Effectively Monitoring and Communicating the Health of the Contact Center Function.*
58. 'Dilbert is a strip cartoon drawn and written by the American Scott Adams. The main character is Dilbert, an IT-er who has problems with the management of his company. The success of the strip probably owes something to the fact that the absurd situations it depicts are not too far removed from the realities of life in many companies.' (Wikipedia)
59. Training for leaders and manager organized by The House of Contact Centers, originally in collaboration with the University of Antwerp Management School, today with an anchoring in the Erasmus University of Rotterdam.
60. See annex 2 for a detailed description of this 'homework', which forms the basis for the research results that follow.
61. Executive Board - Customer Contact Council (2007) *Effectively Monitoring and Communicating the Health of the Contact Center Function.*

62. Covey, S. (1992). *The Seven Habits of Highly Effective People.* London: Simon & Schuster Ltd.
63. Also remember that a similar phenomenon occurred when various leaders and managers within the same contact center did the same exercise. In this in-house exercise 14 people suggested no fewer than 43 different KPIs.
64. The categories are inspired by the previously mentioned report by the *Executive Board.* This gives a useful external marker for comparison purposes. The consistent use of the categories over several years makes it possible to compare the inputs year by year, notwithstanding the underlying evolutions.
65. Extract from a cause and effect diagram from a Vlerick course in Mastering Interim Management.
66. The terms marked with an asterisk are indicators that were not given as such by the participants. This applies equally to the terms marked with an asterisk in the annexes.
67. Kaplan & Norton (1996). *The Balanced Scorecard.* Boston: Harvard Business School Press. Figure 68 is based on www. Patagonia-bv. Com/bsc-balanced-scorecard.
68. *Customer Operations Performance Center,* or COPC®, is an internationally applied management model for contact centers. The model is used to measure quality and performance in contacts with customers and is based on best practices from 200 leading contact centers worldwide. (Source: BRW group)
69. Fluss, D. (2005). *The Real-Time Contact Center.* New York: AMACOM.
70. Wikipedia: '*Myth Busters* is a popular American science program, broadcast by the commercial Discovery Channel. It is presented by Jamie Hyneman and Adam Savage. The program focuses on different myths, which it then seeks to either prove or disprove.'
71. 'Service level' is a stricter indicator than 'accessibility', which shows how many calls are answered, but with no reference to speed of response. 'Answering all calls within a minute' is therefore a service level indicator.
72. Jennings, G. (2005). *The Hitchhiker's Guide to the Galaxy.* Touchstone Pictures, after the books by Douglas Adams.
73. Dixon, M. & Freeman, K. & Toman, N. (2010). 'Stop trying to delight your customer.' *Harvard Business Review.* July-August, 2010. 116-122.
74. Dixon, M., Toman, N. & Delisi, R. (2013). *The Effortless Experience.* London: Penguin Portfolio.
75. Millard, N. & Alcock, T. (2014). *Superagent 2020: The evolution of the contact center.* British Telecom.
76. Nicola Millard at the Frost & Sullivan Customer Experience Exchange, Lisbon 2014.
77. Teunter, L. & Maijers, A. (2013). 'Wat is de beste metric?' *Telecommerce, 05.* 38-39.
78. *9th Annual Customer Contact 2015, Europe: A Frost & Sullivan Executive MindXchange,* Copenhagen, 9-10/6/2015.
79. Vianen, M. & Van Vliet, G. (2004). *Contact centers, een open boek.* Coniche International.
80. Methodology inspired by *La Poste – Automation of contact centers* – Boston Consulting Group, 2005.
81. Metaphor borrowed with pleasure from Cohen Brown, who devote a whole module to this subject in their program Breakthrough Service Performance.
82. Source figure: http://www. shutterstock.com/pic-113447770/stock-vector-ancient-physicians-hippocrates-avicenna-and-galen.html
83. McGovern, G. (2010). *The Stranger's Long Neck.* London: A & C Black Publishers Ltd.
84. Call Metrics (2006). *TelephoneX-Ray: Determinants of call satisfaction.* Research report. Call Metrics/Möbius & University of Ghent.
85. Bart Dietz: 'In contact centers performance comes before employee satisfaction'. Expert Class in Contact Center Management. 06/05/2013.
86. Measurement of satisfaction via an automated answer menu immediately after the conversation, involving customers who had previously agreed to participate.
87. From 'Customer @ the center', the winning bpost entry for the 2014 *World Mail Award in Customer Service.*
88. 'Back office or black office, because no-one knows exactly what happens there.' (Bas Filipina of Tolerating in CCM12, 2009).
89. System and reporting via Klant contact monitor. NL.
90. From 'Customer @ the center', the winning bpost entry for the 2014 *World Mail Award in Customer Service.*
91. Vienne, M. & Van Vliet, G. (2004). *Contact centers, een open boek.* Coniche International.
92. *Essentials of Leadership,* London Business School, 21-26/10/2012.
93. With thanks to Seth Godin's daily blog for mentioning this metaphor.
94. http://www. Joe-ks.com/archives_may2011/HowToDrawAnOwl. Htm
95. Naughton, J. *Zappos Customer Service Story* on Frost & Sullivan Customer Contact 2013. 9-11/6/2013. Cannes.
96. Van Steendam, T. (2018). *Dossier klotejobs (1).* Humo 4071/37 – 11/09/2018, p. 8-10.
97 Bart Dietz in Executive Class in Contact Center Deployment, THOCC. June 2013.
98. Course as part of the Expert Class in Contact center management, year 7, Rotterdam 6/5/2013.

99. In this connection, explicit reference is made to the work of, amongst others, Adam Grant, management professor at the Wharton School, University of Pennsylvania.
100. Codrington, G. *Tomorrow Today* at the CCLA congress. 13/4/2014.
101. I don't like having to explain this, but at a certain moment it becomes necessary, because it otherwise risks becoming dated: this is a reference to the '*Je suis Charlie*' solidarity movement that spontaneously developed following the terrorist attack on the offices of *Charlie Hebdo* in Paris in January 2015.
102. CCLA New Year's reception, Melsbroek, 22 January 2015. 'The Janus perspective".
103. Figure based on a conversation with Michel Delfosse, Genesys.
104. YouTube. First Follower Leadership. Lessons from Dancing Guy. www.youtube.com/watch?v=fw8amMCVAJQ"
105. Stefan Kauck, Genesys in *Beyond the contact center, Genesys user conference*. 24/9/2015.